Also by Madeleine Goss

BEETHOVEN, MASTER MUSICIAN

DEEP-FLOWING BROOK: THE STORY OF JOHANN SEBASTIAN BACH

BOLERO: THE LIFE OF MAURICE RAVEL

UNFINISHED SYMPHONY: THE STORY OF FRANZ SCHUBERT

Also by Robert Haven Schauffler

THE UNKNOWN BRAHMS

BEETHOVEN: THE MAN WHO FREED MUSIC

THE MUSICAL AMATEUR

FIDDLER'S LUCK

FIDDLER'S FOLLY

BRAHMS: THE MASTER

Johannes Brahms
1833 - 1897

BRAHMS
THE MASTER

by

MADELEINE GOSS

and

ROBERT HAVEN SCHAUFFLER

Illustrated by

FREDERIC DORR STEELE

NEW YORK
HENRY HOLT AND COMPANY

Published, November, 1943
Second printing, April, 1945
Third printing, July, 1945

PRINTED IN THE UNITED STATES OF AMERICA

CONTENTS

CHAPTER I

BACON ALLEY

THE SNOW was falling in a thick veil of white. Frau Brahms pulled her shabby old armchair nearer to the window and bent over her sewing. Beside her on the floor a small boy with fair, straight hair and singularly clear blue eyes was playing with some colored beans and a few battered lead soldiers. As she worked she began to sing. The lad listened intently.

"Again!" he cried as soon as she had finished. "Sing it again!"

Frau Brahms put her hand caressingly on the boy's yellow head. *"Na*—do you like that song, my Hannes?" she said tenderly. " 'To Bethlehem let us go' it's called—an old Latin Christmas hymn."

"Will the Christ child come soon?" asked four-year-old Hannes, looking up at his mother expectantly.

The woman's eyes filled with tears. "It's not much the Christ child will have for you this year, my poor lamb, unless your father finds work soon."

Life had not been easy for Johanna Christiana Brahms. She was a frail, careworn woman, with hair already turning gray, and blue eyes that seemed pale reflections of her son's. A crippled foot made it hard for her to walk, and this handicap had not improved her disposition.

"Always the same story," she went on, half to herself. "Jakob expecting every day to get a steady job—lugging his bass-viol and horn all over the city—and nothing ever coming of it!" There was a bitter note in her voice. "When he joined that Soldiers' Band he was sure it would bring him work. Plenty of work—that's right! But no pay. . . . Just a fancy green uniform and nothing else has he got from the Civic Guard." She leaned closer to the light to thread her needle. "I wonder what is keeping him so long?"

Little Hannes ran over to the window and stared out through the snow into the dark, evil-smelling courtyard below. In 1837 the Alley District of Hamburg was a poor tenement quarter. High, half-timbered houses—old and tumble-down—crowded the narrow lanes and shut out most of the light.

The Brahms family lived on the second floor of number 60 Schlüterhof, in a court just off the Specksgang, or "Bacon Alley." Here they had a small apartment of three tiny rooms: a kitchen, hardly large enough to turn around in, a dining-room that served also as parlor, and an alcove bedroom. There were only a few pieces of furniture, all of them old and battered. But somehow, in spite of the poverty and the disreputable neighborhood, the little apartment had a cheerful air. Frau Brahms kept everything immaculately clean; there were always fresh white curtains at the windows, and a pot or two of gay red geraniums.

Through the open kitchen door came a smell of sauerkraut and *Schnitzel*. Johanna rose painfully from her chair and limped into the kitchen to prepare the noon meal. After she had left the room, little Hannes began humming to himself as he played with his lead soldiers.

He was a shy, quiet child. At first he hardly sang above his breath, but gradually the tune came louder. It was the same melody his mother had been crooning: *In Bethlem Transeamus*. He could not say the Latin words, but the notes were clear and accurate.

Frau Brahms came to the kitchen door. "But, Hannes," she called in surprise, "where did you learn to sing so well?"

The boy was startled. He turned away and pretended

to be absorbed in his toys. Then, as his mother went back to her work, he called over his shoulder, "I can sing *all* of the hymns—if I want to!"

A curious thumping noise sounded on the stairs outside. Hannes ran to open the door just as Father Brahms—his large bass-viol strapped to his back and a horn under his arm—reached the landing.

"Blast these stairs!" the man muttered, looking back over his shoulder. "Me and my double-bass will get stuck there sure one of these days. No wonder they had to lower old Schmitz's coffin through the window last week. *Na,* Hannes!" he said, shaking the snow from his thin coat. "Where's your mother? Johanna, come here—quick!"

Frau Brahms limped eagerly in from the kitchen. "What is it, Jakob? What luck this time?"

"Only listen!" her husband announced proudly. "At last—believe it or not—I got me a fine job. Substitute player at one of the grandest restaurants in town, on the Alster Basin."

"It's about time," cried his wife. "God be praised!"

"And what do you know," went on Jakob in his Low-German dialect. He looked around the tiny room for a place to put his instruments. "'Twas our Musicians' Union got me the job! *Ja, ja*—you thought that the Union was just foolishness, now didn't you, my treasure?"

"I don't hold with these new ideas," Johanna said drily. "Who ever heard of musicians joining together in a union? Just an excuse to stay away from home and spend time and money drinking at the tavern."

Father Brahms' round, good-natured face looked rueful. *"Na, na,* Johanna, you don't mind if once in a way I have a drop of beer with my pals, do you? And our union—see now, it's right useful. I shouldn't have got this job without its help." He nodded his head ponderously. "The Pavilion up there on the Alster Basin is a most elegant restaurant, you know. What luck, eh! I'll be substitute at first, and to begin with I'll have to pass the plate around—the newest member of the band always has to do that. But no matter. Lots of chances for advancement there. The bass-viol player—he's so old he can hardly hang on to his bow. Later I might get his job."

Johann Jakob looked around the little room with a sigh of content. "A real Christmas we'll have this year! A tree with paper ribbons, and gingerbread men, even a goose, maybe, eh?" He eased himself into the battered family armchair and stretched out his legs.

"My father always told me: 'You'll never amount to anything with that music-craze of yours.' But if he knew about the fine job I have now he'd say: 'Jakob, you're a credit to our name!' "

Hannes looked up at his father with round eyes, but Johanna, well used to her husband's rambling talk, went back to the kitchen.

"It's a good name, Brahms," Jakob continued. "You—Hannes, did I ever tell you how we got that name?"

The child climbed upon his father's lap. "How?" he asked curiously.

"Well—our family lived in the lowlands of Dithmarsh, in the north. Some day I'll take you up there. In spring the country is covered with the yellow broom plant—*'Bram.'* So we're *'Brams'*—sons of the broom!" Smiling, he poked Hannes in the ribs. "Maybe that's where you got your yellow hair, eh? *Ja, ja,"* he nodded, *"Brahms* is a good name. What's more, it's a king's name too! Why, the royal family of England was once named for the broom. *Plantagenet* they called it there."

Hannes puckered up his forehead. "Does 'Brahms' mean music too?" he asked hopefully.

Jakob threw back his head and roared. "That's a good one! I wish your grandfather could hear that. He had no use at all for music. Such a time I spent trying to make him let me be a musician. He kept a tavern in Heide, you know. I used to listen to the fellows who played dance-music there, and try to catch on to the way they made their instruments work. They all poked fun at me because I was so music-crazy. Father thought it was just a joke—*he* wanted me to be an innkeeper."

Jakob wagged his finger at the child. "It was no joke to me. I knew what *I* wanted. *Ja*—I even ran away from home and went to the nearest Town Piper to beg him to teach me. In those days the *Stadt Pfeiffer* was chief musician in country towns," he added by way of explanation.

Little Hannes couldn't understand everything his

father said, but he listened with absorbed interest as Jakob went on with his story. "My father found me out; he came after me and brought me home by the ear. But I only ran away again. . . . At last he gave up and bound me apprentice to the Town Piper of Meldorf." Jakob smiled with satisfaction at the memory.

"At Meldorf I worked hard. *Ja,* you should have seen how I worked! I learned to play the horn and flute, the violin and even the double-bass. And after two years—only two years, mind you," he paused dramatically, "my teacher gave me the 'certificate of apprenticeship.' Some day when you can read, Hannes, I'll show you that paper. 'Faithful, desirous of learning, industrious, and obedient'—that's what it says, and a lot more. . . ."

Johanna, who had been in and out of the room as she set the table, looked over at her husband with amused scorn. "Till now all that recommendation hasn't done you much good," she remarked.

Her husband sighed. "*Ja,* that's right. Nothing but struggle, struggle, playing on street corners, then in cheap restaurants and sailors' dives—anything to make a few thalers to keep body and soul together." His good, honest face twitched with feeling. "What would I have done without *you,* Johanna?"

In spite of her sharp tongue, Frau Brahms loved her husband dearly. "I often wondered what you saw in me!" she said, with unaccustomed humility. "I am so small and plain, and so much older than you."

"Tut, tut," Jakob said quickly. "Don't talk that way. Why, when I first got to Hamburg—remember how poor I was? No friends, no money. You and your sister were wonderful to me. You let me board free till I could earn something. You were the first person that ever took an interest in me—that's what you were. And such a fine education you had. . . . Of course I had to fall in love with you! What if you *are* seventeen years older than me? Seventeen years wiser, that's what *I* say!"

Johanna turned away to hide her emotion. "In those days I thought you were going to be a great musician," she remarked a little acidly. "Well—life can't be fine for everybody, I suppose. Don't forget," she added, changing the subject, "this is your day for the Soldiers' Band."

Opening the small clothes-press she took out her husband's green uniform. "You know, since you joined that Band, Hannes can think of nothing but soldiers."

"That reminds me. . . ." Father Brahms reached into his pocket. "There was a peddler selling lead soldiers for a penny. I thought—well, since I got me this fine new job, I thought, 'Why shouldn't Hannes have a new soldier?' *Hannes,* where are you?"

From the adjoining sleeping-alcove there suddenly came a strange tooting sound. Little Hannes, seeing his father and mother engaged in their own conversation, had slipped away to experiment with Jakob's horn.

Father Brahms burst into laughter, but his wife silenced him. "Listen!" she said. "Today Hannes was singing—but just wonderfully for a little one of his age. He seems to remember every tune he hears, and you know how he always stops his play when you practice. I believe he has real music in him."

Jakob pursed his lips together and shook his head gravely. "That may be—that may be. I shouldn't regret it. When he's a bit older I'll try him on the violin. Some day," he added a little wistfully, remembering what high hopes he had had in his own youth, "some day our Hannes might be good enough to play in a real orchestra—anyhow, *second* violin!"

From the next room the strange sounds continued. Frau Brahms, listening with pride, imagined she could recognize some of the notes from "To Bethlehem let us go."

Johannes Brahms never forgot the tunes he heard in his early childhood. They stayed with him all through his life, and when he began writing music, a number of these melodies were woven into his compositions.

One of Brahms' most beloved songs—a tender lullaby called "The Little Sandman" (dedicated to the Schumann children) takes its theme from the Latin hymn *In Bethlem Transeamus:*

When Father Brahms began teaching his young son music, he was amazed. Little Johannes mastered the horn and flute as easily as most boys learn to play marbles. Next, Jakob started him on the violin.

Hannes had never seen printed music, but almost before he could write words he tried experiments in setting down the tunes he heard. One day his father found him laboriously busied with pencil and a large sheet of paper.

"What's this, what's this?" Jakob inquired, laughing.

Hannes tried to hide the paper; but his father seized it from him and examined it with growing interest. When the child saw that he was not going to be teased, he tried to explain his invention.

"These are the lines for writing down the notes, you see." He pointed to a crude staff with large black dots sprawling across the page. "And here is the tune. . . ."

Father Brahms could hardly believe his eyes. "You thought this out all by yourself?" he asked incredulously. He was sure now that his young son must be a musical prodigy. "If the boy keeps on," he told his wife, "soon he'll be able to play in the taverns with me."

"What are you saying, Jakob?" cried Johanna in high disapproval. "A dance-hall is no place for a child!"

Jakob sighed. "But we need the money so badly. . . ."

There were now three children in the Brahms family. Hannes had an older sister, Elise, and a younger brother named Fritz. Like her mother, Elise was small and delicate. Even as a child she suffered from severe headaches, and in later years these headaches ruined both her health and her disposition. The poor living conditions in the slums of Hamburg, the lack of fresh air and wholesome food, were hard on all the family. Throughout his childhood Johannes was pale and undersized, and he too was subject to headaches. If it had not been for the strength he inherited from his father's peasant ancestors, he might never have survived those early years.

When the boy was six years old his father sent him to a small private school near by. Hannes proved a good student, and learned rapidly, making the most of what meager formal education came his way. At home he was affectionate and obedient, and especially devoted to his mother.

Johanna, on her side, lavished all the love of a lonely and thwarted nature on her "sweet Johnnie," as she called him. There was a bond between the two which held Brahms to his mother even after he left home to make his way in the world. Long after childhood days he remembered the hours she had spent singing to him or reading aloud from the Bible and the German poets. Her voice was soft and low (Brahms always had a weakness for lovely voices), and the child never tired of listening to the musical flow of the words.

Both indoors and out he was surrounded by music. In those days the streets of Hamburg were filled with melody. Groups of wandering musicians, called *Pannkoken* ("Pancakes"), played on the corners, and barrel-organs ground out the latest waltzes. Whenever a band or a barrel-organ appeared in Bacon Alley, all the children of the neighborhood would gather to sing and dance to the music. Their wooden shoes clattered an accompaniment on the cobblestones—in rhythmical forecast of modern clog-dancing—and their shrill voices echoed the tunes.

Most of the games the children played involved singing. Even the counting out of Hide-and-seek was accompanied by song. Hannes was so fascinated by these melodies that he was more apt to stand on the sidelines, listening, than to join actively in the fun. For always he seemed to be listening, storing away impressions. Now it was the melodious hum of the spinning tops that fascinated him, now the tinkle of small pieces of tin which the children fastened to their hoops and rolled, jingling merrily, through the narrow streets.

More often, however, Hannes could be found seated at the table of the Brahms' little living-room-dining-room, poring over his self-ruled music-paper, or experimenting with new tunes on his father's instruments.

For music—anything to do with music—was what Johannes Brahms loved best of all.

CHAPTER II

HANNES DISCOVERS THE CLATTER-BOX

AT THE Alster Pavilion, Father Brahms' droll humor made him a great favorite with the patrons and the other members of the band. But sometimes he was almost too independent and outspoken. "What do you think?" he told his wife one day after a rehearsal. "That fresh fellow of a band-director said to me this morning: 'Brahms, you're playing out of tune.' But I put him in his place, I did! What do you think I answered back?"

Johanna looked apprehensive. *"What?"*

"I says, says I: 'Herr Direktor, a pure tone on the *Kunterbass* is just a pure accident—just luck, no more, no less. And I am luckier than most!' You should have heard the others laugh. . . ."

Hannes, who was now seven years old and sometimes went with his father to hear the music at the Alster Pavilion, spoke up. "The bass isn't pretty alone," he said thoughtfully; "but when you all play together it sounds like real music."

"Ja, ja, that's right," Father Brahms agreed. "Several instruments, each playing a different part—that's what makes harmony. And it's why some people think so much of the organ and the pianoforte. You can play a lot of notes all at once on those instruments."

Johannes had heard the organ in church, and its mighty volume of sound enchanted him. But the piano—or *pianoforte* as it was called because it could be played either soft (*piano*) or loud (*forte*)—was comparatively rare. Not many people could afford to own such a costly instrument.

Hannes had never heard a pianoforte until one day Jakob took him along when he went to visit a crony from the Musicians' Union. There, to his joy, the boy discovered one of the instruments he was so anxious to know more about.

Jakob's friend was amused at the child's eager interest. "Would you like to hear how it sounds?" he asked, smiling.

Hannes was too shy to say "yes," but his eyes sparkled and he listened with absorbed attention. The piano sounded even better than he had imagined it would. He was quite familiar with the string and brass instruments, but this, now, seemed to him much more satisfactory—almost like a whole orchestra in itself. If only *he* could learn to play the pianoforte. . . .

"My Hannes is very clever at music," Father Brahms announced proudly to his friend. "I'll wager you a good full stein of beer that he can learn the notes in no time at all. Listen here, Hannes—" he called, seating himself at the piano.

Johannes, who had been examining the pedals, looked up.

"This—" said Jakob, striking a note with ponderous precision, "is middle C."

"Yes, Father," the boy answered dutifully.

"Next is this black note—C sharp. Then this—"

Hannes, bored by such elementary instruction, edged away towards the window. "Will you listen to me?" called his father angrily. "I'm trying to teach you!"

"But I know all the notes," Hannes answered absentmindedly as he looked down into the street. Dusk was falling. A group of boys below were playing with lanterns made out of old tin cans and bits of candle. Hannes was fascinated. He wondered if he could make a lantern like that. . . .

"Oh!—so you know all the notes, my fine fellow!" cried Jakob in mocking tones. "What's this then?" He banged a key at the top of the piano.

"G flat," answered Hannes, still watching the children below.

"Boy—are you trying to make a fool out of me?" roared Father Brahms. "Name this—"

"D," called Hannes without hesitating.

"And this—and *this?*"

Each note the child identified correctly. Finally Jakob stopped in sheer amazement. For he had discovered that his son possessed a rare gift. The boy had what is known as "absolute pitch," and could recognize or sing any note that was played or called for.

After this visit, Hannes could think of nothing but the piano. "Couldn't I have some lessons?" he begged his father.

"On the *pianoforte?*" Jakob cried, regarding him with scorn. "Why, that's nothing but a clatter-box full of wires. A plaything for the idle rich, but no good for anything else."

Johannes' face fell. "Oh, but—I think it's a *wonderful* instrument, Father," he urged, with unusual insistence. "Please let me. . . ."

Jakob snorted. "And how do you think you'd make a living out of that old box of wires? The violin now, or the horn—'most any other instrument—they'll get you into a band or orchestra. But the piano . . ."

Hannes, usually so docile, looked ready to cry. His mother came to the boy's rescue.

"Why shouldn't my sweet boy learn the piano if he wants to?" she cried, putting her arm around the child's shoulders. "After all, Jakob, have you forgotten how you had your own way when *you* were young?"

Father Brahms threw up his hands. "Where do you think we'd find a teacher—or money to pay for the lessons?"

Johanna sniffed. "What of your precious Union? You said it was to help the members. Isn't there a pianist there who would be glad to teach a child as talented as our Hannes?"

Jakob couldn't resist an opportunity to justify the value of his Musicians' Union. But still more, the pleading expression in his small son's eyes finally persuaded him.

"There *is* a pianist named Cossel who's a member of our Union," he admitted. "If you're both so set on it, I'll speak to him."

Johannes threw his arms about his father's neck. He knew that no instrument but the piano would satisfy him. But little did he or his parents then dream that he was destined to become one of the well-known piano virtuosos of his day, and that a large number of his compositions were to be written for that instrument.

Otto Friedrich Willibald Cossel was considered a very fine piano teacher. He had studied with the celebrated

Marxsen; it was very doubtful, Father Brahms felt, that he would be willing to accept Hannes as a pupil. But Jakob was a man of his word, so the next week, on an afternoon towards the end of 1840, he took his son to Herr Cossel.

A wealthy young Fräulein was just finishing her lesson when the two arrived. Hannes listened eagerly from the corridor. "It sounds like a machine," he whispered to his father. "How stupid she is to play like that. . . ."

The lesson evidently had not gone brilliantly. "If that girl only had an ounce of talent—just one ounce!" Cossel murmured despairingly as the Fräulein left.

"You may come in now," the servant-girl told the two visitors as she opened the door into the pleasantly furnished sitting-room where Herr Cossel gave his lessons.

Father Brahms was very nervous. He had met the distinguished piano teacher only once before, at a meeting of the Musicians' Union. Little Johannes, however, felt much too excited to be overawed; he looked at once for the piano, and was amazed to see not one but *two* shiny black instruments standing side by side at one end of the room.

"Perhaps the highly-well-born Herr Professor may remember me," stammered Jakob, stepping forward with a self-conscious bow. "I'm a fellow-member of the Hamburg Musicians' Union. I—" he pushed Johannes before him, "I have made so bold as to bring my young son to you. He is—*aber* very talented. Yes, your Honor, really talented, and he wishes badly to study with you."

Cossel looked down at the pale, delicate child. Little Hannes was dressed with painstaking neatness. He wore a fresh blue smock and well-scrubbed wooden shoes, and Johanna had brushed his hair until it shone like pale gold. But what impressed the teacher most of all was the intense expression in the boy's clear blue eyes. As the two looked at each other, Johannes suddenly smiled—a shy but singularly winning smile. Cossel found his heart warming towards this unknown child.

"How old is your son?" he asked the father.

Jakob counted on his fingers and mumbled a little under his breath. "May 7th, 1833. . . . That makes him—let's see—yes, seven and a half, going on eight," he finally announced. "But my Hannes is already a fine musician. He can play horn and flute and violin, and he can even write down music. Only look—" he proudly exhibited a page of the boy's work. "Made it up himself, he did, and invented a way to write it down, too."

Cossel smiled a little. "Remarkable," he agreed politely. "But that sort of thing is only play in a child of his age. He shouldn't waste his time experimenting. Let him first become a skillful performer. Has he a good ear?"

"Splendid!" Father Brahms exclaimed eagerly. "Really extraordinary! Hannes, do you sing for the Herr Professor, and play a little tune for him on your violin."

Cossel was visibly impressed by the boy's performance, and Jakob, quick to follow up his advantage, said: "The Herr Professor must understand, of course—I am only a poor musician; sometimes we hardly have enough to eat. I couldn't *pay* for the boy's lessons. But my Hannes is very talented, and he's a good worker too. Only give him a try! He'd be a credit to you!"

Herr Cossel thought for a moment. The child did show unusual promise; there was no question about that. And in addition he seemed serious and anxious to learn. It would be a welcome change, the pianist thought cynically—remembering the recently departed Fräulein—to have a gifted pupil to teach.

"Are you willing to let the boy stay with me until he becomes a really first-class pianist?" he asked, recalling other pupils who had been taken away from him and exploited before they were finished performers.

Jakob beamed. "But certainly, Herr Professor. If you will only teach my Hannes, then I promise he shall stay with you until—until he knows as much as you do!" He burst out laughing at the absurd idea of his son's ever becoming as fine a pianist as the great Herr Cossel. If only the boy could learn enough to play in the taverns, that would be quite sufficient to satisfy Jakob Brahms.

While the two men were talking together Johannes wandered over to the nearer piano. For a while he stood there looking at it with eager attention. Then very softly he placed his fingers on the keyboard. A lovely chord, full and rich, sounded delicately from the "clatter-box." Hannes could hardly wait to begin his lessons.

Herr Cossel had never known such a serious and ambitious pupil as young Brahms turned out to be. He never had to urge him to work—quite the contrary.

"Hannes, you have practiced enough for today," he said late one afternoon some months after he began teaching the boy. He took him by the shoulders and pushed him away from the piano. "Remember that you still have a long walk home, and the streets are very dark and none too safe after nightfall."

Hamburg was a foggy, dismal city on the northwestern coast of Germany, with much rain and little sunshine. In the days of Brahms' childhood its harbor was crowded with sailing vessels from all parts of the world. Its wharves were piled high with strange, exotic merchandise. Pungent odors of spices and oriental perfumes mingled with that of the boiling tar which was used to calk the seams of the ships. Sailors and travelers from foreign countries swarmed through the streets. Along the waterfront could be heard curious, unfamiliar music—the nasal twang of Japanese samisens, faint tinkling of East Indian cymbals, and even, at times, the dull beat of African drums. All this movement, color, smell, and particularly sound, fascinated young Brahms. He loved to linger along the wharves, and always stopped for a few moments on the way to and from his lessons.

One night when Johannes was a little over nine years

old, a disastrous fire broke out not far from his home. It raged for nearly four days before it was finally brought under control, and an entire district of the city was burned down. Fortunately the house in which the Brahms family then lived was not touched, and curiously enough the Alster Pavilion, although directly in the path of the conflagration, also escaped.

The fire made a deep and lasting impression on young Brahms. Even in later life he always kept a small boy's delight in watching a house burn down, and fireworks were his special joy. Once he wrote in a letter to his publisher:

> Not for a long time have I had such a beautiful treat at a fire. . . . Standing near a hose, on the flat roof of the house adjoining, I looked right down upon it. It was extraordinary! If a house *must* burn, at least one enjoys watching it.

After the great fire in Hamburg, Johannes was obliged to make a long detour to get to Herr Cossel's house. One day as he was on his way home from his lesson, he came upon a small factory building where pianos were made. Over the door hung a sign:

BAUMGARTEN & HEINZ

Someone was at work tuning one of the instruments, and Hannes stopped to listen. Presently his curiosity got the better of him, and he pushed the door open a crack.

"Come in, come in," a voice called. "Why do you stand there?"

Johannes hesitated a moment, then entered the room. Before an open piano stood a little old man in a tight-fitting black skull cap, bending over a mass of wires and small felt hammers. Hannes was so fascinated by this unaccustomed view of his beloved pianoforte that he almost forgot his usual timidity.

"Well, what is it you want?" grumbled the old man.

"Could I—would your Honor allow—" Hannes stammered, "might I perhaps just watch while you work?"

When he saw the genuine interest of his young visitor, the little old man became quite friendly. He explained how the piano was put together and how it was tuned.

Hannes confided to his new friend that he was taking lessons of Herr Cossel and hoped some day to be a fine pianist.

"Do you practice seriously?" Herr Baumgarten inquired in a severe voice.

"As much as I can!" Young Brahms hesitated a little. "You see, we have no piano at our house. Herr Cossel lets me practice on his instrument when I have finished with my lesson—but it is not enough."

"So-o-o," the old man remarked, examining the boy through his spectacles. "How would you like to come and practice here once in a while? Of course—" he hastened to add as he saw the eager light in the boy's eyes—"only when there are no customers to be disturbed."

Hannes took full advantage of this kind offer. Hardly a day passed without his appearing at the piano factory, hoping he might be allowed to practice for at least a few moments. Because these opportunities were rare they became doubly precious. He discovered that by concentrating deeply he could make every minute count.

This ability to focus his attention was one of the reasons why Johannes Brahms became such a great man. Complete concentration is a vital requirement for any outstanding achievement, and this was one of Brahms' strong points. At times it even proved a little disconcerting to his friends. If, for instance, he happened to be talking to someone, and another person broke into the conversation, he would be so completely absorbed that he would not even notice the other's presence.

In addition to his practicing, young Brahms could not resist experimenting with original tunes, even though he knew that his teacher disapproved. One day Cossel arrived a little late for the boy's lesson. As he came in he heard Johannes at the piano, and stopped to listen.

"What were you playing there?" he asked.

Hannes rose from his seat in confusion. "I—I did not hear you come in, sir," he stammered.

"But that piece?" Cossel insisted, frowning a little. "What is it now?" Suddenly the guilty look on the boy's face answered his question.

"Johannes, you have been disobeying me again. How often have I told you not to waste your time trying to compose? Can you ever expect to become a good pianist if you spend your energy on useless things instead of practice?"

The boy hung his head. He could not bear to displease his master. But he knew it would be impossible for him to give up writing music. His mind was always full of tunes. They stayed with him, haunted him until he wrote them down. He simply had to get them on paper to be rid of them!

Young Brahms learned with extraordinary rapidity, and in two years he had made such progress that Cossel decided his own teacher, Marxsen, must hear the boy.

Eduard Marxsen was one of the leading musicians of northern Germany. Although a composer of some note, he was especially famous as a teacher of the pianoforte. He had more pupils than he could take care of, so when Cossel asked if he would hear Johannes Brahms, Marxsen was not much interested.

"There are so many child prodigies in the world," he told his former pupil. "And what ever comes of them?"

"But this boy is really exceptional," Cossel insisted. "If you will only hear him I'm sure you will agree."

Marxsen finally consented. "Bring him if you wish then."

When Johannes played for Marxsen he was so intimidated that he could not do himself justice. He had spent weeks in preparing a difficult Cramer étude, but he was too much concerned with technical perfection, and his playing lacked its usual character and expression.

Marxsen was not particularly impressed. "You have a serious and industrious pupil there," he told Cossel. "Continue with him as you have been doing. The boy could not be in better hands."

Father Brahms was disappointed. It would have been a great feather in his cap if the renowned Marxsen had been willing to teach his son. Hannes, however, was quite satisfied to remain with Herr Cossel. He loved his teacher with all the devotion of a sensitive, ardent nature. At New Year's in 1842 he tried to express a little of his appreciation in a letter. This letter, written on a double sheet, quarto size, is the first bit of Brahms' writing that we possess:

Beloved teacher!

Another year is over, and I remind myself that you have, during this last year, brought me along very far in music. How much gratitude I owe you! Of course I must also remember that sometimes I failed to meet your wishes by not practising as I should. However, this year I promise you by industry and attention to carry out your desires. While wishing you a lot of happiness in the New Year, I remain your obedient pupil,

J. Brahms

Hamburg
1 Jan., 1842

Johannes' family now lived in a slightly larger flat. Elise helped her mother with the cooking and housework, and Father Jakob had begun to teach music to Fritz, the youngest member of the family. He hoped that this son, too, would prove a prodigy like his elder brother; but Fritz never became distinguished, except through his relationship to the celebrated Johannes.

Frau Brahms ran a small shop at the front of the building, where in order to make a little extra money she sold needles, thread, and other notions to the *Hausfraus* of the neighborhood. In her leisure moments she took in fine sewing; but still the family was desperately poor.

Hannes loved all his people, but his mother most of all. To him she did not seem old or plain. On the contrary, he thought her beautiful. Even her lame foot held a certain fascination for the boy. For him her halting walk made an interesting rhythm. Brahms often used syncopation in his compositions. Some believe that his mother's limp may have inspired his partiality for this form of rhythmical irregularity.

Johannes was always trying to find ways to help his mother. Each morning he would rise at daybreak and clean from the family shoes the mud of Hamburg's unpaved streets. He did not in the least mind getting up early. It was the only time he was sure of being entirely alone and undisturbed. Those early morning hours held magic for him. The air then seemed filled with melody.

In speaking of his first attempts at composition Brahms later said: "I was always composing, even in my youngest days, but only in great secrecy. My finest melodies would come to me early in the morning, while I was cleaning the boots. . . ."

Cossel continued to discourage the boy's passion for writing music. "It is a pity," he told a friend; "young Brahms might be such a good pianist, but he will not leave this everlasting composition alone!"

Jakob was immensely proud of his son's progress. Friends who heard the boy were equally impressed.

"Your Hannes should be giving concerts," they told the father. "What is that man Cossel thinking of to keep such a talent hidden? Why, you could make a lot of money out of the boy's playing. Don't you remember what a fortune the Mozarts collected from young Wolfgang's concerts? People are always interested in child prodigies."

Father Brahms, who privately thought that his son played even better than Mozart could have done at his age, began to have ambitions for Hannes. When the boy had almost reached his tenth birthday Jakob learned that a famous impresario was coming to Hamburg in search of new talent. It was quite possible, Father Brahms reasoned, that this music-agent would be impressed if he heard Hannes play, and might want to take the boy on a concert tour through Germany. Or through Europe, for that matter—even, perhaps, to the United States! Jakob had sudden dreams of wealth; for America was even then considered the land where sharp eyes were likely to discover a gold-piece wedged in the cobbles of every other street.

In some way a concert must be arranged, so that Hannes could be heard. But first Herr Cossel would have to be persuaded. . . . Father Brahms was not at all sure that his son's teacher would approve of the plan. A little strategy might be necessary.

The next day Jakob walked over with Johannes to his music lesson.

"Herr Cossel," he began, making his round, good-natured face as guileless as possible, "are you satisfied with my Hannes' progress?"

"I am more than satisfied," Cossel replied. "He has been doing very good work."

"Then couldn't he maybe give a little concert? Nothing important, you understand," he added quickly, noting the teacher's expression. "Just a subscription concert where he could play a few pieces—something to give him a bit of experience. I have a lot of Musicians' Union friends that'd buy tickets."

Cossel thought the suggestion over and decided it was not a bad idea. If Johannes were to play before an audience he would have something definite to work for. It might even prove to him how much more important practicing was than trying to compose.

Young Brahms started at once to prepare several piano solos, including a difficult show piece by a contemporary composer named Herz. He was also to play, with other assisting artists, a piano quartet by Mozart, and a Beethoven quintet.

The main room of the Old Raven Inn was engaged for the concert, and the date decided on. Then there came an unexpected setback which nearly proved fatal to poor Johannes.

CHAPTER III

HANNES MAKES HIS BOW

JOHANNA BRAHMS was just doing up a package of gray yarn and some knitting needles for one of the neighbors, when she heard a sudden commotion outside the door of her shop. An excited friend, hurrying in, called to her: "Now don't be alarmed, Frau Brahms! It's really nothing—just a little accident. Your Hannes—"

Johanna's face went pale. *"Hannes?"* She gave a cry and rushed so quickly for the door that her lame foot nearly gave way beneath her.

A silent group of neighbors came down the street carrying Johannes on a stretcher. He looked so white and still that his poor mother was sure he must be dead.

But the child was only unconscious. On his way back from school he had been run over by a carriage. The wheels passed directly over his chest; for days it was feared he would not live.

Then gradually he began to improve, and in six weeks' time he had recovered enough to begin practicing again. He worked so hard that, in spite of the accident, he managed to be ready for his concert.

That evening an expectant crowd gathered at the Old Raven Inn. Jakob had talked so much about his extraordinary son that all his friends of the Musicians' Union were anxious to hear the prodigy. When Johannes came in for his first number, and bowed before the audience, as his teacher had instructed him to do, there were murmurs of astonishment.

"Why, that child can't be ten years old," they whispered; "not more than six or seven, I should say." The ladies were moved to maternal emotion. "Poor little fellow, he looks very delicate. But they say he really can play. . . ."

"Don't think about the audience," Herr Cossel had warned his pupil. "Just imagine that you are making music for me alone. Your very best it must be!"

And it *was* Hannes' best. He played so brilliantly—even the difficult show piece which would have taxed the powers of a full-grown artist—that everyone was amazed.

Seated in the audience—just as Jakob had hoped—

was the music impresario. Father Brahms watched the man out of the corner of his eye. It was evident that he was impressed.

The day after the concert Jakob and his wife went together to call on Herr Cossel.

"We are in luck, Herr Professor," they told him. "Only think, a concert-agent heard our Hannes play last night, and would you believe it—he wants to travel with him, take him on a tour to the United States, and us with him!"

"Hannes—on tour—giving concerts!" Cossel cried indignantly. "Man, you don't know what you are talking about. Why, the boy isn't ready for anything like that. It would ruin his future career."

Jakob sat on the edge of his chair and cleared his throat nervously. "But, Herr Professor, we must eat! We would make a pile of money—"

"Money!" Cossel exploded. "Is that all you think of?"

"We are so very poor," Frau Brahms broke in timidly. "The Herr Professor cannot realize what this means to us. Why, if we should go to America we could live in hotels, and I shouldn't have to sweep and cook any more."

Cossel began to pace up and down the room. He had been afraid something like this might happen. What could he do to save the boy? A glorious future was in store for Johannes, if only he could be directed in the right way. But to give up his lessons at this point—start out on a concert career—nothing could be worse!

The pianist stopped suddenly in front of Father Brahms and leveled an accusing finger. "You promised," he cried, "that Johannes should stay with me until he knew as much as I do!"

Jakob's face fell. "But, Herr Professor, this is such a colossal opportunity for us—"

Cossel was now thoroughly aroused. "Word-breaker!" he shouted. "That's what you are if you take the boy away now. Word-breaker!"

Father Brahms cringed. At heart he was a good, honest soul. To accuse him thus was to strike at his most vulnerable spot. Then he brightened. "But, my Hannes—he does play—that is, they say he plays as well as . . ." Jakob hesitated to make the comparison, but Cossel understood.

"You may be right—perhaps he does play as well as I do. But you don't understand. Hannes *may* become one of the best pianists in the whole country, if only he gets the right training. Perhaps—" He had a sudden inspiration. "Why, I believe Marxsen himself would be willing to take the boy now. If we could persuade *him,* then Hannes' future would be assured."

Jakob sighed heavily, and the tears gathered in Frau Brahms' eyes. It was difficult for them to give up their dreams of immediate prosperity. But if it really was to Hannes' advantage . . . They finally agreed that if

Marxsen would continue the boy's musical education they would refuse the impresario.

When he volunteered to give up his best pupil, the good Cossel was making a real sacrifice.

"But why do you wish me to take this boy?" Marxsen asked, when the proposition was put before him. "You are perfectly able to go on with his teaching."

"No, your Honor," insisted Cossel. "Young Brahms has made such progress during this last year that I have nothing further to teach him."

Marxsen, who suspected the real reason, raised a suspicious eyebrow; but when he heard Hannes play again he found that Cossel had not exaggerated the boy's talent. Here was a gift that deserved the best instruction.

"If I give you lessons will you work really hard?" he asked the child.

Before Johannes could answer, Cossel broke in. "That I can guarantee, your Honor. Johannes has been a faithful and industrious pupil. His only fault has been a tendency to spend too much of his time in trying to compose."

"So . . . ?" said Marxsen. "The young man wants to compose?" He looked with interest at the boy. "One of these days you shall show me some of your work."

Hannes stared at him in delighted surprise. Was it possible that his new teacher would not scold him for doing what he liked best in all the world? Might even help him with it?

To show his appreciation he worked with even greater industry than usual to prepare his lessons with the new master. Marxsen gave him a difficult *Moto Perpetuo* by Weber to look over and see what he could make of it. When Hannes brought it to his next lesson the professor was amazed to find that the boy could play it almost perfectly.

"I have also practiced it in a different way," young Brahms announced, and proceeded to play the right-hand part with the left hand alone. Then he transposed the composition into another key.

Now Marxsen began to realize his new pupil's promise. At once he started him on harmony and counterpoint, and special exercises in transposition. When Hannes showed him his manuscripts he was astounded to see what the uninstructed child had managed to work out for himself.

"How did you learn to write music so well?" he asked.

Johannes explained that he had trained himself by setting down the music that he heard; then, whenever possible, comparing it with the printed scores to find out what mistakes he had made.

"And sometimes," he went on, "I copy the parts of the different instruments in Father's band. It's like a game to put them down one beneath another, and then see how they can be fitted into a single whole."

In later years Marxsen said:

When I began to teach him composition, he showed an unusual incisiveness of thought which delighted me. And, though his first experiments in creating something of his own turned out insignificant, I was obliged to recognize in them a spirit which convinced me that here slumbered a great, an extraordinary talent of unique depth. Therefore I gladly spared no pains to arouse and form this talent, in order some day to win for music a priest who would, in a new way, and indeed through his own achievement, preach the gospel of the lofty, the true and the eternal in art.

Hannes was a dreamy, sensitive child, living in a world of his own. After music his greatest pleasure was reading. Books he loved with a quiet passion that began in those early days when his mother read aloud to him, or recited long poems. She knew most of Schiller's verse by heart, and countless passages from the Bible. These classics made a deep impression on the boy, and gave him a lasting preference for the best in literature.

Whenever young Brahms had a penny of his own to spare he would hunt up one of the book peddlers. These wandering merchants trudged through the streets of Hamburg selling second-hand books from a wheelbarrow. Hannes gradually acquired a small library of classics. Among them was a story of adventure which the Germans pronounced Róh-been-sohn Crew-so-aýe, and which we call "Robinson Crusoe." It always remained one of his special favorites.

Hannes read a great deal; but even when he was engrossed in a book he did not forget his music. As he read he would silently exercise his fingers on the arm of the chair—unconsciously drumming out the rhythm of his thoughts.

There was still no piano in the Brahms household; but Hannes had managed to get hold of a second-hand silent practice-clavier. Hours daily he worked on this portable keyboard. Although the music sounded only in his head, his fingers were strengthened by the exercise.

Father Brahms still played at the Alster Pavilion, and in addition had occasional engagements in the theaters. But all this brought in only enough to keep starvation away. Because of the visions of sudden wealth which the impresario had dangled before their eyes, the family felt their poverty even more painfully than before. Jakob finally decided on a desperate expedient.

"There is no help for it, Hannes," he told his son. "Since your teachers wouldn't let you go with the music-agent you'll have to play in the dance-halls to earn some money."

Hamburg was overrun with sailors and low-class foreigners. A number of dance-halls and taverns provided them with entertainment, and music—of a sort—was always in demand at these places. The better class boasted a small band. The poorer had only a broken-down piano.

To play in such an environment was a true desecration of art; but, although Jakob knew this, he could see no way out. "It won't be so hard," he said to Johannes.

"All you have to do is sit at the piano and pound out a few popular tunes. Just a mechanical trick. . . ." Father Brahms laughed, but his eyes were sad. "It will exercise your fingers as much as the silent-clavier!"

Hannes shuddered. At his portable keyboard at least he was alone; and, though the notes did not sound, he could hear the harmonies in his head. To spend his nights in a crowded, noisy dance-hall filled with smoke and shouting sailors and their loose women, pounding out cheap tunes to amuse the company—how could a sensitive, beauty-loving child possibly endure such an existence?

But Hannes cared deeply for his family; he was willing to do anything in his power to help them. The sailors' dance-halls were in St. Pauli, the most notorious quarter of Hamburg. So late the next afternoon Jakob took him there to ask for work.

When they saw the small, delicate-looking child, they only laughed. "He is much too young and inexperienced," they told Father Brahms. None of the better places would even consider engaging the boy; so finally father and son ended up in one of the lowest sailors' dives. And here they agreed to give Hannes a chance.

Jakob had to leave the boy and go on to his work at the Alster Pavilion. When Hannes found himself alone, seated before the rickety piano, it was all he could do not to weep with terror. He had to remind himself that he was now a man—a bread-winner for his family.

Drunken sailors sprawled across the tables, or danced

with gaudily dressed women. The air was so thick with smoke that he could hardly breathe, and the piano so out of tune that it hurt his ears to touch it. But he knew he must make good!

The clients of the tavern were amused at the new pianist's childish appearance. Young Hannes was always small for his age. His pale cheeks, intense blue eyes and long fair hair made him an almost angelic apparition—a heart-breaking contrast to the sordidness of the place. The women were especially taken with the boy. They hung over him as he played, dragged him to their tables and took him on their laps. They petted him outrageously, and even tried to make him share their drinks.

At first it was all a horrible nightmare to Hannes. But he soon learned that if he wanted to keep his place he must submit to anything the "patrons" demanded. And gradually he grew used to it, and felt at home with the sailors and their wild companions.

Perhaps because of this early association with women of loose morals, Brahms in later life was never entirely at his ease with the ladies of "high" society.

"At least," he often said, "those creatures had good hearts. They were kind and generous, and that is more than can be said for a lot of others with better reputations."

Dance music was what the people in the taverns wanted, and Hannes would sometimes relieve the monotony by improvising variations on the popular waltzes of the day. But what finally made his work endurable was the discovery that while his fingers were mechanically pounding out familiar tunes on the broken-down piano, he could at the same time read a book.

Night after night—often until the small hours of the morning—little Hannes played on. Propped above the keyboard would be a volume of poems or adventure. And he was not too unhappy, because now he had learned to escape from his cheap surroundings into the realm of imagination, beauty, and romance.

Soon Hannes became quite celebrated for his playing in the dance-halls. His services were in demand even at country hotels and private homes. On Sundays he was often engaged to entertain the patrons of an inn a few miles outside of Hamburg.

One afternoon a youngster named Christian Miller came over and spoke to the boy as he sat there at the piano.

"You play very well," he remarked.

Hannes' pale face flushed with pleasure. "Thank you, *mein Herr,*" he answered. "It is nothing to play dance tunes. I can do classical music much better."

"I thought so," Christian exclaimed. "Because, you see, well—I play the piano a little myself. Wouldn't it be fun to try some duets together? What do you say?"

Young Brahms was delighted. There had not been much time in his life for friendship—he had always had to work too hard. The companionship of Christian Miller was a welcome new experience, and the two boys soon became intimates. They often played the piano together at the country inn where they had met, amusing themselves and the patrons with four-handed variations on popular melodies which young Brahms had arranged in his leisure moments.

Christian sometimes accompanied Johannes on his long walks to and from the country inn. On these excursions Hannes usually carried his hat in his hand. It was a habit that always remained with him; he liked, he said, to feel the breeze blowing through his hair. On these trips, according to Christian Miller, young Brahms seldom spoke, but walked along humming to himself—as if music were more familiar to him than words.

Hannes was not always solemn—far from it! He could be as full of fun and wild pranks as any boy. With Christian he worked out a scheme which they both found hugely entertaining. They would knock at the door of a house where, perhaps a century before, some illustrious citizen of Hamburg had once lived.

"Is Herr Georg Friedrich Handel at home?" they would ask with great seriousness.

"Herr Handel?" The housewife would look puzzled. "Why, no—I don't know anyone by that name."

"Are you quite sure now?" the young rascals would insist with feigned astonishment. "We understood that this was his house. . . ." Then they would hurry off, shaking with laughter.

One Sunday following a long afternoon of playing

at the country inn, Hannes was very tired, and as soon as he got home he went straight to bed.

Late that evening there was a loud knock at the Brahms' door.

"Who's there?" called Jakob in his broad Low-German.

A servant in elegant livery stood outside. "Is the young piano-player at home?" he inquired arrogantly.

"Yes, but he's in bed asleep."

"Then wake him up!" the servant continued, looking with scorn at the humble furnishings of the tiny flat. "My master wants him to come and play for his guests."

Jakob grunted. "What will he pay?"

"Two thalers, and all he can drink!"

Father Brahms scratched his head. That was an offer not to be sneezed at. "Up you get, Hannes!" he called, and pulled the sleepy boy out of bed.

Life was a little easier now for the Brahms family since Hannes brought home his earnings from the dance-halls. But the boy's health began to suffer from the late hours, the smoke-filled air, and the strenuous work. He was none too strong to begin with. Now he began to have violent headaches, like his sister Elise. Some days he could hardly sit at the piano.

Frau Brahms was very much concerned. Even Jakob could see that something must be done. It was near the end of the season, and there would be less demand for Hannes' services during the summer months. If only some way could be found to send the boy into the country. . . .

The Alster Pavilion, where Herr Brahms now played the bass-viol, was picturesquely situated on the shore of the Alster Basin. This restaurant attracted not only the people of Hamburg but also visitors from the country. A certain Herr Giesemann of Winsen, a small village some twenty miles from Hamburg, often came to the city on business, and he usually dropped in at the Alster Pavilion to have a glass of beer and listen to the music.

He and Jakob Brahms had become friendly. "We are all lovers of music in our family," Herr Giesemann told the bass-player. "I myself play the guitar, my wife sings, and we have a small daughter named Lieschen who, one of these days, shall learn to accompany us on the piano."

Jakob at once spoke of his son. "You should hear my Hannes," he said proudly. "*He* plays the piano like a great artist!"

Now Father Brahms, racking his brains to think of a way of sending Hannes to the country, remembered his conversations with the gentleman from Winsen. The next time Herr Giesemann came to the Alster Pavilion, Jakob left his bass at the first intermission and went to sit beside him.

"Once, *mein Herr,* you said you wanted your young Fräulein to learn to play the piano. Is that right?"

"Even so," answered Giesemann, puffing at his pipe. "She is almost old enough to begin now."

"Ach, really?" cried Jakob eagerly. "But that is perfect!" He drew his chair closer. "You know I've told you how wonderfully my Hannes plays. Why, the great Marxsen teaches him for nothing because he is so talented." When he spoke of his son, Jakob's voice trembled with pride. "But lately I've been a bit worried about the boy. He's been working too hard. . . ."

Father Brahms leaned closer across the table and beamed at his companion. *"Ach,* Herr Giesemann, you should know my Hannes. Such a boy!—such a *good* boy; everyone loves him." Jakob's eyes grew moist with emotion. "He is not sick, you understand, just thin and run down. He needs a little country air.

"How would it be now—" Jakob went on, hesitating; "what would you think, for instance, if my Hannes should give your Lieschen piano lessons in return for a little stay with you in the country? He could accompany you too when you play the guitar."

"A splendid idea!" cried Herr Giesemann. "Let me talk to my wife about it. If she is agreeable the boy shall come at once."

Two weeks later Johannes was on his way to Winsen.

CHAPTER IV

INTRODUCTION TO THE COUNTRY

BEFORE he was really awake, Hannes became conscious of unfamiliar and enchanting sounds. It was just daybreak; birds were beginning to sing in the apple tree outside his window, twittering softly as if they too were just waking up. He could hear the bleating of a lamb, and the gentle whinny of a horse.

How different this was from his usual awakening in the slums of Hamburg, where wheels clattered over the cobblestones, and peddlers shrieked their wares! The boy half-opened his eyes. Over his head were the rafters of a peaked gable roof. No—it wasn't a dream after all! He really was in Winsen, on a farm miles away from town.

His arrival the evening before still seemed like a dream. Good Frau Giesemann looked concerned when she greeted him. "My poor child! But how pale you are, and thin. It's plenty of good milk you need, and butter and eggs to fatten you up."

Hiding behind her mother in a starched pink pinafore was little Lieschen. In honor of the occasion she had woven cherry-colored ribbons into her long yellow pigtails. Hannes, however, was too tired to notice much.

Now he stretched himself drowsily in the unaccustomed luxury of a feather-bed. Suddenly, just under his window, a rooster crowed. The city-bred child jumped like a jack-in-the-box. He listened a moment; no one was stirring in the house. It was not much after four o'clock (May dawns come early in northern Germany), but Hannes was too excited to think of going back to sleep. He pulled on his shirt and trousers and, wooden clogs in hand, tiptoed downstairs.

In the orchard below the house, the sun was coming up through a veil of cherry blossoms. What freshness there was in this country air! None of the stench here of decaying food and poor sanitation which lay heavy upon the tenement quarter of Hamburg. Instead, the fragrance of clean growing things, and—silence.

At least it seemed like silence to him after the noisy

streets of Hamburg! But gradually he realized that the stillness was filled with music. There was the wind humming through the orchard trees, the tinkling water of a brook, songs of birds and insects—dozens of new sounds.

For the first time in his life Hannes heard the voice of Nature. He had to listen very carefully to catch the overtones. . . . He stood so still, straining his ears so eagerly, that presently he was no longer conscious of listening, but felt himself actually a part of that deep, melodious silence.

Just then a flock of noisy pigeons flew over the boy's head and broke the spell. He came out of his dream with a start, and tumbled back to earth. The beautiful moment was gone. But it left a never-to-be-forgotten impression. Now Hannes knew where he could go to find inspiration—outdoors, close to Nature! If he could recapture that brief sense of unity, then he felt sure he would be able to write great music.

Still in a daze, Hannes walked through the orchard and out into the fields. He smiled as he saw how the morning dew clung to his wooden clogs like little round notes of music. He began to whistle them softly to himself. Everything, this perfect morning, seemed to make him think of music!

An enticing path sauntered away from the field through a thicket of hazel bushes bordered with daisies and buttercups. Following it he came upon the River

Luhe. The clear water looked so inviting that impulsively he stripped off his clothes and plunged in.

Later, as he walked back to the house, he saw little Lieschen coming towards him. She was skipping along the path, twirling her sunbonnet in one hand and humming a gay tune. Hannes, who was all ears this music-bright morning, listened in delight.

"Morning, Hannes," called the child, forgetting her shyness of the evening before. "I thought I'd be the first one out, but you beat me, didn't you? Have you seen the new lamb, and the baby chicks—and the two spotted calves?"

Johannes had never been on a farm before. Everything fascinated him. But before he went to see the animals there was something important—"You have a nice voice, Lieschen," he said shyly. He drew a notebook from his pocket. "Do you mind if I write down that tune you were singing as you came up the path?"

Lieschen's eyes grew as round as the notes of dew on Hannes' clogs. "Can you *write* music?" she asked. "I thought only great musicians— Oh-h-h, may I see your book?"

Reluctantly Hannes showed her his precious notebook, curiously ruled with the horizontal lines dear to musicians. This he always carried with him. Whenever he thought of something special, down he would jot it. The entry might be just a few words on the margin, or a line of verse that popped into his head as he walked along. But more often it was a musical phrase, which would have been lost if he had not caught it and fixed it at once on paper, as a collector of butterflies impales what he has netted.

By the time the two children went in to breakfast, Johannes was ravenously hungry. Never had anything tasted so good as the crusty chunks of rye bread which he and Lieschen broke into their bowls of foaming milk. Frau Giesemann exclaimed with pleasure at the boy's appetite. As fast as he drained his mug she filled it from the big pitcher.

"Lieschen is off to school each morning," Herr Giesemann told the young guest. "Late in the afternoon when she returns you shall give her a piano lesson." (Lieschen made a face behind his back!) "But during the daytime we have decided that you must be out of doors as much as possible."

Hannes could hardly wait to be off. "Here is some lunch to take with you," Frau Giesemann called, handing him a generous-sized package.

"Thank you, gracious lady!" he cried, in the formal style his mother had taught him.

"Na, na, since you are to be a member of the family we must not be so formal," she answered, beaming on him maternally. "You shall call us 'Aunt Lisel' and 'Uncle Adolf.' "

Hannes started off whistling. On his back was a knapsack with his lunch and a story book to read, in his pocket the precious notebook, and under his arm the silent-clavier. For, while exploring the countryside, he did not intend to neglect his practice. He could sit by the edge of the river, or beneath the trees in the woods, and exercise his fingers while he reveled in this surprising adventure of being out in the country. The very air seemed filled with music. He wanted to write it all down. . . .

Weeks went by, and Johannes grew strong and rosy under Aunt Lisel's motherly care. Every morning he was up at dawn, and down to the river for a swim. Then Lieschen would meet him and the two would walk through field and forest, hunting birds' nests and wild flowers, and exploring new paths.

There were children in the neighboring village who sometimes came over to play after school. The boys were mostly country yokels who cared only for wrestling and other rough sports. Hannes, on the other hand, had a quiet, more imaginative temperament; he was unusually small for his age, and could not hold his own among the husky, overgrown lads brought up in the country. He preferred the society of the girls, and because of this the boys often teased him and took advantage of his weakness.

One evening after a game in the river, when the youngsters had been splashing about and chasing each other along the shallow banks, Lieschen started ahead with some of the girls. Heinrich—the ringleader of the boys, younger than Hannes but a good head taller—pounced on the city visitor with a shout.

"Sissy!" he cried. "You're nothing but a sissy, you are! Here, Otto, let's give him a good ducking and see how he likes it."

Before Hannes could collect his wits the young ruffians pushed him, gasping, into the water. Then while he was spluttering and trying to catch his breath, they emptied his pockets and made off with the contents.

Johannes suddenly realized that his notebook was gone. This was the last straw. "You *devils!"* he sobbed, staggering after the jeering boys. *"Devils!*—give me back my book . . ."

Lieschen heard the commotion and, as fast as she could run, came to the rescue. "Heinrich—Otto—Wolfgang—bring Hannes' things here *quick*. You'll catch it—just you see! My father . . ." Her breath gave out before she finished her threat, but the boys decided it was better to play safe. They dropped Johannes' belongings and vanished.

Lieschen put her arms around her friend and tried to comfort him. "They're gone now—don't you care. And here are your things."

Hannes was already consoled, for the precious notebook had scarcely been harmed at all.

Like most plain country people the Giesemanns did not have much use for books. Hannes had soon read through their limited library. He was in the habit of taking a volume with him on his rambles through the country, and when he sat down to exercise on his silent-clavier he would read at the same time.

"I wish I knew where I could find some more books," he said to Lieschen one day.

She puckered up her forehead and pulled thoughtfully on one yellow braid. "In the village there's a lending library run by Frau Löwenherz."

Hannes' face lighted up, but his expression soon changed. "I suppose it would cost a lot of money to *rent* books?"

"Her boy Aaron is in my class; I'll ask him."

Aaron had an eye to business. "Of course it does come high if you rent them through the library," he agreed. "But—" he winked at Lieschen slyly, "I might be able to find what you want for, say, a penny apiece. Mother need never know."

The children thought they were getting a good bargain. By pooling their small resources they managed always to have a volume on hand. Hannes introduced Lieschen to the delights of reading. The two would sit for hours under a tree in the woods, or fishing from the river bank, reading together from the same book.

They usually asked Aaron to find them stories of adventure. One day he brought a volume entitled *The Beautiful Magelone and the Knight Peter with the Silver Keys.* Hannes and Lieschen found themselves in a new world as they read this romantic story. It made such an impression on the sensitive young Brahms that years later he wrote one of his most famous song-cycles around the tale of Magelone and her knight Peter.

On Sunday mornings Johannes went with the Giesemanns to the Lutheran church in Winsen, to hear Rector Köhler preach. Following the services they returned to a lavish midday dinner, and after that it was the family's custom to gather with some music-loving friends at an inn in the neighboring village of Hoopte. There was a piano in the main room of this tavern, and the afternoon was spent in singing, playing, and dancing.

On Hannes' first Sunday in Winsen Herr Giesemann proudly introduced his small guest from Hamburg. "This young gentleman is a *real* musician!" he announced to his friends. "Johannes is a pupil of the great Marxsen, if you please. He can play anything on the piano."

The assembled company were all properly impressed. They immediately asked Hannes to perform, and when he sat down and gave them a spirited waltz, which he proceeded to weave into endless variations each more complicated than the last, they were as enthusiastic as if a world-renowned artist had appeared among them.

The little village of Winsen and its neighboring sister, Hoopte, seldom had an opportunity to hear good music. One or two of the country people could perform modestly on the guitar or accordion, or pound out a dance tune on the piano; but their main music came from the singing of a small choral society. The twelve members of this group were mostly schoolteachers, with a few tradespeople, including Herr Meyer, the goldsmith of Hoopte, and the master-baker Rieckmann of Winsen.

When these gentlemen saw what a fine musician Herr Giesemann had brought from Hamburg, they asked young Brahms if he would conduct their choral group the following week. Johannes was flattered. . . .

On Saturday they all met at Rector Köhler's home to practice (he was the only member who had a piano). The twelve singers took their place around the billiard table, while little Hannes in a fresh white shirt with turned-down collar, his fair hair hanging almost to his shoulders, climbed upon a chair at one end of the table, so that he could more easily be seen.

The rehearsal went famously. When the group sang on Sunday afternoon at the Hoopte Inn under their new conductor's direction, the members were so pleased at the result that they asked Hannes to continue leading them as long as he stayed in Winsen.

He took his new responsibilities very seriously, beating time with great emphasis, and insisting on perfect pitch, tempo, and expression. He did not spare the singers. "Herr Schröder, that E was a little flat—come now, it must be higher," he would call severely. Or—to the burly baker who loved to make his bass notes sound—*"Nein, nein,* Herr Rieckmann. Not so loud. You drown the others out!"

Herr Schröder, the schoolteacher of Hoopte, sang tenor in the Winsen Choral Society, and knew more about music than any of the other members. He had studied harmony and counterpoint.

"If you need help at any time with your composing, my boy," he told Johannes, "come to me, and I may be able to set you straight."

One morning Hannes decided he would take advantage of this offer and call on Herr Schröder in his nearby village. He thought he knew just how to get there, by a short cut through the woods.

Late that afternoon a group of schoolchildren came to the Giesemanns' to ask a favor of Hannes.

"I can't imagine what is keeping him!" Frau Giesemann said, looking anxiously down the road. "He should have been here some time ago for Lieschen's lesson."

This, Lieschen was not sorry to get out of. The piano bored her terribly. But she was worried about Hannes.

They had almost decided to send out a search party for him when suddenly, with a great clatter of wheels and cracking of whip, up drove a neighbor from Pattenzen.

"Here is your Hannes," he cried. "He lost his way this morning, and as luck would have it I came by and found him asleep by the side of the road, way off towards Lüneburg. His clavier was by his side, and—"

"My notebook!" cried Hannes, feeling in his pocket. "I've lost my notebook. . . ."

The driver's shoulders shook with good-natured laughter. "I knew you'd be looking for that!" he said, handing the book to the boy. "It almost fell off into the ditch; and so did *you,* for that matter."

"A 'committee' has come to call on you, Hannes," said Frau Giesemann. "Some of the schoolchildren want you to help them plan a surprise serenade for Rector Köhler's birthday."

Hannes was secretly gratified to find Heinrich and Otto, his former enemies, in the group. Now that his skill as a musician was known all through the neighborhood, they no longer teased him or made fun of him. They even looked on his famous notebook with respect, for Lieschen had told them it was in this that—wonder of wonders!—he wrote down the songs which later could be sung by whole groups of people. In those days music was held in the highest esteem by everyone—even the children.

Young Brahms arranged several songs and rehearsed the youngsters until they knew their parts perfectly. Herr Köhler's birthday was a very special event in Winsen. All the villagers joined to honor their Rector. It was a holiday for the whole community. Everyone dressed up. The little girls were dazzling in white dresses with quantities of stiffly starched petticoats, and hair in long corkscrew curls; while the boys had paid elaborate attention to polishing their boots (and faces), and felt very important and uncomfortable in their Sunday suits. With Hannes at their head, the children took their places under Herr Köhler's window. Groups of friends who had also come to present gifts and compliments gathered in the background to listen. Then Johannes turned to his chorus and gave the signal to begin. Fresh young voices broke into song—up went the window over their heads, and out peered the Rector's smiling face.

The serenade made a considerable stir, and everyone congratulated Hannes.

One Sunday afternoon, at the weekly singing of the Winsen Choral Society, a distinguished-looking gentleman with white hair came in and took a seat at the back of the room. When the music was over Herr Giesemann drew Hannes aside.

"Did you see who was here today?" he asked, in evident gratification.

"You mean the old gentleman who sat by himself back there?"

Uncle Adolf shook his head reproachfully. "Don't you know? That is the distinguished Judge Blume; and he wants to meet you."

It was Johannes' turn to be impressed. Everyone thought highly of the District Judge. Hannes had heard of him, and had hoped that some day he might make the old gentleman's acquaintance, for he was said to be an excellent musician and he owned the best pianoforte for miles around.

"My wife and I would be glad if you would come over and play for us," Herr Blume told the boy. "Perhaps we could do some duets together. I have a fine collection of Beethoven's music."

Frau Blume took a great fancy to the shy, fair-haired boy. During the latter part of Johannes' stay in Winsen he frequently went over to the old Judge's house to play duets with him (always it was Beethoven), and to practice on the piano.

Weekly young Brahms rehearsed the Choral Society, and on Sunday afternoons led their singing. When the men learned that he could compose as well as play and conduct, they asked him if he would write a part-song for them.

Since the group was made up chiefly of schoolteachers, Hannes used the alphabet as his theme, with musical accompaniment. He started with A, B, and C, and all the following letters; then he put these into combinations of syllables, like a spelling lesson. As an ending to the song the words "Winsen, eighteen hundred seven-and-forty" were sung in full chorus, *lento* and *fortissimo*. It produced a fine effect, and Hannes was so encouraged that he wrote another spirited number for the Society called *The Postilion's Morning Song*.

When Marxsen had first learned that his star pupil was planning to leave Hamburg for a long stay in the country he was disturbed.

"It would never do for the boy to stop his practice and lessons just now," he told Father Brahms.

"Ja, ja, that's right, Herr Professor," said Jakob, who had already thought of a plan. "But it's not necessary he should stop. You know there is a river boat direct from Winsen to Hamburg, and he could come down by it each week for his lesson."

Every Wednesday, therefore, Hannes took the afternoon boat to Hamburg, stayed over night with his family, and spent the day following in study and practice and in going to Herr Marxsen for his lesson. Frau Brahms was overjoyed to have her dear Hannes at home for a weekly visit. She missed him sadly during the rest of the time.

"You must bring Fräulein Lieschen with you whenever her family will let her come," said Johanna. "She can share Elise's room. We should try to repay a little the Giesemanns' kindness to you!"

Uncle Adolf and Aunt Lisel had such confidence in Johannes, and Lieschen begged so hard to go with him to Hamburg, that finally her parents consented. Herr Giesemann's brother was in charge of the restaurant on the river boat, and the two children were placed in his care. The weekly excursion became a real holiday for them.

Lieschen never forgot their first trip down the river to Hamburg. Aunt Lisel gave the two children a bountiful lunch: slices of fresh, crusty bread, with meat and cheese and liverwurst between. In addition, Lieschen's uncle contributed cakes and coffee. The children sat in the stern of the boat and watched the river apparently hurrying back past them to Winsen. Hannes meanwhile practiced on his silent-clavier.

When they reached Hamburg, its noisy wharves and crowded streets intimidated Lieschen, who was not used to cities. She wondered how Hannes could ever find his way home. But he did not hesitate; he took his small companion by the hand, and in a few minutes they reached the Damthorwall, where the Brahms family were then living. Lieschen privately thought it a very poor quarter. She was impressed, however, by Frau Brahms' tiny shop, and when Hannes' mother limped to greet her with arms outstretched in welcome, the girl felt at home.

Lieschen took a great fancy to Frau Brahms. She followed her about, begged to be allowed to wait on the customers in the shop, and tried to help her in every way she could think of. In the evening, when Johanna started down the steep stairs from the apartment to fetch water from the courtyard below, Lieschen insisted on taking the pail from her and filling it.

Hannes began at once to practice. There was now a small upright piano in the Brahms parlor, but not much else. The room seemed very bare to Lieschen, though she was impressed by the shelves of books, and noticed how neat and shining everything was kept.

But she missed the light and sunshine of her country home. The apartment was very dark. Its windows looked out onto a bare, narrow court. What a contrast, the little country visitor thought, to the sunny fields and green trees of Winsen!

"It is sad that your mother has no pretty outlook from her window," she said to Hannes.

The boy sighed. "We are used to that."

Lieschen thought a moment. Then she had a bright idea. "If you had a window-box," she said, "we could plant something that would grow fast—something with pretty flowers, so your mother wouldn't have to look out into that ugly courtyard. I know—scarlet-rambler beans!"

On the next trip to Hamburg the children brought some bean seeds and planted them in a box outside the parlor window, setting high sticks to support the vines. Lieschen could hardly wait for the bower of green and scarlet flowers which were to delight Frau Brahms.

But the sun could not reach the window in the dark courtyard. To the children's great disappointment the beans refused to grow.

CHAPTER V

HANNES HEARS AN OPERA

HANNES found it very hard to say good-by to his friends in Winsen. He hated to leave the carefree country life and return to the drudgery of Hamburg. But Uncle Adolf assured him before he left, "Next year you shall come back to us again." With another summer in the country to look forward to, Johannes felt he could stand anything—even the hateful work in the Hamburg dance-halls.

The boy's health had been immensely improved by his long holiday. During the months spent in Winsen that summer and the year following, Brahms laid the foundation for a constitution of exceptional vigor. In later years his energy was a marvel to his friends.

Johannes found it difficult to settle back into the strenuous routine of life in Hamburg. Every day was filled with practicing and composing. In addition he gave a number of piano lessons, which took a good deal of his time but brought in very little—only one mark each, or about 25 cents in our money. Until the small hours, he played at dance-halls. And this work provided his family, not with luxuries, but with the bare necessities of life.

No wonder that later, in speaking of his youth, Brahms said, "Few others can have had so hard a time." And yet he did not regret those early hardships, for he declared that they had helped to form his character and to train him for serious work.

On his return to the city, however, he missed most of all the bracing country air and the excursions through fields and woods. Whenever he could spare a few hours he would walk into the country beyond Hamburg. Without these occasional escapes he would not have been able to stand the hardships of his life.

Brahms always kept his deep love for the outdoors. It was his daily habit to take long walks alone. These solitary communings with Nature were a necessity to him, for in them he found the chief inspiration for his music.

A few weeks after his return to Hamburg, Johannes found his teacher much upset.

"I have just received terrible news from Leipzig," Marxsen said. "Mendelssohn died last night."

"Mendelssohn!" Hannes was almost as shocked as his teacher. "Why, he was very young."

"Only thirty-eight," Marxsen groaned; "and now—

cut off in his prime, just as Schubert and Mozart were."

Marxsen had often told Johannes that, in his opinion, Felix Mendelssohn-Bartholdy was the greatest composer since Beethoven. Born of a Jewish father and a Christian mother, this composer had enjoyed a life very different from the sordid, poverty-stricken existence of young Brahms. Mendelssohn's family was distinguished and wealthy, and during his childhood he had been given every possible educational advantage.

"Yes—" Marxsen continued, pacing up and down the room; "in a number of ways he was like Mozart and Schubert. He too began to compose when he was a mere child. . . ."

Johannes had heard the story of young Felix Mendelssohn's achievements many times before, but it never failed to inspire him.

"Why, before the boy was eleven he had already written over fifty different works! Then, during his next year, he composed five symphonies and two operas —think of it! And besides this a number of songs, piano pieces, and string quartets. Colossal, eh? He was only seventeen when he wrote that heavenly overture to *A Midsummer Night's Dream!*"

Marxsen shook his head sadly. "The English especially will be heartbroken to hear that he is dead. Every tour to England was a triumph for him. Only last spring he was there. But the trip was too much for him —too many concerts and parties. Then when he came back from England there was the awful shock of his sister Fanny's death, which knocked him out completely. They adored each other, you know."

Marxsen rambled on: "You should have seen him, Hannes! He was the handsomest man that ever lived—fine-cut, sensitive face, large expressive dark eyes, waving black hair. He could draw and paint, too. He had everything!

"Now that he is gone, maybe people will realize how much they owe to Mendelssohn. If it hadn't been for him we might never have known the true greatness of Bach. The old Cantor was forgotten after he died; his music was hardly ever played until Mendelssohn resurrected it. Yes, Felix Bartholdy was a real classicist. Who will take his place now?"

Marxsen stopped suddenly in front of Johannes and stared at him fixedly. "My boy—" his voice was solemn —"*you* are the one who shall carry on!"

Johannes was now ready, his teacher felt, to come before the public as a finished artist. Accordingly, a week apart in late November, two concerts were arranged. There were other performers, but apparently young Brahms' playing created a sensation. One newspaper reported:

> A very special impression was made by the performance of one of Thalberg's fantasias by a little virtuoso called J. Brahms, who not only showed great facility, precision, clearness, power, and certainty, but occasioned general surprise and obtained unanimous applause by the intelligence of his interpretation.

Marxsen's faith in his pupil had justified itself. He had always been sure that a fine future was in store for Johannes. "A great master of the musical art has gone," he said in speaking of Mendelssohn's death; "but mark my words—an even greater will be found in Johannes Brahms."

As long as he lived, Brahms was grateful to both of his teachers, Cossel and Marxsen, and later in life he helped them whenever he could. Marxsen wrote quantities of music, but he was far from being a great composer, and not much of his work was ever printed. Shortly before he died, Brahms gave him a rare pleasure. At his own secret expense he had one of Marxsen's longer compositions published.

Jakob Brahms had now realized his greatest ambition: he was a double-bass player in the Hamburg Philharmonic Orchestra. One day in February 1848 he came home from a rehearsal with good news for Johannes.

"Next month," he announced, "there is to be a concert by that fine violinist you've been wanting to hear."

"You don't mean *Joachim?"* asked Hannes in excitement.

"Ja, ja—the Hungarian fiddler who's been making such a stir."

Joseph Joachim was only seventeen years old, but already he was celebrated throughout Europe. He had begun his career at the age of seven and, by the time he was ten, had given concerts in most of the Continental capitals. He played brilliantly, and everywhere his audiences went wild with enthusiasm.

As soon as Johannes learned that Joachim was to give a concert in Hamburg he began to save up his pennies for a ticket. The top gallery was the best he could afford; but of all the large audience that crowded to hear the violinist, young Brahms was, as he admitted in later years, "surely the most enthusiastic." Sitting there in his gallery seat, worshiping from afar, he would have been overcome with amazement if he had known that this young artist whom everyone acclaimed with such adulation was to become his dearest friend.

Hannes had no money left to buy a program. He heard someone sitting near him say, "Herr Joachim is giving a number of his own compositions this evening," and took it for granted that the concert was to be made up entirely of the gifted young performer's own works; for indeed Joachim was said to be a fine composer as well as violinist.

The Hungarian played magnificently, with dazzling technique. One number, a concerto with orchestra (Hannes could see Father Brahms in the rear, sawing away enthusiastically on his *Kunterbass*), the boy thought a real marvel. He was, in fact, quite carried away by the composition. "I was in a very chaos of emotion," he told Joachim when he met him some years later.

Hannes spoke especially of this number to his teacher, marveling that Joachim could have written such a masterpiece. Marxsen smiled. "You are quite right, Hannes—it *is* a remarkable composition; but Joachim didn't write it. That concerto was composed by Beethoven!"

These days young Brahms spent a good deal of time in writing music. He had discovered that it was profitable to make arrangements of various popular tunes. Though he did not consider it *music* in the best sense of the word, he could sell the stuff for real money (perhaps because it was such trash!), and this was a thing that Hannes desperately needed. As he could not bring himself to put his own name to these arrangements, he compromised by signing them "G. W. Marks."

At the same time he continued to work on his own original compositions. Hardly a day went by that he did not set down some new theme, or variations on waltz tunes (he wrote 150 of these waltz-variations during this period), fantasias of operas, songs, and orchestral potpourris. Some of these were not too bad, Hannes thought (he was always his own sternest critic), but still they were not so good as he expected to be able to write.

Even in his earliest days, Johannes Brahms had exceptionally high standards for his work. Nothing but necessity would have persuaded him to send out anything he considered less than the best he could do. While the original pieces he wrote at that time were a little better than the arrangements of "G. W. Marks," he was still not satisfied with them.

The publishers, however, were willing—even anxious—to accept them. Again Johannes compromised and chose a second pseudonym: "Karl Würth." Before Johannes Brahms had published Opus 1, the number of "Herr Marks'" works had already reached Opus 151! Later he took still another name: "J. Kreisler, Jun."

This constant writing of music had one good effect. It developed a remarkable memory in young Brahms.

One fine morning in May 1848 Hannes packed up his few belongings in a battered old carpetbag, tucked his faithful silent-clavier under his arm, and walked down to the wharf to take the river boat for Winsen.

It came chugging down the river, just as it used to the summer before when he and Lieschen went back and forth every week. And there, waving to him from the deck, was "Uncle" Adolf's brother.

On the Winsen wharf, all Johannes' friends were waiting to greet him. Even old Judge Blume was there. "The piano is ready for you whenever you want to practice," he said; "and how about our duets?" Hannes was so happy to be back in Winsen again that he threw his carpetbag into the air with an exultant whoop.

This summer Lieschen seemed rather grown up, and just a little in awe of her former playmate. Hannes, however, had not changed so much. Although he was now fifteen, he looked much younger, and his voice had not begun to deepen.

He spent a good deal of time with the Choral Society, and wrote for it several clever arrangements of country folk tunes. Brahms always liked to use folk melodies in his music. Those he arranged that summer for the Winsen singers were the first of a long succession which later included his famous Hungarian dances that were based on gypsy folk tunes.

Hannes told Uncle Adolf about Joachim's concert in Hamburg, and how tremendously he had been impressed by the violinist's playing. Herr Giesemann was interested, but not particularly.

"Concerts are all very well," he agreed; "but for my part I prefer singing. Especially the opera. . . ."

Johannes had to admit that he had never been to an opera.

"Never been to an opera!" cried Uncle Adolf. "And you such a good musician. No; I can hardly believe it!"

A few days after, as Hannes was preparing to embark for his usual weekly lesson with Marxsen, Herr Giesemann handed him a little envelope.

"I understand they are giving Mozart's *Marriage of Figaro* tomorrow evening at the Opera House. Lieschen has not heard this opera—nor you either, I take it?" he added, with a wink at his young visitor. "You shall go as my guests, the two of you."

The children were wildly excited at the prospect. All the way down the river they talked about the opera, and Hannes told Lieschen what he knew about Mozart.

"He was the greatest composer of all," said the boy with enthusiasm. "At least, my father thinks so! Mozart began writing music when he was only five years old, and soon after that he was playing in concerts all over

Europe. My father thought *I* was going to be another Mozart." He gave a wry smile, for he had not forgotten the incident of the impresario. "*Figaro* was written in Vienna, six years before Mozart died. He only lived to be thirty-five, you know—not even so old as Mendelssohn; but during those few years he wrote more fine music than any other composer ever had written in such a short time."

As soon as Hannes finished his piano lesson, he and Lieschen went down to the Opera House to get their tickets. It was hours before the theater opened, but since Uncle Adolf could only afford to give them unreserved places in the gallery, they wanted to be sure of front-row seats. Frau Brahms had provided packets of sandwiches, and they ate supper as they waited in line for the box-office to open.

The two children were in the seventh heaven. Everything interested them. They had never before been in an opera house. On their way up the long flights to the fifth gallery, they peeked into the restaurant where, during intermissions, the more elegant patrons refreshed themselves with beer and sausages.

From their high seats they looked down into the grand boxes of the First Tier, brilliant with jewels, gleaming with white bosoms and whiter shirt-fronts. Lieschen admired the painted curtain that hung before the stage, and the enormous gas chandeliers so close over their heads. But Hannes was more interested in the people around them. None but music-lovers were willing to climb so high for the privilege of listening; for, back of the first two or three rows, little of the stage was visible. Hannes and Lieschen thought themselves lucky to be in the front row.

Then the lights were dimmed and the music of the prelude began. Mozart was at his best when he wrote *Figaro,* and the overture is a masterpiece of rollicking melody. Hannes was familiar with the music, but now, in the hushed dimness of the vast theater, it took on an added beauty and glamour.

"Lieschen, Lieschen!" he whispered during the applause that followed the overture. "Did you ever listen to such music?"

But his companion did not even hear him. For the curtain was just rising, and she sat on the edge of her seat, breathless with anticipation.

Now Johannes' second summer at Winsen was drawing to a close. Sadly he realized that in the future he would probably never again have time for such a long, carefree, happy holiday. Marxsen now considered young Brahms a fully trained musician, equipped to go out into the world and earn a living for himself and his family.

Just before he left Winsen, the Choral Society planned a special farewell party for its young conductor. All the friends and relatives of the singers were invited, and a large party gathered at the inn in Hoopte. The concert that opened the evening was devoted chiefly to the songs that Johannes had written for the Society. First the "A B C" chorus ("Winsen, eighteen hundred seven-and-forty"—only this year they sang it "eight-and-forty"), and then the folk-song arrangements which he had composed that same summer.

An elaborate feast followed, to which each house-mother of the community had contributed some specialty. After this there were speeches by various members and by Herr Giesemann and the old Judge. Then, rising, Hannes drew a rolled paper from his pocket, cleared his throat, and—in his still childish treble and with fine dramatic style—read a poem he had written specially for the occasion:

> Farewell, farewell, ye friends upright and simple . . .

It was not much of a poem, but it touched the good citizens of Winsen. When Hannes finished, there was silence for a moment. Then came a tremendous clapping and shouting and stamping of feet. Herr Rieckmann, the big master-baker, took the boy on his back and marched him around the room, while the rest of the company followed, all of them singing at the top of their voices.

Johannes was to leave by the next day's boat. As he walked back to the farm with the Giesemanns, his heart was heavy. Lieschen knew how he felt. She was sad too. She slipped her hand into his, but no one said a word.

Later, just as the little girl was starting upstairs to bed, Hannes called to her. "Here is something for you," he said, thrusting a manuscript into her hand, and running off before she could even say "thank you." "It's a farewell present," he called over his shoulder.

When she opened the manuscript she found it was a copy of the four-part songs which Hannes had composed for the Choral Society. It was written in his neatest style and embellished with scrolls and fancy lettering. On the title page stood Lieschen's name with a special dedication. This manuscript always remained one of the girl's most treasured possessions.

When Hannes went back to his little room under the eaves, he stood for a while looking out of the window. A full moon shone over the orchard and meadows, and laid a wide band of silver across the distant stream. The crickets made a soft, chirruping music; fireflies sparkled under the trees, and the fragrance of new-mown hay filled the air. Hannes wondered if ever in his life again he would be as peaceful and happy as at that moment.

Twenty years later, in a letter to his old playmate he wrote:

> The remembrance of your parents' house is one of the dearest that I possess. All the kindness and love that were shown me, all the youthful pleasure and happiness that I enjoyed there, lie secure in my heart with the image of your good father and the glad, grateful memory of you all.

CHAPTER VI

"A GREAT COMPOSER, MY HANNES!"

"A SECOND concert my Hannes is to give!" Jakob announced during the intermission of a Hamburg Philharmonic rehearsal. *"Ja,"* he went on; "the first one, last fall after his second summer at Winsen, was such a success that Herr Marxsen insists he give another. You shall see, my Hannes will be the greatest pianist in the world. *Ja,* already—"

The men in the orchestra nudged each other. Jakob Brahms was really tiresome about that sixteen-year-old of his. "I suppose you never heard of Rubinstein," they jeered. "And what about Liszt?—one of the finest pianists that ever lived, and a great composer as well!"

Jakob was a little crestfallen; then he brightened. "My Hannes—*he* writes music too! He's going to play one of his own pieces at that concert. See—" he pulled out a copy of the program his son was to give, and read aloud, laboriously: " 'Fantasia for Piano on a Favorite Waltz, composed and performed by the concert-giver.' And just see this," the proud father continued, pointing to another line, "he's to play Beethoven's *Waldstein* Sonata! Only a great artist can master *that* piece. *Ja, ja,* he's coming up in the world, my Hannes is. Last fall the tickets to his concert cost only one mark each; but this time Herr Marxsen says we must charge two, because the first concert was such a hit."

The second appearance of young Brahms—now sixteen years old—proved quite as successful as the first. The hall was so crowded that some people even had to sit on the stage. But in spite of the good attendance Hannes made very little actual money; too many expenses had been involved. After this second attempt he did not give another concert, at least entirely his own, for nearly ten years.

Meanwhile he continued to play at the taverns and to teach. Also he had occasional engagements as accompanist at the Town Theater, and was sometimes asked to assist on the programs of other artists, or to play at the homes of wealthy Hamburg citizens.

At the same time he kept on going to the piano factory of Baumgarten & Heinz, where, since first starting his lessons with Herr Cossel, years before, he had been given the privilege of practicing. Here he was free of the interruptions that made working at home difficult, and he was sure of finding a good instrument to play on.

One day, about a year after his second concert, Johannes, thinking himself completely alone at the factory, began playing a new fantasia that had recently been taking shape in his mind. Twilight was falling and the big, half-empty wareroom with its rows of silent pianos (some already crated and ready to ship away) was filled with shadows.

Suddenly, as he looked up from the keyboard, Hannes saw one of the shadows move a little, and discovered a young girl standing there. She was watching him intently. In confusion he broke off.

"Oh—please don't stop!" said the girl, stepping forward.

"I didn't know anyone was listening," Hannes began.

"But, please—don't let me interrupt you. I've listened to you often before, you know."

"No—I didn't know," Johannes murmured, abashed.

"Oh, yes." The girl came nearer. "The first time was years ago; I remember Herr Heinz said you were only eleven. You were playing something you had composed yourself. It sounded very well. A sonata, I think it was."

Hannes was still more confused, but not a little gratified. "You are a musician, Fräulein—"

"Japha. Louise Japha is my name," the girl answered

in a friendly voice. "Yes, I am a musician. That is, I play a little, and try to compose now and then." She came to the piano and stood, smiling.

Johannes had been too busy with his work to notice young ladies much, but he thought the girl attractive. She was evidently older than himself (seven years, he later learned), her dark hair piled high with puffs and curls, sparkling brown eyes, and a smile that was full of humor and good nature. She was simply gowned, and wore a frilled muslin kerchief tied across her breast and fastened with a cameo brooch.

"Perhaps you will play for *me* then, Fräulein," Hannes suggested politely, fearing the worst. But he need not have been alarmed.

"I would much rather listen to you." Louise smiled back at him. "Herr Heinz says you have composed some really fine things. That piece you were playing, for instance. It was *beautiful!* Did you write that?"

Young Brahms felt quite at his ease now. "Yes," he admitted. "It's something new I'm just working on. But it is really meant for two pianos. Look—" a happy thought struck him. "Perhaps you would play the second part with me, so I can hear how it sounds?"

Fräulein Japha was willing, and soon the big warehouse vibrated with an unaccustomed volume of sound. Hannes discovered that his new friend was an excellent pianist; indeed, she later became famous all over Europe as a concert artist.

Johannes also learned that Fräulein Japha had composed some charming songs. After that, the two young people met frequently. They would spend hours playing together, or discussing their favorite books, authors, and musicians. Often they compared their music manuscripts, and Hannes sought eagerly for Louise's commendation. She was usually enthusiastic about everything that he wrote; so much so that he became a little suspicious.

One day he brought a new duet. "Do you like it?" he asked, when they had finished playing it through.

"It's wonderful, Hannes," she answered politely.

"But this theme now—" He pointed out a passage that did not please him. "Do you really think it is properly developed? It seems rather ordinary to me."

"Well—perhaps you are right," Louise admitted.

"Then why didn't you say so at once!" Johannes exclaimed with sudden sharpness. "Why do I have to keep on asking you?"

The girl looked at him in surprise. For all his gentleness, Hannes could be almost rough at times, especially if he suspected the least lack of sincerity. It was a habit that was to grow on him with the years, until finally the gruff side often overbalanced the genial part of his nature.

Partly because of his dread of insincerity and partly because of his natural shyness, Brahms never, even as a youth, went out of his way to be agreeable or diplomatic. "Why should one 'put on' what one doesn't feel?" he argued. Several times Louise Japha took him to see her family, but he was so taciturn and apparently unfriendly that he did not make a very favorable impression.

One evening after a visit to the Japhas, a friend who had been calling there asked Johannes if he might walk home with him, since they were both going in the same direction. Johannes much preferred being alone, but he could hardly say no. During the walk, however, he obstinately refused to talk to his companion. The latter tried in vain to make conversation. Not a word would the boy say.

The next day Louise, who had heard of the episode from her friend, took Johannes to task. "Why were you so unsociable last evening on the way home?"

He looked at her in surprise. "Unsociable? You mean because I wouldn't talk to your friend? Well, I didn't feel like talking; so why should I? If one has nothing to say it is better to keep quiet, isn't it?"

Louise could not help laughing at his expression. "No," she insisted; "you should always answer when you are spoken to. You were very rude!"

Hannes shrugged his shoulders with pretended indifference. "In the years when I should have been learning good manners I had to spend all my leisure hours playing in taverns and cheap dance-halls," he said. "You don't learn social deportment in those places!"

Even at that early date, Louise Japha had vision enough to realize the real genius of Johannes Brahms. She admired him fervently, both for his musical talent and for the sincerity and frankness which shone from his candid blue eyes. And when he talked to her of his mother and his good, honest father, she knew how warm and loving his nature really was. "It went to one's heart when he spoke of his old mother," she said; "he was so utterly devoted to her."

Louise's friendship and encouragement meant a great deal to Johannes. He was then just beginning to experiment with the larger musical forms which later were to make him so famous. Marxsen was amazed to see how easily he mastered whatever he undertook. The boy no longer had regular lessons, but his former teacher still supervised his work and gave him advice when he needed help.

Johannes' spare moments were, as usual, devoted to books. He realized his lack of education and tried to make up by reading and study for what he had missed in earlier life. Through persevering and concentrated effort he succeeded so well in educating himself that in later years he could hold his own with the best minds of the day.

As we have seen, whenever he could spare a little money he would buy books for his library. These were usually second-hand volumes from the outdoor stalls in the Jewish quarter of Hamburg. Nearly all his books were classics; they included Sophocles and Cicero, Dante, Goethe, and Schiller.

Brahms often found inspiration for his music through this reading. When Louise Japha would ask him where he got the idea for a certain work he would sometimes tell her, "It came into my head after reading so and so." During this period he wrote a number of songs. "I generally read a poem through very slowly, and then, as a rule, the melody is there. I only have to set it down on paper."

For some time after his return from Winsen, Johannes did not see his friends the Giesemanns. Then one afternoon, when he came home from a session at the piano factory, his mother met him at the door of her shop.

"There are visitors waiting for you upstairs in the parlor," she told him, smiling.

"Who is it?" asked Johannes. But his mother only smoothed the folds of her black alpaca apron. "A surprise for you!" she said mysteriously. "They told me not to tell."

Hannes rushed up the steps, two at a time, and burst into the tiny sitting-room. "Why, it's Uncle Adolf!" he cried, "—and Lieschen!"

He hardly recognized his little country playmate in the demure young Fräulein who curtsied before him. She was dressed in formal city clothes instead of the familiar gingham pinafore; her yellow braids were wound around her head in a tight coronet; and a stylish poke bonnet gave her the appearance of a young lady of fashion.

"What have you been doing with yourselves?"

Hannes inquired. "And how goes Lieschen's music?"

"Well," said Herr Giesemann, "the piano is not so good. . . ." (Lieschen blushed a little and turned away from Johannes' reproachful look.) "But singing now—" he went on proudly; "our Lieschen really has a voice, you know!"

Hannes remembered how he had loved to hear the child sing during their rambles together around Winsen. "It is time she began taking lessons," he said. "She should have a really good teacher."

"Yes," agreed Herr Giesemann; "and that is what I came to ask you about. Can you recommend someone?"

Johannes thought a moment. "There are many professors of singing in Hamburg, but she must have the best. I'll tell you—let me take Lieschen to Herr Marxsen. She shall sing for him and then he can judge of her voice. He will know the teacher she should have."

Lieschen was dreadfully frightened when she sang for the great Marxsen. She had a small, sweet voice, but there was nothing exceptional about it, and the older musician told them, as diplomatically as possible, that it would be useless to spend time and money in trying to develop it.

Herr Giesemann was very much disappointed, and so was Lieschen. But Hannes was the most disappointed of all, for he had hoped he could do something for the Giesemanns in return for all their generosity.

Many years later he was able to repay a good part of

this debt. Lieschen's daughter—as sometimes ironically happens—was endowed with the beautiful voice which her mother had always longed for. Brahms took charge of the girl's musical education, and himself paid for her singing lessons.

When Johannes first met Louise Japha she was studying with Fritz Wahrendorf in Hamburg.

"Why don't you go to Marxsen?" he urged her. "He is one of the best teachers in all Germany."

Louise raised her eyebrows. "In all Germany? That's a big order! No, Hannes, I can't agree with you. What I should really like to do is to study with the Schumanns in Düsseldorf."

"You mean Robert Schumann?" Hannes stiffened. "Herr Marxsen doesn't care for *him* at all. Says he's too romantic. Worse, he's a modernist!" The mind of the famous pedagogue was too closed against new impressions to realize the worth of one of the greatest composers then living.

Louise laughed. "Listen—your teacher is such an ardent classicist that he can't see anyone later than Beethoven."

"That's not true. He adores Mendelssohn."

"Well, Schumann has written just as good music as Mendelssohn ever wrote—better, *I* think. Look here—" she added as she noted his disapproving expression, "do you really know much about Schumann?"

Young Brahms had to admit that he didn't. "Then

let me tell you what *I* know," Fräulein Japha volunteered.

The two young people were alone in the piano warehouse. They had permission to stay as late as they pleased. Louise usually brought along a cushion for the hard piano bench when they were playing; now she tossed it to the floor and made herself comfortable beside Hannes, her back propped against the piano.

"Well, to begin with, Schumann was born in 1810. He's only forty now, you know. His father was a bookseller, author, and editor, who died when Robert was sixteen. The boy was given the finest kind of education at the universities of Leipzig and Heidelberg. His mother wanted him to be a lawyer. That's just about like expecting a nightingale to become a kingfisher." (Louise chuckled at her own comparison.) "No—Robert was much too dreamy and imaginative to stick to dry things like the law. First he wanted to be a poet; but he always loved music, and finally he knew he must become a musician.

"Of course his widowed mother was against the idea. But when Robert Schumann makes up his mind. . . . Anyhow, he decided to be a concert pianist. Imagine trying to prepare for a career like that at the age of twenty! Usually musicians begin in the nursery. He knew he had to make up for lost time, so he invented a machine to stretch his fingers."

Louise shook her head over such folly. "Anyone could have told him that was dangerous. He ruined his right hand, and had to give up all his hopes of the concert stage. But it was a lucky accident at that, because it made him turn to composition instead."

Hannes looked down at his own hands. "You think a concert career interferes with composing?" he asked anxiously.

"Oh, not necessarily," Louise replied. "But Schumann might never have known he could compose if he had concentrated entirely on playing. At first he was dreadfully disappointed. Fortunately, though, he married a wife who could do all the necessary playing for the family. . . ."

"I've heard that Frau Schumann is a very fine pianist."

"She is *wonderful!*" his companion exclaimed with enthusiasm. "Beautiful, magnetic, plays like a man, but still remains a perfect wife and mother. The Schumanns have five children and have lost another; yet Frau Clara finds time to play often in public. She is her husband's greatest interpreter, you know—and the inspiration for most of his music. There's romance for you!" Louise sighed sentimentally.

"She was the daughter of Schumann's piano teacher, Herr Wieck. Robert loved her for years—from the time she was a little girl, and already a famous child pianist. But her father had selfish ambitions for his daughter. He forbade Schumann to see her, and threatened to shoot him if he did. When they met on the street, the old man would actually spit at him!" Louise shook her head angrily.

"Then, when the two young people persisted in being faithful to each other, and Clara asserted her independence by going off on a concert tour, Wieck tried to ruin her reputation with slanderous letters. He even bribed the piano dealers to give her bad instruments to play on!

"But it didn't do a bit of good. Robert and Clara finally applied to court for permission to marry. The father fought the suit with venomous lies and underhand tricks; but they won out!"

As the two young people sat silent for a moment, the door opened and little old Herr Heinz, the factory owner, poked his head in. "Oh—you're still here!" he exclaimed. "I was about to lock up."

Louise scrambled to her feet. "I was just telling Hannes about the Schumanns. He doesn't like Robert Schumann's music."

"Herr Marxsen thinks he is too romantic—" Johannes began.

"Schumann too romantic?" cried the old man. "I don't agree. No one is more devoted to the classics than he is. Bach is his god. In fact—" Herr Heinz shook his grizzled head—"Robert Schumann is a champion of all that is best in music. He can't stand anything insincere or superficial. Pretense and sham make him rise right up. Have you read his articles in the *New Magazine for Music?*"

Hannes shook his head.

"You don't know the paper? I'm surprised," Herr Heinz exclaimed. "It has a real influence in the musical world. And Robert Schumann is the man who founded it."

A few days later, when Louise Japha came in to practice with Johannes, he could see that she was excited about something.

"What do you think?" she cried. "Robert Schumann and his wife are coming to Hamburg to give a series of concerts! It has just been announced. He will conduct the orchestra, and Frau Clara will play his great concerto and a number of his piano compositions. Now you will have a chance to hear Schumann's music!" she went on. "You might even meet him. Why don't you call on him? I wish he could see some of your work. His opinion would be valuable."

Johannes was much too shy to seek out Schumann himself, but Louise's suggestion about showing the composer some of his works seemed a good one. He made up a package of what he felt were his best compositions, and left it with a note at the hotel.

Schumann had always been absentminded. He was gentle and lovable by nature, but extremely temperamental. At times he would be feverishly gay, at other times gloomy and depressed. While in Hamburg he was engrossed with his concerts and other problems, and had no time to look over young Brahms' work. He sent the package back unopened. Johannes, too young and inexperienced to appreciate the demands of a public career, took the matter personally and was offended.

However, he did not let this incident discourage his music-writing. "G. W. Marks" and "Karl Würth" went on furnishing the publishers with scores of compositions. At the same time "J. Brahms" was beginning to try his wings.

When Louise Japha asked Hannes what he did with all his manuscripts, he told her, laughing: "My room is papered from top to bottom with songs and quartets, sonatas and trios. I have only to lie down and I can enjoy a whole concert by just looking at the walls!"

But when, later, she asked to see this strange collection, Johannes only shrugged his shoulders indifferently. He told her that he had taken them all down and destroyed the sheets.

"I took a whole packing case full over to the factory near our house and burned them in the furnace there."

Louise cried out in horror. "You *didn't!* But why—?"

"Better that I should do it than another!"

In a letter to Clara Schumann forty-three years later, Brahms wrote: "Now I should like to be as wise after my 60th birthday as I was before the 20th. In those days the Hamburg publishers could not by any means induce me to let them print anything of mine."

Whenever Father Brahms saw his talented son spilling notes with unbelievable speed over the music-paper before him, he would tiptoe silently around like one awe-struck in the presence of genius.

"Ja, ja," he would whisper ecstatically to himself (or to anyone who would listen to him). "A great composer, my Hannes!"

CHAPTER VII

MUSICIANS ERRANT

JOHANNES lifted the knocker on the door of an imposing mansion in Hamburg's fashionable residence quarter. At once the door was opened by a footman in foreign livery who looked surprised when he saw the short, fair-haired boy. "I have come—to play," Hannes stammered, quite taken aback by the servant's manner. "To play the piano," he added.

"You mean, to entertain the guests?" said the footman, staring at him haughtily. Hannes nodded. The man pushed him insolently to one side. "Will the young —er—pianist—be so good as to apply at the rear entrance? Quick now—don't you see that the guests are already arriving?"

Hannes' face flushed with anger, but he moved hastily away to make room for an elegant couple, the lady in stiff brocade and the gentleman with a flowing cape and high silk hat, who were just stepping down from a shiny black victoria drawn by two bay horses.

As the young musician made his way to the rear door he shook his head resentfully. It was quite true that he should have known better than to go to the front entrance—what *had* he been thinking about to be so absentminded? Oh, yes, that phrase in the new quartet! To be sure, in those days musicians were little better than servants; at least, when hired to entertain in wealthy homes. Nevertheless Hannes felt that the footman had been unnecessarily high and mighty.

Still smarting under the rebuff, he was ushered into a small study adjoining the drawing-room. A lanky young man was standing in front of the fireplace. He appeared to be a good deal older than Johannes (actually just three years). He wore a black velvet jacket and flowing tie, and had long, dark hair and eyes as brilliant as the high lights on the violin he was holding. With thin fingers he nervously plucked the strings.

"Are you the accompanist?" His manner was haughty, and he spoke with a strong foreign accent.

"At your service."

"Well, I hope you know how to read music," continued the violinist, reaching for some sheets on the table beside him. "I have some rather difficult native airs here. The effect is quite lost if the accompanist doesn't keep time."

"I can manage," answered Johannes. He glanced through the pages and then looked up with sudden interest. "Hungarian music! Are you from Hungary?"

The violinist, busy resining his bow, nodded.

"Do you perhaps know the great Joachim?"

"Oh, yes," the fiddler replied nonchalantly. "I know him well. We studied under the same teacher at the Conservatory in Vienna."

"I heard Herr Joachim in a concert here two years ago," said Johannes with enthusiasm. "He plays marvelously. . . ."

"Fair," conceded the violinist with an air of generous condescension. "We Hungarians are born with music in our fingers. My name is Remenyi," he added, looking expectantly at his companion.

Brahms had heard of the eccentric young violinist, whose wild playing was the talk of Hamburg. "I am delighted to meet you, Herr Remenyi," he exclaimed warmly. "My name is Brahms."

The footman who had been so rude to Johannes appeared at the door. "If Herr Remenyi is quite ready," he said in a manner far different from the one he had used to the younger musician, "the guests would like some music now."

The two young men filed into the large drawing-room, Hannes well to the rear. He seated himself at the piano as inconspicuously as possible.

Remenyi first played some of the conventional favorites of the day, and Johannes, while noting that he was an able violinist, did not see anything exceptional in the performance. But when the young Hungarian started on his native airs and gypsy melodies, he was suddenly transformed. All the turbulence and passion of his wild temperament found expression in these stirring rhythms. He played with such fire and abandon that his audience was quite carried away. Likewise his accompanist! Brahms was captivated by this fascinating music. It awakened a deeply responsive chord in his heart, and was the first inspiration of the much-loved Hungarian Dances which he wrote in later years, and of such exciting movements as the finales of the first piano quartet, and of the G major quintet for strings.

Remenyi was delighted with his accompanist, so sensitive to every nuance of tempo and rhythm.

"You have a fine feeling for this music," he said. "We must play together often."

During the following weeks the two young musicians saw much of each other. Remenyi had fled from Hungary as a political refugee, and was hoping to get to the United States; but certain papers were necessary before he could leave Europe.

Summer came. Johannes had planned to spend his holidays (a couple of weeks were all he could spare now) with the Giesemanns.

"Why don't you come with me?" he asked his new friend. "They are crazy for music, the good people of Winsen. They would like your playing."

Remenyi did not need much persuading. The two young men took the river boat to Winsen, and there, as Hannes had predicted, everyone received the violinist cordially.

All but Lieschen. She mistrusted the flashy, handsome young Hungarian.

Hannes did not make friends easily. He had an exceptionally shy, modest, and reserved nature, and was engrossed in a world of his own. Louise Japha was one of the few people with whom he felt at ease. The two had so much in common. Her friendship meant a great deal to the sensitive, lonely boy. He was quite heartbroken when she told him that she was leaving Hamburg.

"You know how I have always longed to study with the Schumanns," said Louise, her eyes gleaming exultantly. "Now at last they have written that I may come to them in Düsseldorf."

"Why are you so set on going there?" Hannes asked petulantly.

"I believe you are still prejudiced against Herr Schumann because he sent your manuscripts back to you without looking at them," she remarked.

Johannes would not admit it, but the incident still rankled.

"Herr Schumann was terribly busy at the time; don't you realize that?" Louise continued. "If he had known about you—if you had had some sort of introduction to him—things would have been very different, I'm sure. You must come to Düsseldorf while I am there, and I will introduce you."

Young Brahms was not at all sure that he cared to meet Schumann. He was still too much under the influence of Marxsen to admit that his teacher's opinion could be wrong. He begged Louise not to go.

"I shall be so lonely without you," he told her with pathetic insistence. "You are the only person who has ever taken an interest in me!"

"You should get out into the world, Hannes," Louise answered firmly. "You mustn't stay buried forever in this town. You ought to be giving concerts of your own right now."

Johannes shrugged his shoulders slightly. He knew only too well that it took money to start out on a concert career. As a matter of fact, the world's acclaim did not mean so very much to him. If only a few appreciated what he was trying to express in his music, that was all that he would ask for.

Soon after Louise Japha left Hamburg, Remenyi returned, and lost no time in looking up his former accompanist. Although Johannes did not entirely like the boastful young violinist, he was fascinated by his Hungarian gypsy music, and enjoyed playing with him. Spring was just coming on, and Remenyi, remembering the previous spring's pleasant voyage to Winsen, suggested that they go again to visit the Giesemanns.

Uncle Adolf and Aunt Lisel were always delighted when Hannes could come to them, and they were honored to have so famous an artist as Remenyi in their home. The latter enjoyed showing off. "Why don't we give a concert for these good people?" he suggested to Hannes. "We should be able to sell quite a few tickets among your friends?"

Just as he had surmised, everyone was delighted at the prospect. News of the coming event spread far and wide. Remenyi and young Brahms began practicing. Each morning they went over to work at Herr Köhler's house. The weather suddenly turned hot, and Johannes discovered, now that he was working regularly with Remenyi, that the latter was even more temperamental than he had suspected. He was terribly exacting and often unreasonable, and would fly into a fury if anything displeased him.

It was especially difficult to suit the violinist in accompanying his native Hungarian melodies. He never played them twice alike, but according to his mood, now slowly, with sentimental languor, now in wild rubato. To emphasize the tempo he would sometimes bring the violin bow sharply down across Hannes' shoulders.

Young Brahms was usually fairly tolerant of these outbursts, but one morning the worm turned. "I'm sick of this!" he cried, closing the piano with a bang. "Go find an accompanist who can suit you; for *I* shan't play another note!"

"Sorry!" the Hungarian muttered with a surly frown. "I didn't mean to be so rough. Let's forget about it and go on."

Hannes was not too easily persuaded, but he knew how much his friends were counting on the concert, so finally he gave in and the practicing continued.

People came from all the outlying districts to hear the young artists. Their concert was the greatest musical event that Winsen had witnessed in years. All of Johannes' friends were there excepting Herr Schröder—the schoolteacher from Hoopte and tenor of the Choral Society; he was ill and could not leave his home.

Hannes knew how disappointed Herr Schröder must be to miss the concert. "Why couldn't we—" He looked questioningly at Remenyi, but for once the latter was in an amiable mood. "How would it be if we stopped by Herr Schröder's house on our way to the boat and played a few of our numbers for him?"

Johannes had not forgotten what a help the schoolteacher had been to him during his first summer at Winsen. He always treasured in his memory any kindness or service that was shown him, and tried in some way to repay it. Some years later, to celebrate the silver-wedding anniversary of Herr Schröder and his wife, Brahms dedicated to them two of his compositions.

In the Winsen audience, one of the most enthusiastic listeners was Herr Blume, the old District Judge. He had followed young Brahms' career with the greatest interest.

"Since this concert has been so successful," he told the two musicians, "I should think you young men would give a series. You could go to Lüneburg. My son lives there, you know, and I could write him to make the necessary arrangements. Then at Celle we have another good friend, Dr. Köhler, a cousin of our Rector here, who is a great music-lover."

When Remenyi and Brahms counted up their profits from the Winsen concert, they were jubilant; nearly $45 had been taken in.

"We have quite enough for traveling expenses!" they congratulated themselves. "Let's start at once."

First it was necessary to return to Hamburg and pick up a few belongings; no more, however, than they could each carry comfortably in a small bag. Hannes packed a few of his own compositions, but he did not include any of the pieces that he and Remenyi expected to play; all of this music he carried in his head. Marxsen once said, "Brahms had such a wonderful memory that it never occurred to him to take printed music with him on his concert tours." He could reproduce an entire score if it happened to be lost.

This was the first time that Johannes had traveled any distance from home, or had been away from his family for more than a few days at a time. During his summers at Winsen he had returned frequently to Hamburg. Now he expected to be gone for several weeks—perhaps even months.

"Please, little Mother, write to me often," he begged.

Frau Brahms nodded her head doubtfully. She was growing old and stooped from her long years of hard work. There had never been much time, or occasion, for correspondence. It would be a real undertaking for her to grant Hannes' request. But she agreed to send him a weekly letter.

It was a promise which Johanna Christiana faithfully kept. Not a few lines, but three whole pages were mailed to her Hannes each week. Envelopes were then not yet in use; the fourth page of the double letter sheets was folded over, sealed and used for the address.

When Frau Brahms could not think of anything else to write, she would copy extracts from the Hamburg newspapers. "What is she to do when she has no more news?" Brahms said to Louise Japha. "She cannot write a philosophical treatise, but she always sends me three whole pages."

To Remenyi the proposed trip was of no great importance. He had been traveling and playing in concerts for years, so the tour would be only a matter of routine. But to Hannes it was a glorious adventure.

May Day in 1853 came on a Sunday. A tapestry of many shades of green covered the banks of the River Luhe. Cherry and wild hawthorn flowered luxuriantly; while here and there were clumps of the yellow broom—the "Bram" from which Johannes' family took its name.

A throng of pleasure-seekers waited at the river landing to board the paddle-boat bound for Celle. Among the crowd were two young men who presented such a contrast in appearance that people turned around to look at them.

The first was tall, thin almost to emaciation, very dark in coloring and with the world-weary expression of one who has known too much adulation. The other, on the contrary, seemed completely unspoiled. There was an eager, child-like look in his clear blue eyes. He was short and slender, with long fair hair, and no one would have thought him twenty years old.

Aware of his youthful appearance, Brahms held himself with a stiff dignity which still failed to convince people of his real age. To his annoyance, his voice persisted in retaining its high register. He tried his best to deepen it, forcing the tones down to a gruff alto. This strained his vocal cords so much that the gruffness stayed with him all his life. Some believe that it was the result of a bad cold caught in early youth, but it is more likely that the unnatural forcing of his voice at this early period was responsible.

The first concert was scheduled for Monday, May

second, at Celle. Some days before, Dr. Köhler, Judge Blume's friend, had inserted a notice in the local paper:

> Next Monday evening at seven o'clock the concert of the Messrs. Remenyi and Brahms will take place in the Wierss'sche Hall. The subscription price is 12 g.gr. [A "*Guter Groschen*" was worth about 2½ cents.] Tickets may also be obtained of Herr Wierss, Jun., at Herr Duncker's hotel, or on the evening of the concert at the room for 16 g.gr.

Early Monday morning Remenyi and young Brahms went to the Wierss'sche Hall to rehearse. Hannes took one horrified look at the decrepit piano.

"But this is impossible!" he cried in dismay.

"Try it," suggested Remenyi with more hope than he felt.

The instrument sounded even worse than it looked. Some of the notes refused to work at all, and a number of the strings were broken.

"I can't possibly play on this," Johannes said. "They will have to find us another piano, or there won't be any concert tonight."

Pianos were scarce in Celle, and it was almost time for the concert to begin when another instrument was finally set up in the hall. Johannes played a chord which roughly jarred his sense of "absolute pitch." "Ouch!" he cried. "It's almost a half-tone too low!"

Remenyi stared in consternation. "What shall we do? I couldn't possibly tune down to that; it would spoil the quality of my violin."

Johannes had already thought of a way out. "I know what. You tune just a little higher. Then I will transpose the piano parts up half a tone."

"Without any music to go by?" Remenyi asked incredulously, remembering the printed sheets left behind in Hamburg.

"I can do it," said Hannes with confidence.

He managed the transposed accompaniments brilliantly. Even the difficult piano part of Beethoven's C Minor Sonata went off without a hitch. Marxsen's strenuous training in transposition served Brahms on more than one occasion during his career.

Remenyi was so impressed by the feat that when the two young musicians were bowing before an enthusiastic audience, he made a little speech:

"The credit is really due to Herr Brahms," he said, with generous condescension. "The piano here was tuned too low, so—from memory, mind you, with no music to go by—he transposed the music a half-tone higher."

The concert in Celle was such a success that Brahms and Remenyi were invited to return later and repeat the program. First, however, they had promised to go to Lüneburg, where they were to be the guests of Herr Blume, son of the Judge in Winsen. The old man had often written to his son about the talented young pianist from Hamburg, so Brahms was already known there by reputation.

Herr Blume's wife wanted to give a party for the two visitors. "It will be good advertising for you to meet the musical circle of our town," she told them.

Johannes looked uncomfortable. "Will there be ladies present?" he asked.

Frau Blume stared at him in surprise. "Do you object?"

Young Brahms stammered with awkward shyness. "Would you mind? Don't you think—well, now—wouldn't it be nicer without them?"

Brahms was never completely at his ease in the society of women of the upper classes. This may have been due to his early association in dance-halls with women of a far different character. But it was probably also because of the modest environment from which he sprang. He was never able to forget this class distinction; often he tried to make up for a certain feeling of inferiority by assuming a gruff, boorish manner.

At Lüneburg the young artists scored another triumph, and again were asked to repeat the performance. The local newspaper (mentioning specially the fascinating Hungarian melodies) announced that two days later, "by general desire," the program would be given again.

By this time the two musicians were so elated over their success that they decided to try a concert in the city of Hildesheim entirely on their own. They had no one there to herald their coming, write advance notices, and prepare the way. Since they were unknown, the concert hall was almost empty. When the program was ended, Remenyi packed up his violin and turned ruefully to his companion. "Let's go to a tavern and celebrate."

"Celebrate?" repeated Hannes ironically.

"Yes—celebrate the big audience we'll have *next* time!"

When they opened the tavern door they heard a gay chorus of singing. That was the place where the young blades of Hildesheim spent most of their evenings, draining endless steins of beer and making merry. The merrier they grew, the louder they sang.

"Hail, hail! Here comes a *musician!"* they cried when they saw the violin under Remenyi's arm. "Join our group, gentlemen, and give us a tune on your fiddle."

Johannes and his companion soon found themselves the center of an animated circle. Remenyi played some dazzling gypsy melodies that swept the young Hildesheimers so far off their feet that they responded in a burst of choric song.

"Why—you are first-class musicians!" cried the leader of the company.

Hannes and Remenyi exchanged glances. "You have probably heard my name, gentlemen," said the Hungarian importantly. "I am the violinist Remenyi, and this is my accompanist, Herr Brahms. We just gave a concert here this evening."

"Pity we weren't there to hear you," said one of the young men, draining his stein of beer.

"Yes, it *was* a pity," answered Remenyi. "We didn't have much of an audience. . . ."

"Tell you what," exclaimed another; "why don't you repeat the program tomorrow evening? We'll tell all our friends about it. I know!" He banged his stein down on the table. "Let's go and serenade the Baroness. She's the wealthiest person in Hildesheim, and a great music-lover."

Everyone was enthusiastic about the idea. With one accord the merry crowd left the tavern, and presently found itself under the window of a large house on the outskirts of Hildesheim. Remenyi first played a *czardas* and a *furiant;* then the young men cleared their throats, and Hannes gave the signal for a choral explosion.

The scheme worked perfectly. Not only was the Baroness enchanted, but all Hildesheim heard about the serenade. Next evening the two musicians appeared before a packed hall.

Johannes' and Remenyi's new friends begged them to stay longer in Hildesheim. But the two had other plans. Now was to come what Hannes had most looked forward to on this trip: Remenyi had promised to take him to Hanover and introduce him to the musician he admired so greatly—the violinist Joseph Joachim.

CHAPTER VIII

HANNES MEETS JOACHIM

DURING the greater part of the 19th century, Germany was made up of a number of small states. There were almost a hundred of these separate duchies, principalities, and kingdoms; and it was not until 1871 that Bismarck unified them into one empire with King Wilhelm I of Prussia as Emperor. Up to this time, each small state had been ruled over by its own King or Grand Duke: Saxony, with its capital at Dresden; Bavaria, with Munich the principal city; Prussia, focused in Berlin (later to become the capital of the German Empire)—these, and many others, including Hanover.

The small kingdoms were, for the most part, no larger than the separate counties which make up some of our own States in America. But each felt itself vastly important and kept up an elaborate court with all the pomp and ceremony observed at the great European capitals. Music was an important part of this court life. The rulers usually maintained their own private orchestras and opera singers.

Hanover was noted for its music. Here the King had gathered together some of the finest musicians in the country, and Joachim was concertmaster of the orchestra.

Late in May of 1853, two young travelers presented themselves at Joachim's door. One of these was a fellow countryman. Joachim remembered Remenyi, but with no especial liking. The brilliant and conceited young Hungarian was too sensational to suit his more conservative taste. The other visitor was a stranger; he seemed much younger than his companion. Joachim was at once attracted to the boy.

"I have brought my accompanist with me," announced Remenyi, introducing young Brahms. Then he added, half disdainfully, but with a touch of envy, "Johannes admires you most extravagantly, my friend."

Joachim looked with penetrating eyes at the slight, fair boy, and thought to himself: "Here is a strange companion for this wild compatriot of mine." Aloud he said, with a cordial smile: "You must be a good musician to satisfy our friend here!"

Hannes smiled back with eager response. He could hardly realize that this was the artist he had so long hoped to meet. He took in every detail of the violinist's appearance. Joachim was wearing a voluminous dressing-gown, and a red fez was perched on the back of his head. Beside his armchair stood a table with a strange-looking affair which Johannes later learned was a Turkish water-pipe, or "hubble-bubble." (Joachim's friends called him "Yussuf" because of his fondness for Turkish things.)

Hannes thought the violinist a very imposing figure, and he found it difficult to believe that this young man, already world-famous and a veteran of the concert stage, was only two years older than himself.

"I studied under Eduard Marxsen," he said, answering Joachim's questions.

The latter raised his eyebrows. "Marxsen is a great teacher. I must hear you play, Herr Brahms."

"Ask him to give you something of his own," suggested Remenyi, stretching himself lazily in Joachim's most comfortable chair. "Johannes composes music—good stuff, too. How about that new sonata?"

Joachim led young Brahms to the piano and stood beside him as he played. He listened attentively and with growing astonishment. Why, this boy was a remarkable pianist! He could see that at once—and still more remarkable was the music he was playing. His own composition, Remenyi had said? Joachim recognized at once a talent far above the ordinary.

In speaking later of this first visit Joachim said:

> The dissimilar companions, the tender, idealistic Johannes and the self-satisfied, fantastic virtuoso, called on me. Never in the course of my artist's life have I been more completely overwhelmed with delighted surprise, than when the rather shy-mannered, fair-haired companion of my countryman played me his sonata movements, of quite undreamt-of originality and power, looking noble and inspired the while. . . . His playing so tender, so imaginative, so free and fiery, held me spellbound.

In a letter Joachim spoke of Brahms' "exceptional talent for composition." He had, he said, "a nature which could have been developed in its integrity only in close retirement, pure as the diamond, tender as snow."

Remenyi was not entirely pleased by Joachim's evident interest in young Brahms. He felt that *he* should be the center of attraction.

"I understand your King here is quite a music enthusiast," he said pointedly. "If his Highness knew of my presence in Hanover he would no doubt wish to hear me play."

Joachim looked at his compatriot with distaste. Certainly he would not go out of his way to arrange a concert for Remenyi. But for young Brahms he would do much. . . .

"I am leaving shortly for Göttingen," he answered. "But, before I go, I will see what can be done."

On Joachim's recommendation a concert at the court

of Hanover was arranged. The King was greatly impressed by young Brahms' playing. He nicknamed him "the little Beethoven."

Joachim felt that Johannes' talents should be brought to the attention of Germany's leading musicians. One of the most outstanding of these lived in Weimar.

"Had you thought of going to Weimar?" he asked the boy.

"Weimar!" broke in Remenyi. "To be sure—that is where lives our great compatriot Liszt. I have long wished to know him better. Perhaps you could give us a letter of introduction?"

Joachim hesitated—but only for a moment. Liszt was often helpful to younger musicians. It would probably be to Johannes' advantage to meet him.

Franz Liszt was then forty-two years old. Born in Hungary, he had spent most of his life in Vienna, Paris, and of late years in Germany. His father was steward to Prince Esterházy, of the family celebrated for its patronage of music. Both Haydn and Schubert had, years earlier, been in the service of an Esterházy. When Liszt was young the Prince took an interest in his musical education, and sent the precocious boy to Vienna to study with Salieri and Czerny. Beethoven heard the child play there and predicted a great future for him.

When he was twelve, Liszt gave a concert in Paris and immediately became famous. From then on his career proceeded from one spectacular triumph to another. He was one of the greatest piano virtuosos the world has ever known, and equally renowned as a composer. He wrote quantities of music—most of it in florid virtuoso style.

Joachim, who had lived in Weimar for two years, knew Liszt fairly well. On more than one occasion the latter had tried to convert the young violinist to the "New German" school. But Joachim, while admiring the master greatly, could not entirely accept his musical ideas.

He was not at all sure that Brahms would care for the artistic atmosphere of Weimar. "The master himself is generous and noble-hearted," he told him; "but he is surrounded by a group of almost fanatical worshipers. Most of them are there to win some sort of musical advantage from the association. Our friend Remenyi is sure to be in his element."

Joachim was unable to understand how the fine and sensitive young Brahms could put up with such a swaggering, quick-tempered companion as Remenyi; it would have been hard to imagine two natures more widely different.

"If you should decide to part from Remenyi," he remarked, before leaving Hanover for his summer holiday, "perhaps you might like to join me in Göttingen."

Hannes flushed with pleasure. Nothing could please him better than to be with Joachim. His new friend possessed all the qualities that he most admired. And the violinist, for his part, wanted to see more of the younger musician.

This was the beginning of a lifelong friendship.

Weimar, a picturesque town in middle Germany, had long been one of the foremost cultural centers of the country. Here for many years lived the poets Goethe and Schiller. Their rooms are still to be seen. (In Schiller's study the desk where he wrote many of his masterpieces stands just as he left it when he died in 1805. The right-hand drawer is stained; he kept it full of rotten apples because, he said, their odor stimulated him to creative activity.) During the middle of the 19th century Weimar was chiefly noted because the "New German" school of music had its headquarters there.

At the death of Mendelssohn, music in Germany became divided into three factions: First, the "Classicists," who followed the old masters and cared only for traditional forms (Marxsen belonged to this school); next came the so-called "Romanticists," with Schumann at their head, professing reverence for the past, yet tending towards a modern, more romantic type of expression; and finally there were the "Neo-Germans," champions of the new and the "music-of-the-future."

The leader of this last group was Franz Liszt. (At that time he had not yet taken Church orders, acquiring the title of Abbé.) One of the great romantic figures of the 19th century, he was to music what Byron then was to literature. Passionate and temperamental, he was gifted with great talent and feeling for music, a keen sense of showmanship, and an ardent nature which found expression in a succession of romantic, almost legendary, love affairs.

At the age of twenty-three he fell in love with the Countess d'Agoult, a woman six years his senior. She left her husband and three children to follow Liszt, and stayed with him for eleven years. Three years after they parted, he met the German Princess Caroline von Sayn-Wittgenstein and went to live with her in her palace at Weimar.

There Liszt was established in state and surrounded by the greatest luxury. The Princess granted his slightest whim, while an adoring circle of disciples, pupils, young composers, and musicians who professed devotion to modern music, gathered around him and hailed him as their High Priest. It was surprising that he was not ruined by so much adulation. Fundamentally, however, Liszt was a great soul, charming and affable in manner, generous and kindly to everyone, especially to younger musicians.

Joachim's letter of introduction obtained a speedy interview for Brahms and Remenyi. They were invited to call on Liszt, and Brahms was asked to bring some of his compositions.

Johannes felt a little dismayed when he found several other musicians there. When Liszt came in—slender, eagle-beaked, with a large wart on the side of his nose, and long, fair straight hair falling to his shoulders—all the young men rose to their feet and stood until the master seated himself. Brahms viewed this ceremony with secret contempt.

Remenyi pushed eagerly forward, but Liszt turned first to Johannes. "I have received an interesting report of your talents from our young friend Joachim," he said genially. "I should like to hear some of your compositions if you care to play them."

Hannes was suddenly paralyzed with self-consciousness. Everything here was new and strange to him—the luxurious surroundings, the servile attitude of the young sycophants, the pontifical manner of their leader. For the life of him, he could not possibly sit down and play before such an audience.

Liszt saw the boy's confusion and did not insist further. He looked through the manuscripts which Hannes had brought with him, then took them over to the piano.

"If you will not play, then I shall have to do it myself," he said with a humorous shrug.

Johannes never forgot the following moments. Unhesitatingly, with amazing power and brilliance, Liszt read the difficult E flat minor Scherzo, all the while keeping up a running accompaniment of comment.

Young Brahms was staggered by the performance. Long after, in speaking of Liszt he would say: "Of course we others can play the piano too; but we have only a few fingers in comparison with his."

Liszt was pleased with the newcomer's compositions.

But the "disciples" were more interested in flattering their master.

"How marvelously that was played!" one of them exclaimed. "And from such a poorly written manuscript. There were parts of the composition, you know, that reminded me strongly of Chopin."

Brahms frowned. "Chopin? I don't know the gentleman, or his music either."

The other smiled incredulously and turned to Liszt. "Will the master favor us with some of his own music now? Possibly our young friend here has not heard *that* either."

There was a discreet titter among the company. With a slight bow Liszt began to play a new sonata he had just completed. Young Brahms pressed his lips together and leaned his head against the wall. It was not a type of music that appealed to him.

The famous musician was always conscious of his audience. He threw himself into his playing with a fervor that seldom failed to rouse enthusiasm. In the midst of the sonata he glanced over to see what impression he was making on the young newcomer. Brahms appeared singularly unresponsive. The master could hardly believe his eyes. . . . Joachim's protégé seemed to be asleep. Liszt finished his playing with a few abrupt chords, rose from the piano, and left the room without another word.

Remenyi smiled a little to himself. Young Brahms had certainly cooked his goose in musical Weimar! He,

Remenyi, would know better how to approach the master. Already the Hungarian was composing a letter in his mind: "This scribbler ventures to address the great man. . . ."

Remenyi decided to stay. The polished elegance of Liszt's entourage was wholly to his liking. To Hannes he remarked: "I have no desire to wander as a musical beggar from village to village. You may try your luck alone."

Nothing could have persuaded Johannes to remain in Weimar. Liszt, who was at heart too noble to harbor resentment, sent for him again and tried to persuade the youth to join the "Neo-Germans." When he saw that Brahms was definitely not interested (for Marxsen and the classicists still held sway over that young man's mind) he made no further effort to detain him. In token of their meeting, he presented Johannes with an autographed cigar-case.

To rest up from his strenuous winter concert tours, Joachim usually spent several summer months at the little university town of Göttingen. There he attended the lectures at the University, made music with his friends, and shared the jolly, carefree life of the students. He was delighted when Brahms, having left Remenyi and the Weimar circle, joined him in Göttingen.

At once the young men became devoted companions. Each had characteristics that complemented the other's, and they shared the same interests. Friendship was a necessity to Joachim's nature. Since the death of Mendelssohn, who had been first a patron and then his closest friend, he had not found the companionship that he craved. As motto he had adopted the musical theme "F A E." Only his friends knew that this stood for *Frei aber Einsam*—"Free but lonely."

Joachim's life had been a continuous triumph; he had never known failure. Brahms, on the other hand, had until recently faced nothing but hardship and struggle. With the exception of Louise Japha he had never had a close friend. It was a new experience for him to find someone to whom he could open his heart, who was sympathetic, responsive, ready to meet his efforts with warm appreciation.

Joachim was completely won over by the sincerity and childlike freshness of Johannes' nature. He wished he could keep the boy always with him. Hannes was a perfect accompanist. The two played duets, criticized each other's compositions, walked, talked, and ate their meals together.

Only one thing Johannes would not share with "Yussuf": he refused to go to the lectures at the University.

"All that stuff can be found in books," he insisted. "I prefer to get my information through reading!"

Their evenings the two friends spent in the taverns

with a group of merry student companions from the University. They made music, played games, and sang rousing choruses of college songs. Brahms was always attracted by folk-music. The college melodies were filed away in his amazing memory, to be later woven into one of his most popular compositions: the *Academic Festival Overture*—a joyous, rollicking medley of students' songs.

"I can't see why you should have chosen 'Free but *lonely*' as your motto," Hannes said to Joachim. "Freedom is a *glad* thing! *Frei aber Froh*—'Free but glad'—it should be. I think I shall have to take 'F A F' for *my* motto!"

"F A F" remained Brahms' "theme-song" all through his life. Freedom meant more to him than anything else. And in his freedom he was *glad*.

Although life at Göttingen was so pleasant, Johannes felt he must not linger there. Before returning to Hamburg, he wanted to take a walking trip down the Rhine Valley.

Joachim hated to lose his companion. "I shall let you go only on two conditions," he insisted. "First that you visit me in Hanover this winter, and second that you promise to end your walking tour at Düsseldorf and call on the Schumanns there."

Johannes was surprised to find that Joachim was a great admirer of Robert Schumann; while Joachim could not understand his young friend's disapproval.

"I'm sure you would change your opinion if only you would take the trouble to study his compositions," Joachim protested. "And aside from the music, Herr and Frau Schumann are such delightful people to know. You really must make their acquaintance."

Johannes did not promise, but he was more than half persuaded. Louise Japha had been urging him to visit Düsseldorf. At least he would see her again there.

Before they parted, Joachim arranged a concert for the two of them; and enough money was taken in to provide for Hannes' Rhine journey. Joachim also gave him a number of letters of introduction to friends along the way. Everywhere Hannes went he was cordially received.

In Mehlem the Deichmanns, ardent music-lovers, insisted that he must make them a visit. Brahms let himself be persuaded because in their music library he found a complete collection of Robert Schumann's works. While there he made a thorough study of these scores, and found to his surprise that Joachim had been right: Schumann did have his roots deep in the classics. But in addition his music had a freshness, charm, and flexibility not often found in the older masters.

Johannes decided that he would go on to Düsseldorf and present Joachim's letter of introduction to the Schumanns.

CHAPTER IX

SCHUMANN'S "YOUNG EAGLE"

As Johannes approached a low, rambling house on the outskirts of Düsseldorf, he heard someone playing the piano. He looked again at the address on the letter in his hand. Yes, this must be where the Schumanns lived. When he knocked, the playing ceased, and presently a servant-girl opened the door.

"Is Herr Schumann at home?" Hannes asked.

The girl hesitated a moment. "Yes—but he is working. He doesn't see many people."

"Then don't disturb him," said Johannes. "I only wanted to leave this letter from Herr Joachim."

The girl took the letter. "Will the gentleman please wait a moment?" she said, showing him into a large, comfortably furnished living-room.

Hannes looked about with interest. There were flowering plants, books, and piles of music everywhere. It was a pleasant, home-like house, radiating the spirit of the kindly people who lived there.

One of Schumann's manuscripts stood open on the piano. Johannes would have liked to examine it, but just then the door opened, and the Master himself came in. He was tall, rather thick-set, with fair hair worn long in the style common among musicians of the day. There was a piercing expression in his blue eyes, and his mouth was pursed into a perpetual pucker, as if he were about to whistle.

"Herr Brahms?" he said gravely.

Hannes flushed a little, and stammered that he didn't want to intrude.

"Not at all," murmured Schumann abstractedly. "Joachim has written about you before. He wants me to hear some of your compositions. Perhaps you will play for me?"

This time Johannes did not hesitate. There were no supercilious young disciples here to disconcert him, as at Weimar; no overpowering personality like Liszt.

He sat down and began the sonata which had so impressed Joachim. As he played, a swift change transformed Schumann's impassive features. The Master listened with growing interest, then suddenly sprang to his feet.

"Please," he cried. "Will you wait just a moment? Clara—" He hurried to the door and threw it open. "Clara, come here—quickly!"

Nonplused, Johannes stopped playing. Frau Schumann, a handsome woman in her mid-thirties, came hurrying in. "What is it, Robert?" she asked anxiously.

Laughing with excitement, the Master pushed his wife into a chair. "You must hear this, my dear. Something quite extraordinary, I assure you. Music such as you have never listened to before. Young man, begin again."

After he had finished the sonata, Brahms was made to play all of his compositions, one after the other, and both Robert and Clara became more and more enthusiastic. Hannes was quite overwhelmed by their praise.

"Truly, you are the one I have been waiting for!" Schumann cried, patting the young musician on the shoulder. "My boy, you and I understand each other."

The lady of the house suddenly realized that it was growing late. "Why, it's dinner-time!" she exclaimed. "Herr Brahms, you must stay and share our meal with us."

There was such a friendly, gracious expression on her face that Hannes fell at once under the spell of her compelling personality. Clara Schumann was a remarkable woman. Devoted to her husband, whom she idolized, a loving mother, and an efficient housewife, she was also one of the most eminent pianists of her day. Few women have combined so many admirable qualities in such superlative fashion.

At the table Johannes found himself surrounded by a bevy of little people. The Schumanns now had six children (one son had died when only a year old). Marie, the eldest, was twelve, and the youngest—Eugénie—not yet two. They made friends with the visitor at once. Hannes forgot his self-consciousness when he was with youngsters. His own childlike nature responded immediately to their companionship, and he was always a great favorite with the little folks in the households he visited. In Brahms' later years, this love of children was one of the main compensations for his solitary existence.

Before the meal had ended, Hannes felt almost one of the family. He had never known real home life. His early struggle for existence had been too strenuous to allow leisure for gracious living. Now, at the Schumanns', for the first time he was to know the joys of a cultured, well-ordered environment.

That evening, when Brahms returned to the inn where he had taken a room overlooking the rear court, there was a glow in his heart. He felt quite ashamed to think how he had misjudged Robert Schumann. And as for Frau Clara . . . He could see her, sitting at the head of the dining-table, the lovely oval of her face framed with thick brown hair which she wore parted in the middle, drawn over her ears, and braided into a knot at the nape of her neck. Never had Hannes met anyone so charming, so beautiful, so . . . He fell asleep with the vision of a gracious lady. She was listening with rapt attention as he played music more beautiful than had ever been heard before. Dream music. . . .

"I think if I were younger," Schumann wrote to Joachim, "I could make some polymeters about the young eagle who has so suddenly and unexpectedly flown down from the Alps to Düsseldorf. Or one might compare him to a splendid stream which, like Niagara, is at its finest when precipitating itself from the heights as a roaring waterfall, greeted by the fluttering of butterflies and by nightingales' voices. . . ."

Albert Dietrich, one of Schumann's favorite pupils, who was in Düsseldorf when Brahms arrived, later wrote a description of his first impressions of the young composer:

Soon after Brahms' arrival in September, Schumann came up to me before the commencement of one of the choral society practices with a mysterious air and a pleased smile. "Someone is come," he said, "of whom we shall one day hear all sorts of wonderful things; his name is Johannes Brahms." And he presented to me the interesting and unusual-looking young musician, who, seeming hardly more than a boy in his short gray summer coat, with his high voice and long fair hair, made a most agreeable impression. Especially fine were his energetic, characteristic mouth, and the earnest, deep gaze in which his gifted nature was clearly revealed.

Schumann was surprised to learn that none of young Brahms' music had yet been published. "I shall recommend you personally to my publishers," he said. "I think Breitkopf and Härtel in Leipzig are the best in Germany."

To the publishers he wrote: "A young man has just presented himself who has most deeply impressed us with his wonderful music. He will, I am convinced, make the greatest sensation in the musical world."

Johannes had expected to stay only a short while in Düsseldorf; but life there was so pleasant that he could not bring himself to leave. At first he hesitated a little about going to the Schumanns', for fear of forcing himself on his new friends. But when Frau Schumann herself came over to fetch him, and insisted that he must have his meals at their house, he lost his reserve and entered into the family circle as if he belonged there.

Johannes was delighted to find his old companion, Louise Japha, among the group of eager students surrounding the Schumanns. There were other young ladies too. The quiet, aloof young musician from Hamburg now discovered, for the first time, that the society of the opposite sex could be quite pleasant, rather than the bore he had always thought it. His happiest hours, however, were spent in Robert Schumann's library.

One day Louise Japha discovered him there. "Only see what I have found, Louise!" he cried, holding up a battered copy of his old favorite *Robinson Crusoe*. "It is marvelous what a fine collection of books the master has gathered. And he has given me permission to come to his library whenever I wish—even to borrow these precious books!" His voice was solemn, almost contrite. "He is a very generous, a very lovable man, Robert Schumann. And to think that once I believed him proud, affected, self-important! Only imagine," he continued, "when he found out that I was pretty hard up, he even offered me his purse!"

At the Schumanns' home Hannes met some interesting musicians and painters. A whole new world of culture opened up to him. The sensitive child from Hamburg's slums found an environment here that was really stimulating and congenial.

Naturally music held the place of honor in this household. Clara and young Brahms often played together, while Robert listened with keen appreciation. There were times when Schumann seemed oblivious of his surroundings, wrapped up in a gentle melancholy and completely abstracted from the world. Then he would rouse himself to applaud the performers.

Much of his music was written for, and inspired by, his wife. Young Brahms could understand how such a woman might inspire a man! Daily his admiration for Clara Schumann increased.

When Johannes, fearing he might be outstaying his welcome, began to talk of leaving Düsseldorf, the Schumanns cried out indignantly.

"You cannot possibly go until we decide which of your compositions you must take to Breitkopf and Härtel," said Robert.

"And you know," Clara added, "in just a week or so the Lower Rhine Music Festival begins; and surely you don't want to miss that. Joachim is coming, you know."

That day Schumann was in one of his bright moods. "Let's plan a surprise for the honorable Yussuf," he cried gayly. "He really should have a musical welcome! Together we could compose a pasticcio. What shall it be? A sonata for violin and piano?" He turned to young Dietrich. "You, Albert, shall do the first movement. Johannes can take the scherzo. And I shall write the other two. Then we will make Joachim guess who is responsible for which."

Putting their delighted heads together, they decided to base the composition on Joachim's musical signature: "F A E." Schumann himself wrote the dedication page, using the famous signature in reversed order, E A F.:

> This sonata has been written in Expectation of the Arrival of the honored and beloved Friend Joseph Joachim by Robert Schumann, Johannes Brahms, Albert Dietrich.

When Joachim arrived, on October 26th, he was greeted by a large group of friends. Little Julie, Schumann's third daughter, was dressed in an old-fashioned costume, with poke bonnet and folded kerchief; and as the violinist stepped from the train she handed him a basket of flowers. Beneath the flowers he found a rolled manuscript inscribed: "To our beloved friend, Joseph Joachim."

That evening a merry crowd gathered at the Schumanns' house to hear the new composition. Joachim took out his violin and Frau Clara seated herself at the piano. Before the sonata was finished he had correctly guessed the authorship of each movement.

Jakob Brahms was just about to leave for a rehearsal at the Stadt Theater one morning when the postman came. Now that Hannes was away, the arrival of the mail had become an important event in the little household.

Old Jakob talked so incessantly of Hannes' triumphs that his cronies grew a little bored by his panegyrics. Fritz Becker, his next-door neighbor, had even dared to insinuate that Herr Brahms might be given to exaggeration.

Since word had just come from Hannes, telling of his joy in meeting the Schumanns and of the wonderful welcome they had given him, Jakob did not really expect the postman to leave anything that morning. To his surprise the man stopped him as he was going down the stairs with his double-bass.

"A letter for you, Herr Brahms," he said, thrusting a stamped, folded sheet into his hand.

Jakob hurried into his wife's little shop. "Johanna," he cried, "is it *luck*, I ask? Another letter so soon!"

Frau Brahms looked at the address. "This is not our

Hannes' handwriting. Who could it be from?" She opened the seal and found the signature. "Heavens—it can't be—yes, it is—from the great Herr Schumann himself!"

A few moments later Herr Brahms burst into the shop of his friend Fritz Becker. In one hand he brandished the letter, and he was quite breathless with excitement.

"You, Fritz—now what do you say to *this?* Schumann himself has written to me! He says that my Hannes is a great, important artist—and he'll be a second Beethoven!"

Fritz was outraged. It was all very well for Jakob Brahms to brag about his son; but to compare him to Beethoven—that was going a little too far! "What?" he cried. "That foolish, tow-headed young urchin is to become a second Beethoven? Have you gone off your head?" He fixed the excited father with a severe eye. "How can you believe such nonsense? Hannes will never turn into a great man."

Jakob was crestfallen. Fritz always floored him in an argument. Then he remembered that this time he had proof. He withdrew proudly from Herr Becker's presence. At the door he fired a parting shot: "But *Schumann* SAYS SO!"

Soon after his marriage to Clara Wieck, Schumann wrote in his diary: "One thing makes me happy—the consciousness of being still far from my goal and obliged to keep doing better, and then the feeling that I have strength to meet it."

Now, thirteen years later, he felt instinctively that his strength was spent. There were goals that he could never reach. Others, however, would carry on. *One* other . . .

This one, whom he called the "young eagle," he wanted to help in every way within his power. "I should wish to assist him on his first flight through the world," he wrote to Joachim. Now he thought of a way to speed that first flight.

In 1834, a year after Hannes' birth, Robert Schumann had founded a musical review entitled the *New Magazine for Music.* He had always been an ardent champion of the finest in music. Unfair criticism roused his anger, and so did overindulgent praise. Impartial and constructive judgment was, he felt, the only kind that was justified. In an attempt to foster such criticism he started the musical review. One of the finest critics music has ever known, he had written many admirable articles for the magazine. But for the past ten years he had contributed very little.

Now, in his enthusiasm for the genius he had discovered, he decided, with more of impulsive generosity than of wisdom, to introduce Brahms to the world through an article in the *New Magazine*.

Schumann wrote in glowing terms:

I have thought that someone must and would suddenly appear, destined to give ideal presentment to the highest expression of the time, who would develop his mastery, not step by step, but would spring forth fully armed as Minerva sprang from the head of Jove. And he is come, a youngster by whose cradle graces and heroes kept watch. He is called Johannes Brahms, and came from Hamburg. . . . He bore all the outward signs that proclaim to us, "This is one of the elect."

Schumann went on to speak in terms still more glowing of the "young elect," and closed:

There is in every age a secret union of kindred spirits. Bind closer the circle, you who belong to it, that the truth of art may shine ever clearer, spreading joy and blessing throughout the world.

Little did Schumann realize how much bitter controversy and criticism, and what actual damage to Brahms, this article was to provoke.

CHAPTER X

TRIUMPHANT HOMECOMING

THE BRAHMS apartment in Hamburg wore an air of unaccustomed festivity. Sprigs of holly and mistletoe decorated the windows, and in one corner of the small living-dining-room stood a little fir tree gay with strings of colored paper and white wax tapers. From the kitchen came a delicious odor of roasting goose. Frau Brahms limped about with such energy that Elise was afraid her mother would be completely worn out. Even Jakob could hardly contain himself.

It was Christmas eve, 1853, and now Hannes, after eight months away from home, was coming back to his family. When he had left them in April he had been only a boy, not quite twenty, bashful, awkward, and unknown. And now—"*Ja, ja,* it is a genius we have, another Beethoven," Jakob never tired of repeating. "He's made friends with all the musicians. They honor him. Think of it!—my Hannes! Joachim, Schumann, Liszt—" Jakob rolled the famous names on his tongue.

When Johannes finally arrived, Father Brahms was so overcome with emotion that words failed him with which to greet his son. He could only stand and look, awestruck, at the young swan he had so unexpectedly fathered.

Elise hung back too. Life had not favored Johannes' sister. She was small and plain like her mother; her only beauty, a head of long, thick hair. And although she was not yet twenty-three, lines of pain from constant headaches made her look much older.

Fritz, two years younger than Johannes, stared at his brother with more envy than love. Jakob had tried to make a musician of this son too, but genius seldom strikes twice in one family. Poor Fritz was always to be known as "the wrong Brahms"; and how bitterly he did resent it!

Only Johanna remained completely herself. She alternately held her Hannes close and pushed him away from her that she might see how he had changed during these eventful months.

Johannes carried a package under his arm. After the first greetings, he opened it carefully.

"Here is my Christmas gift, little Mother—for you and Father too. See—my first printed compositions! Schumann insisted I must go myself to the publishers, Breitkopf and Härtel in Leipzig. They took my works at once."

Jakob was ready to burst with pride. "A great composer, my Hannes!" he murmured, tears in his eyes.

Dinner that day was an event. Several friends (including the skeptical Fritz Becker, who had so laughed at the idea of Hannes' ever amounting to anything) had been invited to hear young Brahms tell of his travels and triumphs. They all sat around the table until late in the afternoon, listening wide-eyed.

"Late in October," Hannes told them, "I left the Schumanns and went to Hanover to visit Joachim. Then to Leipzig to see the music publishers. Herr Schumann was kind enough to send them a personal recommendation."

There were murmurs and shaking of heads around the table, for Jakob had already proudly displayed Hannes' Christmas gift.

Young Brahms went on to tell of playing two of his own works at a Leipzig concert; but he was too modest to mention the sympathetic notices he had had from some of the critics; or how they praised his appearance. ("The slender, fair youth—so shy, so modest," they wrote, "with Raphael head, Schiller profile, eyes of forget-me-not blue.")

Johannes spoke of meeting the French composer Berlioz. "He was very kind to me," he said. Actually Berlioz had been so enthusiastic over his concert that he had embraced young Brahms, and had exclaimed prophetically: "There is one who will suffer!"

Hannes, however, did not care for the French composer's music. "They call it 'program music,' because it is supposed to tell a story. That seems to be the style now, at least among the composers of the 'New German' school—Liszt especially. But as for me, I think that to tie music down in this way to a single idea is nothing short of blasphemy!"

The lad was silent for a while. "I saw Herr Liszt again in Leipzig," he said presently. "He called on me several times, and wanted me to join his group in Weimar. But the music he stands for—well, it doesn't appeal to me."

Brahms was not interested in cults or schools. Only one thing was important to him: music itself. All through life he remained uncompromising when it came to his beliefs and ideals. He had been brought up in the tradition of the classics, and although he often treated the old forms with rare originality, such work had its roots firmly planted in the training of his early youth.

"That was a nice article Herr Schumann wrote about

you in the *New Magazine for Music,"* Jakob said proudly.

"Nice!" thought Hannes, remembering how hard it had been for him to express his appreciation of such praise. After several attempts he had finally sent Schumann a letter:

Honored Master,

You have made me so immensely happy that I cannot attempt to thank you in words. God grant that my works may soon prove to you how much your affection and kindness have encouraged and stimulated me. The public praise you have bestowed on me will have focussed people's expectations so sharply upon my performances that I do not know how I shall be able to do some measure of justice to it.

"I'm afraid Herr Schumann's praise did more harm than good," Johannes admitted, a little ruefully. "Everyone expects far too much of me now."

"But as soon as they hear your compositions they will know that he did not exaggerate!" the mother exclaimed with pride. "Why, in those articles you sent me—listen only to this . . ." she cried, limping over to the desk and taking out some newspaper clippings:

Schumann's article caused much discussion among the uninitiated, but all doubt has been dispelled by Brahms' public appearance, and we concur with all our heart, and with the warmest satisfaction, in Schumann's opinion of the unassuming and richly endowed young artist.

Johanna looked around the table with a proud nod of her head. "Here's another:

There is something forcible, something transporting, in the works which Brahms performed the other evening. A ripeness rare in one so young, a creative power springing spontaneously from a rich artist-mind, are revealed in them. We find ourselves in the presence of one of those highly gifted natures, an artist by the grace of God."

Hannes was terribly embarrassed to hear such praise read aloud. "That critic was a friend of Herr Schumann's," he murmured deprecatingly. "He and Joachim have been too kind. Now Liszt, I fear, would be less indulgent."

Jakob looked around the table with a deep sigh of satisfaction. His Hannes uttered great names as if they were no more than—well, than the name of his friend Fritz Becker, for example, who sat there with his mouth open. Fritz would be obliged to admit that the "towheaded urchin" had not turned out so badly after all! It was a great day for Jakob Brahms. All the disappointments and failures of his own life now seemed vindicated and fulfilled in the triumphs of his beloved son.

The day after he arrived in Hamburg, Johannes went to see his old teacher Marxsen. The latter had heard all about young Brahms' success in Leipzig. To a friend he had written: "There was probably but one man who was not surprised—myself. I knew what Brahms had accomplished, how comprehensive his acquirements were, what exalted talent had been bestowed on him, and how finely its blossom was unfolding."

Hannes' second visit was to Cossel (he was later to stand godfather to Cossel's baby daughter), and then—by way of celebrating his emancipation from the hated drudgery of earlier years—he made the rounds of the taverns where he had been obliged to play as a youth.

It was a happy vacation, that Christmas of 1853. "My parents, my teachers, and myself are in the seventh heaven," he wrote to Joachim, "and I can only wish that you may have spent the festival season as gloriously as we did."

Soon after New Year's, Brahms returned to Hanover to see Joachim again, and there he also found a new friend, Julius Otto Grimm, whom he had met that fall in Leipzig. Grimm was known as "Ise" to his intimates. Joachim ("Yussuf"), Albert Dietrich, and "Ise" became Brahms' closest young friends.

The three spent most of their evenings together discussing, arguing, and making music until all hours. Joachim and "Ise" smoked like chimneys. Johannes had never tried tobacco, but finally in self-defense he too began. Soon he was the greatest smoker of them all. In later years Brahms was seldom seen without a cigar.

Hans von Bülow, gifted concert pianist and close friend of Liszt, came to Hanover in January, and Brahms made his acquaintance. "A very lovable, frank nature," Bülow wrote of the young composer, "and a talent that really has something God-given about it."

Thin, elegant, with a sensitive face and small, pointed beard, Bülow was the first artist (aside from the composer himself) to play Brahms' music in public. A month or so after their first meeting, at a concert in Hamburg, he performed part of the C Major Sonata. Johannes was touched at this mark of esteem. "I shall hold it in the heart's memory," he told the pianist. He wondered how Bülow had managed to memorize the difficult composition, for it then existed only in manuscript form. But Hans von Bülow's memory was prodigious: he could read through a piece on the train during an afternoon, and then the same evening play it by heart without ever having tried it on the piano.

At that time Bülow was too much under the spell of Liszt and the "New German" program type of music, really to appreciate young Brahms' work. After his first enthusiasm he decided that this composer was too severe and academic for his taste. Years were to go by before he finally gave him his whole-hearted approval. "I respect and admire him," he wrote, "but—at a distance!"

Eventually, however, Hans von Bülow was to become one of Brahms' most devoted interpreters. He it was who later coined the phrase "The three B's: Bach, Beethoven, and Brahms." It is interesting to realize that all three of these imperishable names had their origin in nature. Beethoven means "beet-garden"; Brahms, "broom-plant"; and Bach, the "brook" which, deep-flowing, waters the other two.

Late in January 1854 Robert and Clara Schumann came to Hanover for a series of concerts. Joachim conducted the orchestra and also played the master's violin *Fantasie,* while Frau Schumann performed a number of her husband's piano compositions. It was a gay and festive time; there were parties and much champagne. Schumann was in high spirits, happy and carefree. Little did his friends realize that these high spirits were the last he was destined to enjoy.

A month later, tragedy struck.

In Hanover, on the morning of February 28th, Joachim was preparing to go to a rehearsal, when Johannes, pale with emotion, burst into the room. He thrust a newspaper at his friend.

"I can't believe it—only read what a terrible thing has happened. The master—" He stopped for breath, then went on as Joachim seized the paper from his hand: "Herr Schumann has suddenly gone out of his mind. He tried to drown himself in the Rhine, but some fisherman rescued him. Now he is to be committed to an asylum."

"How horrible! Poor Frau Clara!" Joachim began.

"I must go to her at once," Johannes exclaimed. Before the day was ended he had started for Düsseldorf.

He found Clara beside herself with grief. "Only for a moment was Robert left alone!" she cried, clinging to her young friend's hands. "He was in his bathrobe and slippers. How could anyone dream . . . The keeper at the bridge said that Robert had no money to pay his toll, and so left his scarf with him. Then he threw himself over the edge. Oh, it is too terrible!"

In vain Johannes tried to comfort the poor woman, but she was too distraught to listen. "We had no idea that his condition was so serious," she went on. "But I should have known! He kept talking about a certain note that he heard all the time. And then the last composition he wrote—he insisted that Schubert had come to him personally and given him the theme. . . . I just thought he was overwrought!" The tears rained down her cheeks. "They would not let me see him before they took him to the asylum in Bonn. They were afraid. You see"—she looked up at the young musician with anguished eyes—"I am to have another child soon."

On June 11th Clara Schumann's eighth child was born. He was named Felix, after Mendelssohn, and Johannes Brahms was chosen godfather.

All through the trying months that followed Schumann's breakdown, Johannes stayed close by the distracted Clara. "Brahms is my dearest, truest support," Frau Schumann wrote in a letter to a friend. "Since the beginning of Robert's illness he has never left me, but has gone through everything with me and shared my sufferings."

Schumann's condition varied. At times the report would come that he seemed quite normal, and then it was pathetic to see how Frau Clara's spirits revived. But soon the unfortunate man would become violent again, or sink into a deep melancholy from which it was impossible to rouse him.

Johannes' devotion was touching. He visited Robert

in the asylum, being one of the few people allowed to see him; even Clara was not permitted to go to her husband. He sent him books and music, including a new composition, "Variations on a Theme by Robert Schumann," dedicated to Clara. Johannes also carried messages to the musician from his wife. "I have learned to love you and your splendid wife more than ever," he wrote to Schumann.

In spite of the shadow that hung over the household, Brahms was happy, for each day he became more deeply attached to the sorrowing Clara.

Schumann continued in his sad state for more than two years. During most of that time Brahms stayed in Düsseldorf. Clara was obliged to give concerts, wherever she could get engagements, in order to support her family and pay the heavy asylum expenses. She often included some of Brahms' compositions in her programs. Occasionally he played concerts with her, and sometimes Joachim also joined them with his violin. But for the most part Brahms stayed in Düsseldorf, giving lessons to Clara's pupils during her absence, and keeping an eye on the children.

He was devoted to the young Schumanns, and in some ways was as much of a child as they were. He loved to amuse them by sliding down the bannisters, or doing acrobatic tricks. They often begged him to make songs for them, and he did so. Later these were gathered into a collection and published anonymously under the title "Children's Folk-Songs, with added accompaniment, dedicated to the children of Robert and Clara Schumann." In this collection is found "The Little Sandman," based on the theme from *In Bethlem Transeamus.*

Joachim came occasionally to Düsseldorf, and he and Johannes wrote to each other frequently, sending compositions for criticism.

> I want to remind you of what we have so often discussed [wrote Brahms], and beg you to let us carry it out, namely, to send one another exercises in counterpoint. Every fortnight each should return the other's work . . . with remarks and his own work, this to continue for a good long time, until we have both become really clever. Why should not two sensible, earnest people like ourselves be able to teach one another far better than any professor could?

In order to make the bargain binding, the two young men invented a system of fines to punish irregularity in the sending of work, the money to be spent for music and books. Johannes, who had fewer claims on his time and attention, profited the more by the arrangement.

Although Robert's sad condition was always present in the minds of those who loved him, there were occasional happy times at the Schumanns' home in Düsseldorf.

On the morning of May 7th, 1855, Johannes noticed a strange air of mystery in the house. As he came in for dinner, Elise and Julie were giggling and whispering in a corner, and little four-year-old Eugénie shrieked and nearly dropped a basket of flowers when he suddenly came upon her from behind and lifted her high into the air.

Then the door to the dining-room was thrown open, and a chorus of voices greeted him: "Happy birthday, dear Hannes!"

He had quite forgotten that it was his twenty-second birthday. At first he was so confused that he failed to notice a familiar figure standing beside Frau Clara. Then—"Yussuf—is it *you?*" he cried, as Joachim advanced, smiling broadly.

"I came as a surprise for your birthday, my friend," said the violinist. "And what's more, I've made plans to spend some time in Düsseldorf!"

Nothing could have pleased Johannes more, though he did not realize what a far-reaching effect this visit of Joachim's was to have on his work. In the same house where the violinist was staying, there lived a 'cellist named Van Diest. Joachim, hard at composition, was disturbed by his neighbor's playing, and asked the landlord to protest. Herr Van Diest amiably toned down his instrument, and Joachim was so grateful that he invited the 'cellist to join him with two others in quartets.

Soon they were meeting regularly. Johannes was always present. When he was not playing with them, at the piano, he would sit in a corner, hand over eyes, listening intently. It was his first opportunity to hear chamber music well performed, and it so inspired him that he soon began writing it himself.

That birthday morning Johannes had no more than recovered from his surprise at seeing Joachim, before he found his two other friends, "Ise" Grimm and Albert Dietrich, who had also been summoned to the celebration. It was a merry reunion. Little Eugénie presented her basket of flowers; Marie and Julie recited a poem they had written in Johannes' honor; and even the baby, frail little Felix, was brought in to stare, round-eyed, at his godfather.

Frau Clara sat behind a fine new coffee-machine that Joachim had brought from Hanover, and she motioned Johannes to a seat beside her. There he found a pile of music. From Robert came the manuscript copy of his Overture to *The Bride of Messina.* Beneath this was a sheet of music that pleased Johannes more than anything else: a composition written by Clara herself, *Romance for the Pianoforte,* with a special dedication to her beloved Hannes.

"And now," announced Ise with mock importance, "comes the real *pièce de résistance*—the masterpiece of all! A musical birthday cake—and, if you please, *I* am the author!"

When Johannes opened the package he found no cake, but—more music! *Brahms Polka* it was entitled, a farcical take-off on the favorite dance-tune of the moment, based on the musical letters in the name "Brahms."

Three weeks later the yearly Lower Rhine Festival took place in Düsseldorf. There Johannes met Jenny

Lind, the favorite prima donna of the day and one of the greatest singers the world has ever known. He also made the acquaintance of the Viennese music critic Hanslick, who was later to become one of his close friends.

During the summer of 1855 Robert Schumann seemed much better, and it was sometimes hoped that he might entirely recover. Brahms planned to take a walking trip along the Rhine, like his first journey—was it but two years ago? He could not help thinking how enormously his life had changed since then.

"Why don't you come with me, dear Clara?" he asked Frau Schumann. "You have grown pale and thin with worry. Now that our beloved Master is nearly well again, surely you can allow yourself a short holiday!"

Clara was eventually persuaded. Accompanied by her maid, she and Johannes spent a leisurely ten days walking along the banks of the Rhine. Brahms was completely happy. This journey proved to be one of the most joyous experiences of his whole life.

The following spring Frau Schumann traveled to London to give a series of concerts. It was her first visit to England; she was anxious to make a good impression, and not a little nervous over her début there.

On the day of her first concert a letter from Johannes arrived. Clara was always hopeful there would be news of an improvement in Robert's health. The doctors, however, had of late seemed less sure that he would recover. She sometimes wondered whether they really told her the truth about his condition. . . .

Suddenly she gave a cry. Brahms wrote that he had just returned from a visit to Schumann. He had not been allowed to see him for several months, and now he was terribly shocked at the change in the master. As gently as possible Johannes had to tell Clara that her husband's end was very near.

The poor woman was prostrated. "It can't be true!" she cried in anguish. Always she had believed that sooner or later Robert would get well. Surely *something* could still be done! Perhaps they ought to find a new doctor. She must return at once. . . . But the concert that evening! Impossible—her fingers were like wax; she could never play.

Then she remembered the children at home who depended on her for their daily bread. She *must* play, even if her heart was breaking!

That evening few people in the audience, listening to the superb performance which Clara Schumann gave, suspected what a tragedy had occurred. The concert proved such a brilliant success that she was engaged to play again at the following Philharmonic concert.

A few weeks later, on July 29th, 1856, Robert Schumann passed away at the asylum in Bonn.

His wife, Joachim, and Johannes Brahms—whom the master had "loved like a son"—were in the building; but nobody was with him when he died.

CHAPTER XI

TWO LOVES

AFTER the death of her husband, Clara Schumann was prostrated with grief. The years of anxiety over his condition, the strain of her incessant concert engagements, and the problems of caring for her family, all affected her health so seriously that her friends—Brahms especially—began to fear that she might have a breakdown. He told her: "You must go away for a long holiday this summer; Switzerland, with its bracing air, would be just the place."

The idea appealed to Clara. Johannes must come with her. "And why not take your sister Elise too? I shall write her at once."

When the invitation reached Elise the girl could hardly believe her good fortune. She had seldom been away from Hamburg. Always she had longed to go to Switzerland. During the long hours when she sat, bent over the fine sewing that strained her eyes so badly, she would dream of the beautiful Swiss lakes and flower-filled meadows. And sometimes, when she lay in a darkened room, suffering from one of her constantly recurring headaches, the thought of snow-covered mountains would be like a cooling touch on her brow.

In August a considerable party set out from Düsseldorf. There were Clara and several of her children, Johannes and his sister Elise, and Joachim, who stayed for only part of the summer.

In the quaint little village of Gersau they found a picturesque chalet overlooking Lake Lucerne. Here they settled down for several leisurely weeks. Elise's headaches soon disappeared; her health improved, and her pain-sharpened tongue lost its edge. She was in raptures over this enchanted country. Never had she seen anything so blue as the lake, so green as the lush mountain meadows, so white as the dazzling snow peaks surrounding them.

There were frequent day-long excursions from Gersau. With lunch-filled knapsacks on their backs they climbed the neighboring mountains, walked up to the famous "Ox Road" whose galleried arches are hewn out of solid rock, and made a pilgrimage to the William Tell shrine at the edge of the lake. Elise was filled with sentimental emotion as she stood on the spot where the Swiss patriot (celebrated for shooting the apple from his son's head) leapt to freedom from a tossing rowboat in the midst of a violent storm.

Best of all, Elise Brahms loved the quiet evenings at Gersau. There was always music: Frau Schumann at the piano, or Hannes, or Joachim with his violin, or a group playing chamber music. To these people, whose whole life was bound up in the world of sound, music was a natural and necessary part of existence. They might well have paraphrased the French motto: "A day without wine is a day without sunshine," and said instead: "A day without music is a day without light."

As they played, Elise would sit listening on the gallery of the chalet and look out over the twilight-stilled lake. The music made her dream of all the things that had been denied her own poor life. Dimly, with sentimental yearning, she would be conscious of the unspoken romance at her side. . . .

Johannes was very happy. Just to be near his beloved Clara was joy enough for him. She represented everything that he most admired. Always she remained his greatest inspiration. "How unhappy I should be if I did not have you!" he once wrote her. "It is from you that I am constantly learning that one cannot obtain vital force out of books, but only out of one's own soul. One must draw inspiration not from without, but from within."

He admired Clara for her courage and nobility of character, her tenderness and understanding. Everything that Brahms loved in his mother he found in

Clara Schumann—indeed, there was not a little of the mother-complex in his feeling for her. The difference in their ages did not matter to him. What if she was fourteen years his senior? Was not his own mother seventeen years older than his father?

"I grow more and more joyful and peaceful in my love for you," he had written that same spring. "I miss you more every time, but my longing for you is almost joyful—it really is; and I have known the feeling before, and never was my heart so warm." And again: "I wish I could write to you as tenderly as I love you, and do all the kind and loving things that I desire for you."

In music he could speak to her more eloquently than in words. "I hope you will hear something beautiful and endearing in this," he wrote, sending Clara a composition. "I think a true spirit and a heart aglow with love can make itself heard in music. . . ."

Just what Frau Schumann's feelings were for the young composer has never been fully known. Ise Grimm wrote: "He was to her as a careful friend, a loving and protecting son." At any rate she wisely decided not to marry again. Her first duty was to her children, and next in importance came music.

So when fall arrived, Brahms went on his way into the world alone, while Clara Schumann continued her career. The deep affection that bound the two never changed for long. During life they remained devoted friends.

While Schumann was ill and his wife away on concert tours, Brahms had taken over a number of Clara's pupils. In this way he made the acquaintance of Fräulein von Meysenbug and her family. The spring following the trip to Switzerland he was invited to visit them at their home in Detmold.

The Meysenbug ladies proved very prim and conventional. Brahms was ill at ease. He was so afraid of shocking his aristocratic hostesses that he hardly knew what to say or how to behave. Their young nephew Carl, however, with whom he soon struck up a friendship, was ready for any fun.

The family had close connections at the court of Detmold, and the evening after his arrival Brahms was invited to play at a court concert. His performance made a fine impression on the royal family. But Kapellmeister Kiel, who was director of music at Detmold and a pompous old soul, decided that the twenty-three-year-old visitor was much overrated. Did this young upstart imagine that no one else could compose music but himself?

"I have been occupied with setting a number of Bible texts to music," Herr Kiel announced importantly. He fixed Johannes with a haughty stare. "Some of the Scriptural expressions elude me. *Githith,* for instance. Herr Brahms, you seem to know so much. Could you tell me what a *Githith* is?"

Johannes knew his Bible backwards and forwards.

He winked at young Carl. "Probably it means 'a pretty Jewish girl,'" he answered solemnly.

After the concert, Brahms and a number of others went to a tavern. Carl von Meysenbug was supposed to be at home, in bed. But he had managed to escape from his aunt's watchful eyes and wanted to make the most of his freedom. When the party left the tavern at dawn he said: "It's too late to go to bed now. Let's walk into the country and see the sun rise. I've never stayed out all night before," he added gleefully. "Wouldn't my aunts be scandalized!"

Brahms was always ready for a walk. Just as they were, in full evening dress, they started out. After sauntering for some distance they came to a small wayside inn. Adjoining it was a trellised arbor with table and benches. By this time Carl's enthusiasm had worn off. "What do you say to a little rest?" he asked.

The young men stretched out on the benches and fell fast asleep. Presently the sun rose; still they slept on. A small brown spaniel trotted by and looked inquiringly at the two sleepers. He stood up on his hind legs and gently licked the nose of the fair-haired stranger.

"Heavens!" cried Brahms, sitting up suddenly. He shook his companion by the shoulder. "Do you realize it's broad daylight? We're far from home—and look how we're dressed!"

They hurried back to Detmold. Just as they arrived at the Meysenbugs' house, hoping to slip in by a side door unobserved, "there—oh, horror!" wrote Carl describing the adventure, "we suddenly came upon my aunt setting out for her morning walk. A cold glance of righteous indignation traveled up and down the two night-enthusiasts; for our attire betrayed but too clearly that we had not been back since the previous evening. During the day a stormy atmosphere prevailed in the house of the hospitable ladies, who were not only unused to visits from men, but could never have imagined that the ideal artist would commit himself to such extravagances. I was severely censured by grandmother and aunts as the harebrained youth who had led the honored guest astray. Brahms left the next day, not having been very warmly pressed to prolong his visit!"

However, in spite of this adventure, Brahms' short stay in Detmold proved rich in consequences. His playing had made such a favorable impression at court that he was invited to return the following autumn and stay through the season. This lasted until the New Year. He was to give piano lessons to one of the princesses, play at court, and conduct an amateur choral society.

This was Brahms' first official post. He felt that now, at last, he was launched on an independent career.

Detmold was a pleasant little city. Its picturesque castle had been built in medieval times, when moats and portcullises were a necessary protection against covetous neighbors. But now the moats were overgrown with grass, and the turrets ivy-covered, while trees shaded the enclosed courtyards.

The country around Detmold was mellow and full of charm. The rolling hills and cool green forests, which came up close to the city walls and shut away the outside world, appealed especially to the nature-loving visitor from Hamburg.

Brahms found the place much to his liking. At the City-of-Frankfort Inn opposite the castle he was installed by his royal patrons in comfortable rooms; meals were included and a daily half-bottle of ordinary wine. On Sundays, with Carl von Meysenbug and other friends, he usually went into the country on picnics. By forgoing his daily allowance of wine, Johannes was enabled to bring along as his contribution a fine bottle of Malmsey.

Mornings at Detmold he always gave to practice and composition. Also he spent much time in reading. "Whoever wishes to play well must not only practice a great deal, but must also read a great many books," he often remarked.

His duties at Detmold were not too heavy, so he was able to do much composing. He now began to be conscious of his own powers, and to glory in creative work. "I really believe, dear Clara, that I am growing," he wrote to Frau Schumann. And in other letters: "Now I feel that I can take in my stride many things that I previously had to toil over. How fine it is to create with unimpaired strength!"

Brahms spent the fall of three successive years at Detmold, and while there he composed a number of chamber music works, two Serenades for small orchestra, and a piano concerto. This concerto gave him more trouble than almost any other of his compositions.

Some years earlier he had begun to sketch out a symphony in D minor. Then for the first time he heard a performance of Beethoven's great Ninth in the same key. It made such an overwhelming impression on him that he could not bring himself to go on with his own symphony. Not until twenty years later did he find the courage to attempt this form of music-writing. Meanwhile the material he had thought to use thus was woven into a sonata for two pianos. Again he was not satisfied. After much working over, the sonata finally became the concerto in D minor for piano and orchestra.

During his second season at Detmold, Brahms finished the concerto, and, shortly after the New Year, Joachim arranged to have it performed in Hanover. Brahms played the piano part, and his friend conducted the orchestra. A few days later the work was repeated in Leipzig.

In Hanover the piano concerto had a moderate success, but the Leipzig performance proved the greatest fiasco of the composer's entire career. The critics were almost venomous in their abuse:

> It has nothing to offer but waste, barren dreariness truly disconsolate. Its invention is neither attractive nor agreeable. . . . And for more than three-quarters of an hour one must endure this rooting and rummaging, this dragging and drawing, this tearing and patching of phrases and flourishes! Not

only must one take in this fermenting mass; one must also swallow a dessert of the shrillest dissonances and most unpleasant sounds.

Brahms took all this in his stride.

> My concerto here brilliantly and decisively—fell down! [He wrote to Joachim.] The first and second movements were listened to without the slightest display of feeling. At the conclusion three pairs of hands were brought together very languidly, whereupon a perfectly distinct hissing from all sides forbade any further demonstration of approval.

The following words from this letter should be taken to heart by all struggling young artists who are too often crushed by adverse criticism:

> This failure has made no impression on me. . . . In spite of everything, the concerto will succeed when I have improved its form; and the next one will be quite different. I believe this is the best thing that could happen to one; it forces one to concentrate his thoughts and increases his courage.

Only one little phrase showed how wounded Brahms really was: "But," he concluded, "the hissing was a bit too much?"

It was during the summer of 1858 that Brahms met Agathe von Siebold. He had gone to visit Ise Grimm at Göttingen, the university town where Joachim spent his holidays. Ise had recently married, and his home was a meeting place for the younger musicians.

"I have invited some people in this evening," he told

Johannes on the latter's arrival. "Not a party!" he hastened to add, knowing his friend's taste. "There will be music. Unfortunately Joachim doesn't get back from England until next week, but we have a fair quartet, and perhaps Agathe von Siebold will sing. She is one of my harmony pupils, and she has a good voice too."

Fräulein Agathe was shy and rather plain. When he was first introduced to her, Hannes was not particularly attracted to the girl. But when she began to sing (one of his own songs, too!) he saw her in a different light.

"You have a beautiful voice, Fräulein," he said earnestly. "And you sing with such delicate feeling!"

Agathe flushed with pleasure. To have a compliment from Herr Brahms—a really well-known musician! Her heart beat so fast that she could find no words with which to answer.

"I shall have to write some songs for you," the young composer continued. "Will you sing them with me?"

Brahms always had a weakness for lovely voices—particularly if they belonged to young and charming girls. All the women he loved could sing. Even Clara Schumann was a fair contralto, and on more than one occasion joined his women's choruses.

During the weeks following, Johannes and Agathe saw much of each other. One day he found her struggling over an exercise in composition which his friend Ise had given her. Music-writing was not Agathe's strong point. "Herr Grimm scolds me for making so many mistakes," she admitted to her new friend.

"He *does!*" cried Johannes mischievously. "Well—let's astonish him this time."

He sat down and wrote out the exercise for her. Agathe copied it and proudly carried the sheet to her teacher. But Herr Grimm's reaction was not what she expected. Instead of showing pleased surprise, he cried indignantly: "But this is *terrible!* How on earth did you ever come to write such pitiable rubbish?"

Poor Agathe blushed and finally stammered: "What if Johannes wrote it?" "Then," answered Ise, "it would be still worse!"

Suddenly the two looked at each other and burst out laughing. They realized that Brahms had been fooling them both.

The more Johannes saw of Agathe the better he liked her. Now he could almost put out of his heart the hopeless passion for Frau Schumann. Clara had recently come to Göttingen to spend the summer there with her children. Woman-like, she was inclined to be jealous of her younger rival.

Johannes and Agathe were now so constantly together that everyone began to think they must be engaged. But it came time for the young composer to return to Detmold, and still he had not asked her to marry him. The truth was, he could not bring himself to give up his liberty.

"I love you! I must see you again!" he wrote from Detmold. "But fetters I cannot wear. . . ."

Poor Agathe was broken-hearted.

Brahms himself knew that he had not been quite fair to the unfortunate girl. "I have played the scoundrel towards Agathe," he confessed remorsefully. Not until six years later did he dismiss her completely from his mind. At that time, in writing his G major sextet, he included the musical anagram of her name in the score. As our scale is not very strong on correct spelling, the nearest Brahms could come to TH was D. So that the melody read: "A G A D E." In pointing this out to a friend he said: "Here I have emancipated myself from my last love."

In later years Agathe was able to reach a sane and courageous view of her brief association with a man of genius.

> The memory of her great love for the youth [she wrote somewhat impersonally in her memoirs], of the young days transfigured by poetry and loveliness, has never been quenched in her. . . . His immortal works have often and often been the joy of her life. He himself went forward on the path of his fame, growing greater and greater. And as he belonged, like every genius, to humanity, she also learned little by little to understand that he was in the right to burst the bonds which bade fair to fetter him; that she, with her great love, would never have been able completely to fill his life.

When Brahms was much older, he ascribed his falling out with Agathe to the early failure of his music before the public.

At the time when I would have best liked to marry, my things were hissed off the concert-stage, or at least accepted with icy coldness. I myself could endure this sort of treatment well enough. . . . But if, in such moments, I had had to go to my wife and see her questioning eyes anxiously fastened on mine, and been obliged to confess: "Another fiasco!"—I couldn't have borne that! But the way it has turned out has also been good . . . !

Music was the only thing that really mattered to Johannes Brahms. And he knew instinctively that for its expression he must have complete liberty. "I am in love with music," he said. "I think of nothing else—or if I do, it is only if it can heighten the beauty of music for me."

CHAPTER XII

THE SINGING GIRLS

BRAHMS struck a match to light the oil-lamp in his sitting-room. It was late in September of his second season at Detmold, and he had been out all day on an excursion into the country with his friends. Suddenly, as the wick flared up, he gave a gasp of surprise. "Yussuf! Where on earth—how ever did *you* get here?"

Joachim, who had been asleep on Johannes' couch, sat up and rubbed his eyes. "I thought you'd never come," he growled. "Been here all day waiting for you, and I have to leave early tomorrow morning. Thought we might have a chance to look this over. . . ." From under his overcoat he fished out a bulky manuscript. Hannes pounced on it with a cry. "The *Hungarian* concerto? Have you really finished it? I say, that's great! We'll try it at once."

That night there was not much sleep for the other people at the inn. Several of Brahms' friends came in, and they made music until nearly daybreak. Joachim had to play his concerto several times. Johannes was especially taken with the Hungarian themes. These reminded him of his early travels with Remenyi, and the excitement he had felt on first hearing gypsy tunes. Yussuf had drawn from the same background of native folk melodies for his concerto.

Now the younger composer decided that he too would experiment with these gypsy folk dances, with their insinuating and exciting rhythms. Inspired by Joachim's concerto, he wrote the first few of his famous Hungarian dances. Who does not know the fiery one that starts?—

A number of exceedingly gypsyesque themes found their way into the concluding part of Brahms' first published quartet (the Piano Quartet in G minor), which he called *Rondo alla Zingarese.* (*Zingara* is the Italian word for gypsy.) Joachim was so enthusiastic about this finale that he said, "Hannes, you have beaten me on my own ground."

Any folk music had a stimulating effect on Brahms. While at Detmold he arranged a number of old German melodies for his local group of amateur singers. He always enjoyed directing choruses. Had not his first experience in conducting been with the Winsen choral society, at the age of fourteen?

A few months after his return to Hamburg he organized a new singing group—his famous "Ladies' Choir."

The musical season at Detmold ended with the New Year; and early in 1858 Brahms went home to stay with his parents. Thanks to a generous slice of his salary, they now occupied a fairly spacious flat, where Frau Brahms could take in two or three boarders. Hannes had a comfortable room with sleeping couch, small piano, and shelves for his books.

But in spite of this it was not easy for him to work. There were constant interruptions, and the noise from the streets was disturbing after his quiet inn at Detmold. So when spring came he moved out to the suburb of

Hamm, where he found rooms with a Frau Doctor Rösing, an elderly lady who loved music. She put the whole house at his disposal, including a fine grand piano and a study where he could work undisturbed. Some years later, in grateful remembrance of her help, Brahms dedicated his A major piano quartet to this good woman.

At the back of the house there was a large garden, and in fine weather Johannes often walked up and down the graveled paths, hands clasped behind his back (a habit that remained with him all his life), his mind busy with some musical theme. One day as he was strolling about in this way, he suddenly stopped short. From the other side of the garden wall came the sound of girls' voices. Brahms listened a moment in delight. Then he hurried in to Frau Rösing.

"There are four young ladies singing together in the next garden," he cried. "Do you know who they might be?"

The Frau Doctor smiled. "I have an idea it is my two nieces—Marie and Betty Wölckers; they live there, you know. Perhaps some of their friends are with them."

Brahms was not long in making the girls' acquaintance, and soon he was writing four-part songs for them.

At a wedding in St. Michael's Church, in May of 1859, he heard a chorus of young women sing. He was so impressed by their voices that he asked them to try over an *Ave Maria* which he had just composed for female voices with organ. Their interpretation so delighted him that he immediately organized them into a special choir of his own. Eventually this was expanded into a group of fifty singers, including the two Fräulein Wölckers, and was called the "Ladies' Choir."

"Fix oder Nix" was the motto he coined for them—"Bang-up or nothing"; and he promised to write all the music they could sing if they would meet regularly, and always on time. He even drew up a long set of humorous rules. *"Avertimento"* it was called:

Pro Primo, it is to be remarked that the members of the Ladies' Choir must be *there.*

By which is to be understood that they must oblige themselves to be *there.*

Pro Secundo, it is to be observed that the members of the Ladies' Choir must be *there.*

By which is meant, they must be there precisely at the appointed time.

Those who were late must pay a fine, the *Avertimento* continued, and the money was to be given to the poor. "And it is to be desired that none of them get too much. . . ."

The document concluded:

I remain, in deepest devotion and veneration of the Ladies' Choir, their most assiduous ready-writer and steady time-beater,

JOHANNES KREISLER, JUN.
(*alias* Brahms)

Brahms made his chorus work hard; but the meetings were usually spiced with nonsense as well. Sometimes they all went on country picnics. One warm summer evening a special party was planned in a large garden in Eppendorf, just outside of Hamburg. The place was illuminated with Japanese lanterns hanging from the trees; there was special music and, as climax, a display of fireworks.

Johannes, always conscious of his short stature, found an apple tree in the garden which he decided would make an ideal podium. Like that other sawed-off character in the *New England Primer:*

> Zacchæus, he
> Did climb a tree,

Brahms clambered up to a low-growing branch and, gathering below him his "dear girls" (as he called them), broke off a twig for a baton and signaled for the concert to begin.

When the fireworks started, Johannes was in his element. As each rocket went up he gave a great *Oh!* of ecstatic delight. His pleasure was so keen that he almost yodeled at the spectacle.

Brahms was very happy with his Ladies' Choir. After leaving Hamburg he rhapsodized about them in a letter to a friend:

"Oh, my dear girls, where are you? I shall certainly not stare about me when you are here singing me the pretty things which I have written for you; all forty of you shall stand before me, and I shall see you and hear you in my mind's eye. I tell you that you are one of my most endearing memories. . . ."

One member proved especially "endearing." This was Fräulein Bertha Porubszky, a young Viennese girl recently come to visit her aunt in Hamburg. Brahms found the girl so fascinating that he almost forgot poor Agathe von Siebold. The affair did not last long, however, for Bertha returned a few months later to Vienna.

When Johannes finished his first season with his fascinating chorus, the girls, to show their grief, all came to the last meeting dressed in black. They sent him a large bouquet of flowers, and buried in its midst was a silver inkstand. He had never been willing to accept pay for his work with the singers, but the gift of the inkstand was a welcome tribute. He wrote in thanks:

I think constantly of the glad surprise with which I perceived the inkstand, the remembrance from the Ladies' Choir, under its charming covering of flowers.

I have done so little to deserve it that I should be ashamed were it not that I hope to write much more for you; and I shall certainly hear finer tones sounding around me as I look at the valued and beautiful present on my writing-table. Please express to all whom you can reach my hearty greeting and thanks.

I have seldom had a more agreeable pleasure, and our meetings will remain one of my most welcome and favorite recollections. . . .

With best greetings to you and yours,

Your heartily sincere,

JOHS. BRAHMS

He always kept the silver inkstand on his writing-table, reminding him of one of the happiest experiences in his life.

By the end of Brahms' third season at Detmold he had had enough of court life and etiquette. Like Beethoven he was impatient of empty forms; he too felt that noble birth was purely a matter of chance, that real nobility was shown by character and achievement. Intelligence and, most of all, the power to create, were more important to Brahms than worldly position.

Society—that is, social gatherings with no serious purpose—also irritated him, striking him as just a waste of time. He coined the expressive word, *"Pimpkram,"* to describe this artificiality. If he was forced to attend a social function he would probably sit silent, or resort to sarcasm.

Detmold had far too much social life for his taste. At the close of his third season there, he refused an offer to go back the following year. Early in 1860, when he was twenty-seven, he went to establish himself (as he then thought permanently) in Hamburg. That spring he met Fritz Simrock, who was to become his music-publisher and lifelong friend.

One spring day a year later, an unexpected visitor knocked at the door of the Brahms apartment. When Johannes' mother first opened the door she did not recognize the stylish young lady who stood there, smiling. Then—

"Why, if it isn't Lieschen Giesemann!" she cried.

"Lieschen Denninghof," the visitor answered, pressing Frau Brahms' hand affectionately. "It's been so many years since I last saw you! I was afraid you might have forgotten me."

"But never—never! We often speak of you and your good father and mother, and of all your kindness to our Hannes. Why, just the other day he was saying—" She broke off and shook her head regretfully. "Now isn't it a shame that he's not here today? He will be so sorry to have missed you. Perhaps you will come back?"

"What a pity!" said Lieschen, disappointed. "I am in Hamburg only for the day." She noticed some manuscript music standing on the piano. It always gave her a strange feeling to realize what a celebrated musician her old playmate had become. Suddenly she gave an exclamation of surprise. "Is it possible—?"

Frau Brahms looked over her shoulder. "These are some new songs Hannes has just been composing. See—" she put the music into Lieschen's hand.

Now the past came crowding into the girl's memory. She saw herself sitting on the bank of the river at Winsen, with Hannes beside her, reading aloud from a book "borrowed" from Frau Löwenherz's library by the wily Aaron: *The Beautiful Magelone and the Knight Peter with the Silver Keys.*

Evidently Hannes had not forgotten those days either, for the songs that Lieschen held in her hand were entitled *Magelone Romances.*

This important cycle was not completed for some years. It was a musical interpretation of the romance and adventure that had so stirred Brahms' imagination as a young, just-awakening musician.

Each time Brahms heard Liszt's music he disliked it more. It seemed to him pompous, exaggerated, and over-ornate, meant for showing off rather than as an expression of sincere inner feeling. "I have a perfect horror of all that smacks of Liszt," he wrote to Clara Schumann.

Joachim, too, had grown away from the New-German group. A number of his and Johannes' friends felt as they did. So when an article came out, extolling the excellence of the Weimar school and announcing that all the important musicians of the time had accepted the tenets of the "Music of the Future," they were up in arms.

"We can't let *that* pass!" Johannes exclaimed angrily.

"What nerve to say 'all the important musicians'! There are a few left who don't think as they do," Joachim added.

"I believe we should make a public statement to that effect," Brahms insisted. "Here, Yussuf, let's write it out. I know a lot of 'important musicians' who will want to sign this document."

They drew up a strongly worded statement criticizing the article severely for daring to state that all musicians were in accord with the Music-of-the-Future school at Weimar. It was planned to send this Manifesto to the Berlin *Echo* as soon as they should have secured the other signatures. In some way, however, the newspaper got hold of the document and published it when only one other besides Brahms, Joachim, and Ise Grimm had put their names to it.

The consequences were disastrous to Johannes. Added to Schumann's over-enthusiastic article it made him—if not ridiculous—at least the target of much criticism. And it brought him many enemies.

"Why don't you move to Vienna, Hannes?" Joachim suggested. He had often spoken to his friend of the gay city on the Danube. "*There* is a place," the violinist continued, "where good musicians are really appreciated! Vienna has the best music of any city in Europe. Think of the great masters who have chosen it for their home: Mozart, Haydn, Beethoven, Schubert. . . ."

Brahms had often wanted to visit Vienna. Still—"After all, Hamburg is *my* home, Yussuf."

"It's your birthplace, all right. But do you think Hamburg really appreciates your music? What have its people ever done for you?"

"One of these days I may be appointed director of the Philharmonic," Johannes insisted. "Wilhelm Grund is growing old, you know. He will probably resign soon."

Brahms had every right to expect that he would be chosen the next conductor of Hamburg's orchestra. But, as so often happens, his native city did not know how to value native products. A prophet is a loss in his own country. Stockhausen, a singer and friend of Johannes', was nominated to the post.

Although confirmation of Stockhausen's appointment would not be definite until the following spring, Brahms suddenly decided to follow Joachim's advice. "I am leaving on Monday for Vienna," he wrote to Albert Dietrich. "I look forward to it like a child. Of course I do not know how long I shall stay. We will leave that open."

Brahms was not at all sure that he would remain long in Vienna; but he must have had some premonition that his Hamburg life was nearly over. He found it hard to say good-by to his old father and mother; though this time he could leave secure in the knowledge that they would lack for nothing.

"Father," he said, with a twinkle of his blue eyes, "remember that music is the best remedy for any misfortune." He pointed to the shelf where his music scores were stacked. "If things ever go badly with you, if you need help, just look through my old copy of *Saul*. I think you will find comfort there."

Some time later Father Brahms had occasion to remember his son's parting words about the music-cure. When he opened the score of *Saul* he found it stuffed with German banknotes!

CHAPTER XIII

ON THE BEAUTIFUL BLUE DANUBE

THE TIME was a late afternoon in September 1862. The place, a picturesque old house near St. Stephen's Cathedral in Vienna where Mozart had once written *The Marriage of Figaro* and the great D minor piano concerto. Herr Epstein's servant came in and announced, "There is a young gentleman waiting to see you, sir."

The professor sighed. He had just returned from his day's lessons at the Conservatory, and had hoped for a quiet hour before supper to look over some new music. Joachim had recently sent him a composition by a new composer in Hamburg. What was his name? Bahm—no, *Brahms*. It must be the same "young eagle" that Schumann had written about in that wild article which had caused so much indignation a few years before.

Julius Epstein was always interested in younger musicians, quick to recognize genius and offer a helping hand. He was abrupt in manner—his loud "ha!" was sometimes intimidating—but he had a rarely generous nature and was one of the best-loved men in Vienna.

Now he hung up his hat, smoothed his beard—which he wore parted in the middle, in Emperor Franz Joseph style—and opened the door to his sitting-room. A short, slender young man with flaxen hair and cornflower-blue eyes rose to meet him.

"Herr Professor Epstein? Joachim suggested that I call on you. My name is Johannes Brahms."

"Brahms—*Brahms?* Ha! Are you by chance from Hamburg?"

Johannes smiled. "By chance I am, sir, and only just arrived from that city."

"Well, well!" exclaimed Herr Epstein cordially. "Heard a lot about you—ha! Delighted to make your acquaintance. Sit down, sit down—ha! Tell me all the news from Hamburg. How is my friend Marxsen? Do you expect to stay long in Vienna?"

Before Brahms could answer, the Professor began to bombard him with questions about his own work. "Joachim tells me—ha!—that you have written some really interesting music. Sent me your piano sonata in F minor to look over. Bring any new compositions with you?" he added, noticing Johannes' portfolio.

"I have two piano quartets here," the younger musician began.

"Quartets?—splendid. Ha! Must hear them." He took out his watch and looked at it. "Believe there's still time. . . . Hellmesberger lives just around the corner. His quartet always rehearses at this hour. Frieda—" The impulsive Herr Epstein called his servant. "Run over and tell Herr Hellmesberger I've got a surprise for him here—ha! Tell him to bring the whole quartet."

Joseph Hellmesberger was concertmaster of the Court Opera orchestra (that is, he headed the first-violin section), leader of the city's chief string quartet, and witty czar of Viennese violindom. Each winter his quartet gave a series of concerts for the "Friends of Music" (the society sometimes mischievously referred to as the "'Fiends' of Music").

"Got something interesting to show you!" cried Epstein when the men arrived. He introduced the guest from Hamburg and then thrust Johannes' manuscript under Hellmesberger's nose. "Like to try it over? Ha! Herr Brahms is no doubt willing to play the piano part."

As the music began, the old professor listened with

growing excitement. Hellmesberger, exchanging nods of astonishment and delight with his fellow quartet members, was equally impressed. At the close of the stirring finale *"alla Zingarese"* he cast down his violin, rushed to Johannes and threw his arms around the startled composer's neck.

"Magnificent!" he cried. "Music like that hasn't been written since—" He broke off and his round face suddenly grew solemn. "Gentlemen," he said, turning to the others, "this is Beethoven's heir!"

Epstein and Hellmesberger were so enthusiastic that they wanted everyone in Vienna to hear Brahms' music. "At our next concert we shall play the G minor quartet," the violinist assured him.

They introduced the young composer to the leading musicians of the city. Old Nottebohm, who had won fame by editing Beethoven's notebooks, and a singer named Gänsbacher, became his special friends. He was touched by his warm reception; he could not help contrasting it with the cold, almost hostile attitude of his own city. Hamburg's fellow-musicians had never quite been able to forget that Johannes Brahms had started life as a child of the slums, clattering about its tenement lanes in clogs, and playing in cheap dance-hall dives.

On Nov. 16th, at a concert of the Friends of Music, Hellmesberger's quartet, with the composer at the piano, played Brahms' first piano quartet. The critics were not particularly complimentary; but the audience seemed to like it, and several Viennese music-publishers asked him if they could print his works. Brahms, however, had promised them to Simrock of Berlin.

Epstein felt that the success of this first performance warranted the newcomer in giving a concert of his own. Johannes, however, was a little doubtful. "I know so few here in Vienna. Who would come?"

"More people know more about your music—ha!—than you think," his new friend assured him. "Besides—" the good professor cleared his throat gruffly—"I have—ha!—already reserved a hall for you." When Johannes tried to thank him he added quickly: "Nothing at all! Hellmesberger is really responsible. He has promised—ha!—to play your second piano quartet."

Epstein was right. Brahms' fame had already spread through the city, and the concert was well attended. Enough money was taken in to pay all expenses. In addition to the quartet in A, Brahms played his recently composed *Variations on a Theme by Handel,* which was much better received than the quartet.

In the front row Johannes could see the critic Hanslick with his bald head and bushy eyebrows. Hanslick was soon to become one of the most ardent Brahmsians, but at this early date he had not yet been won over, and his verdict was lamentably wide of the mark:

> The quartet by no means pleased us, and we are glad that the unfavorable impression it created was obliterated by the variations which followed. . . . The composer chooses themes

rather with a view to their capacity for contrapuntal treatment than on account of their intrinsic merit, and those of the quartet sound dry and flat.

Hanslick once remarked: "Brahms has the same fault as Bach and Beethoven: he has too little of the sensuous in his art both as composer and as pianist. I think it is rather an intentional avoidance of everything sensuous than a fault."

Brahms, for his part, never had a very exalted regard for Hanslick's musical taste. In later life he caustically remarked that this critic "prefers his Bach in the form of Offenbach!"

The newcomer was well pleased at his reception by the Viennese public. He wrote enthusiastically to Hamburg:

Dear Parents:

I was very happy yesterday. My concert went quite excellently, much better than I had hoped.

After the quartet had been sympathetically received, I had much success as a player. . . . Every number was warmly applauded. I think there was great enthusiasm in the hall. . . .

Now I could very well give concerts, but I do not wish to do so, for it takes up so much time that I could not do anything else.

I played as freely as though I were sitting at home with friends; one is certainly influenced quite otherwise by the public [here] than by ours [in Hamburg]. . . .

I think my Serenade will be given next Monday.

Although he had been in Vienna only a few weeks, Brahms was already making a name for himself. After the performance of his First Serenade, Hanslick wrote more favorably, calling the work "one of the most charming of modern compositions."

A few months later, the leading Viennese orchestra played the Second Serenade. Though this was even better liked than the First, it caused a minor riot in the orchestra. The musicians complained that the work was much too difficult. At the final rehearsal a clarinetist rose suddenly from his seat.

"This music is no good to play," he said defiantly. And a number of the others nodded their agreement.

Concertmaster Hellmesberger looked around in high indignation. The conductor, who was one of Hellmesberger's friends, rapped sharply with his baton. "Gentlemen, gentlemen, what does this mean?" He fixed the clarinetist with a stern eye. "Am I the leader of this orchestra, or are you?"

The rebellious player still stood his ground. Conductor Dessoff laid down his baton and stepped from the podium. "Very well, then. I resign."

"And I too," cried Hellmesberger.

"And I," echoed the first flute player.

Listening from the back of the hall, Brahms shivered in his seat. The situation threatened to become serious. However, the firm stand of Dessoff and Hellmesberger eventually convinced the men that they had better go on.

The final performance of the Serenade was such a success that the players forgot their resentment over its difficulties. This time Hanslick's criticism was much more enthusiastic:

> He [Brahms] has shown himself . . . as an independent, original individuality, a finely organized, true musical nature, as an artist consciously ripening towards mastery by means of unwearied endeavor. . . . The work had an extremely favorable reception. The hearty applause became proportionately greater at the close as the modest composer made himself even smaller in his seat in the gallery.

Richard Wagner had already written a number of operas. A large following of ardent admirers hailed him as the greatest musician the world had ever known. To them he was a veritable Messiah. But on the other side a group of equally earnest objectors could see nothing good in his music, and pronounced him a pretentious upstart.

Shortly after Brahms' arrival, Wagner conducted in Vienna three concerts of his own works. At that time the younger composer had not yet heard much Wagner. He attended the first concert with a friend who was a fervent follower of the older master.

All through this concert Johannes sat in stony silence. At the close, when everyone was applauding vigorously, he still made no move or comment. Finally his companion—beside himself with enthusiasm—cried: "What music! Wasn't it marvelous?"

The composer raised his eyebrows a little. Then he

asked drily, "Aren't you afraid you will spoil your new kid gloves—clapping so hard?"

Brahms did, however, appreciate Wagner's genius, and always respected him as a musician. When they first met in private, the older composer received him cordially. He asked Johannes to play for him, and at the *Handel Variations* exclaimed: "These show what can still be done with the old forms, provided one knows how to treat them. I should like to hear more of your compositions."

Evidently he did hear more of them, for in the *Meistersinger,* on which he was then at work, there is a distinct echo from Brahms' F minor piano sonata.

But the temperaments and ideals of the two men were too widely diverse to allow any intimacy between them. Wagner saw music in highly dramatic, spectacular form, while Brahms never lost the classic austerity of his early training. "Pure" music always appealed to him more than that which was diluted by literature, as in opera or in the tone poem which Liszt invented and Richard Strauss later popularized.

As time went on, followers of Brahms and Wagner magnified still further the difference between the two. Eventually this grew—on Wagner's side, at least—into open hostility. The younger composer seldom expressed himself. Brahms' earlier ill-timed "manifesto" against Liszt and the "New German" school had cured him of trying to force his musical opinions upon the world.

Bertha Porubszky, the girl who had so captivated Johannes in Hamburg, had recently married and now lived in Vienna. He was glad to find that she had not, as poor Agathe had, taken his attentions too seriously. He became very friendly with the young couple, and often visited them. When Bertha's second child was born he sent her a charming lullaby, which has since become one of the most celebrated of all cradle-songs. It was especially dedicated to her "for joyful use on every occasion." In the accompaniment the composer slipped in an allusion to a waltz that Bertha knew. Perhaps they had once danced to it together. Like so many of the greatest songs, this one is even better without the words:

Perhaps in sentimental remembrance of his earlier attachment this melody was based on an Austrian folk song which Bertha used to sing for him in the Hamburg days. The old words had their meaning then!

> You think perhaps, you dream perhaps,
> That love will ever yield to force . . . ?

Johannes' love never yielded to force! If he suspected any woman—no matter how fair—of designs on his affections, he would fly in the opposite direction. His friends conspired (more or less subtly) to throw him into the company of eligible young ladies. Even the good Epstein was not without guile.

"Johannes," he remarked some months after the composer's arrival in Vienna, "I—ha!—have a new pupil for you. Been working with me for some time. But—ha!—believe you could do more for her than I can. She has great musical gifts—ha!—and she's beautiful, sympathetic, charming."

Brahms was growing a little mistrustful of charming young ladies. But, of course, pupils brought in money. He began giving lessons to Elisabet von Stockhausen.

He found her all that old Epstein had said and much more. She really had extraordinary musical ability, with a memory second only to his own. Her sense of humor was delightful, and she had a genuinely kind and thoughtful disposition which drew everyone to her. Small wonder that the old professor said (with a sigh for his own years!), "No man could possibly keep from falling in love with her!"

Brahms did not prove to be any exception to the rule. But soon he again beat a hasty retreat. "I really don't feel that I should keep Fräulein Elisabet from you," he told Epstein. "It is not right for me to take away one of your finest pupils."

Johannes always felt a sentimental affection for the fair Elisabet, even after she married the composer Heinrich von Herzogenberg. For years her picture was the only woman's photograph on his desk.

Brahms sometimes joked about his single state. Quoting a quip of the witty Hellmesberger, he would say: "Unfortunately I never married; and am—thank the Lord—still single!" To an inquisitive young lady he remarked, "No one would have me!"—then added, "And if one had—well, I never could have stood anyone with such bad taste as to choose a man like me!"

Until late in the following April, Johannes stayed in Vienna, and then went back to spend the summer with his parents. On the way he stopped for a visit with Joachim. Yussuf had recently become engaged to Fräulein Amalie Weiss, contralto at the Court Opera in Hanover.

"You are a lucky fellow," said Johannes, "to have found a bride so beautiful and charming, and a fine musician as well."

"You should marry too," Joachim replied, with a friendly clap on Brahms' shoulder.

Johannes sighed a little. It was all very well to joke about his single state; but there were times . . .

"Occasionally I think of marriage—that's true," he said, his blue eyes full of melancholy. "It would be pleasant to have a wife and home, and little ones to gather around one's knees. Every respectable man should have a home and family. Perhaps I'm not respectable." He smiled wryly.

While Brahms was in Hanover he heard Fräulein

Weiss in a performance of Gluck's *Orpheus,* and was greatly impressed by her voice.

"It is the last time I shall sing in public," Amalie said a little wistfully. In those days it was not considered proper for a married woman to appear on the stage.

"You mean, my dear, the last time in *opera,*" Joachim corrected her. "There will always be *concerts,* you know."

"And I shall write music for you to sing!" added Johannes. He composed a number of his loveliest songs for Amalie. She always included some of these in her concerts, and her singing helped to make them popular.

Brahms reached Hamburg on his thirtieth birthday, May 7th, 1863. His old parents were overjoyed to see him, but almost at once he knew that something was wrong. A little later Jakob took him aside.

"It's no use, Hannes, we can't get along together, me and the old lady."

Johannes looked shocked. "You don't understand," his father explained. "After all, she's an old woman of seventy-four now, and me, I'm still young. What's fifty-seven years to a hale and hearty man like me? But Johanna, now, all *she* wants is to sit in a corner and maybe sew a little. And she nags at me all the time. . . ."

When Father Brahms had married a wife seventeen years older, he had not stopped to realize what a difference this would make as time went by.

"She's getting so she can't even stand music any

more," Jakob continued, scratching his head resentfully. "Makes me practice in the attic, she does. It's cold up there! I don't like it. Fritz is never home; he gives piano lessons to fashionable young ladies. But Elise, she's under foot the whole time. She's even worse than her mother."

Poor Elise! The headaches were worse than ever now. She tried to earn her living by sewing, but the handwork was a great strain on her eyes. It was her fondest ambition to own one of the recently invented sewing-machines; and that Christmas, Hannes fulfilled his sister's wish by sending her a fine one from Vienna.

He was much disturbed by the trouble between his parents. He tried to reason with Jakob. "You two have lived together for nearly thirty-five years now," he said. "Mother may not be with us much longer. Surely you can make allowances?"

Jakob heaved a deep sigh. "Well—I'll try. But I wish you'd tell your mother not to nag so much."

The Hamburg Philharmonic had now definitely installed Stockhausen as conductor. "Vienna seems to think more of me than my own native city does," remarked Johannes, as he handed a letter to his mother which he had just received from Vienna. "Here they don't think I am good enough to conduct an orchestra, but"—he pointed to the letter—"the *Singakademie* of Vienna has invited me to become its director."

Brahms was not sure that he wanted to tie himself

down to any sort of fixed position; but, putting one thing with another, he finally decided to accept the post.

Brahms took his duties as conductor of the Vienna "Singing Academy" very seriously. In recent years this organization had lost much of its standing, and he was determined to restore it to its original excellence.

He made the chorus work very hard. He was exacting, and demanded the utmost co-operation from his singers. If they failed to follow his directions he was inclined to grow sarcastic. Once, at a rehearsal of Haydn's *Creation,* the somewhat elderly sopranos had difficulty in keeping up with the tempo. "But, my dear ladies," cried their director, "why do you drag so? Surely you took this much faster under Haydn!" (The good Papa Haydn had been in his grave since 1809!)

In his choice of music for the Singing Academy chorus, Brahms was equally strict. Bach, Handel, Beethoven, and Haydn formed the main part of his programs. Perhaps prophetically, he started the season with Bach's long cantata, "I Had Much Grief."

The members of the Academy were not very pleased with their new conductor's selections. They had been accustomed to lighter music, more in keeping with the pleasure-loving temperament of the Viennese. Brahms eventually compromised by including folk songs on his programs, some of which he arranged specially for the chorus. These proved most popular of all with both public and singers.

Three concerts were given. The first was a great success; the next two, less so. To close the season Brahms was asked to give a fourth program devoted entirely to his own works. He was invited to continue as director the following year, but he decided not to accept. Any regular obligation irked him, for he needed complete liberty for his work.

Was not his motto: "F A F"—"*free* but glad"? Freedom he must have, and in it he was glad.

When Brahms returned to Hamburg in the spring of 1864, he found that the break between his parents could no longer be averted, and that he would have to set up separate establishments for the two. He wondered if he would be able to meet the added expense. Now that he no longer drew a salary from the Singing Academy, the royalties from his compositions were his only income.

"Can't *you* help a little, Fritz?" he asked his younger brother. "Elise does what she can with her sewing, you know."

Fritz glared resentfully. "Why should I help? I never had the advantages that *you* had! Besides, I have a position of my own to keep up. I can't go around giving lessons in fashionable homes and look like a tramp."

"Very well," Johannes answered shortly. "I'll manage somehow."

He found separate lodgings for his father, and a smaller flat for Frau Brahms and Elise. When the time came for him to leave Hamburg, the old mother could hardly bear to let him go. She leaned her gray head against her Hannes' shoulder and the tears streamed down her worn face.

With a sudden tightening of the heart, Hannes realized how old and feeble she had grown during the past year. "In a few months I'll be back again, little Mother," he reassured her.

But that was the last time he was to see her alive.

CHAPTER XIV

BLACK FOREST MAGIC

"TODAY Johannes took us by surprise," wrote Clara Schumann in her diary on July 30th, 1864. Frau Schumann and her family now spent the summers at Lichtenthal, a suburb of the famous watering resort of Baden-Baden. Her family was rapidly shooting up. Marie, the eldest, was nearly twenty-three. She never married, but always remained her mother's devoted companion. Julie, the third child, was nineteen. She was the most attractive of all Clara's daughters.

Each time Brahms saw her he became more conscious of the girl's rare charm and beauty.

Now, returning to Vienna from his visit to the old parents in Hamburg, he stopped off at Lichtenthal to spend a few days with the Schumanns.

"Only a few days?" Clara exclaimed. "Why, you must stay for the rest of the summer. Rubinstein has gone away on a concert tour, and I'm sure he would let you stay in his villa."

Johannes was not so sure. Anton Rubinstein, the brilliant concert pianist, had not been especially cordial when the two had met. To Liszt, the pianist, he had somewhat malevolently written:

> As regards Brahms, I hardly know how to describe the impression he made on me. He is not graceful enough for the drawing-room, not fiery enough for the concert-room, not simple enough for the country, and not general enough for the town. I have but little faith in this kind of nature. . . .

What put Rubinstein's nose out of joint was the feeling that the younger man did not sufficiently appreciate the vain virtuoso's compositions. He was, however, quite willing to let Brahms use his house, and the latter did not need much urging to stay in Lichtenthal.

This little town stands in the midst of Germany's famous Black Forest—those vast, deep woods of pine and oak which have been the inspiration of so much fairy lore and legend. Johannes, always sensitive to beauty in nature, found it an enchanting spot. He loved to walk in the dim, cool shadow of the black pines. The fallen needles made a soft carpet of silence. He could imagine himself in a huge, pine-incense-filled cathedral, where tall trunks were pillars, arched boughs the roof, and distant mountains glimpsed through trees, the stained-glass windows.

In her biography of Brahms, Florence May has written of the composer's intimate relation with the outdoor world. It was in this same Lichtenthal that she first met him.

> Brahms knew that not alone his intellect, but his mind, [*sic!*] spirit and fancy, must be constantly nurtured if they were to bring forth the highest of which they were capable; and he so arranged his life that they should be fed ever and always by poetry and literature and art, by solitary musing, by participation in so much of life as seemed to him to be real and true, and, above all and in the highest degree, by the companionship of Nature.
>
> "How can I most quickly improve?" I asked him one day later on. "You must walk constantly in the forest," he answered; and he meant what he said to be taken literally. It was his own favourite prescription that he advised for my application.

This "prescription" he passed on to many others. Eugénie Schumann remembers his once saying to her, "You have no idea what you are missing if you don't go into the woods early."

While he was in Lichtenthal, Brahms would always rise at dawn and go for a long walk through the forest.

But first he made himself a cup of good, strong coffee. At any hour of the day or night he could drink coffee, and the stronger it was, the better he liked it. For years one of his admirers sent him a special blend of his favorite Mocha. In making it he would commonly use, for one cup, "as many coffee-beans as would ordinarily make ten cupfuls."

After his morning walk, Brahms worked until mid-afternoon, with time out only for dinner. Four o'clock found him at the Schumanns' villa for the inevitable afternoon coffee, and this was followed by an hour of music, a visit with the family and their guests, or a walk with Clara. He was usually persuaded to stay for supper. A place was always laid for him at her right hand.

There were many interesting people in Lichtenthal. "You will find artists and writers here as well as musicians," Clara told Johannes when he first came. "For instance the Russian novelist Turgenieff comes every year. He writes librettos for Mme Garcia's operettas."

Brahms raised an inquiring eyebrow. "Mme Garcia?"

"Yes, the famous singer, Pauline Viardot-Garcia. She has a fascinating place here, with a gallery full of beautiful paintings and a miniature theater where she gives plays and concerts, and even operas. I must take you to call on her."

Mme Viardot-Garcia was one of the great singers of the 19th century. Although not beautiful, she had an exceptional voice (it could reach F above high C) and great personal magnetism. Later she became even more renowned as a teacher of singing.

At her luxurious villa in Lichtenthal, Mme Garcia held a court all her own. She was surrounded by pupils and ardent admirers. Most of the celebrities who came to the Black Forest were entertained in her home. At that time she was much interested in writing operettas, and these enjoyed something of a reputation. She was delighted to make Brahms' acquaintance. Personally she showed him through her gallery of paintings. At one end, on a table of lovely marquetry, stood a silver casket set with precious stones.

"This," said the lady with a dramatic gesture, "is my most cherished possession! Not the chest," she added, laughing at her guest's expression, "but what it contains."

Inside the box lay the manuscript score of Mozart's *Don Giovanni*. Reverently Johannes gazed at the faded writing. He wished he were fortunate enough to possess even a single page of Mozart's original work. It was a wish soon to be fulfilled.

Mme Garcia introduced the composer to a group of her young lady pupils. Brahms, always ill at ease in the company of strange young women, edged away. But one of the girls followed him and drew him to one side.

"Herr Brahms, you are a composer—yes?" Johannes, vaguely surprised, bowed briefly. "We were wondering," she continued. "You see, in a couple of weeks Mme Garcia will celebrate her birthday. As a surprise we wanted to serenade her. Would you be willing, now, to write a little song for the event, and perhaps direct us in singing it?"

Brahms was reminded of his early youth, when he composed a chorus for Herr Köhler's birthday in Winsen, and conducted the singing children outside the Rector's window.

He could not resist the pleading Fräulein. The very next day the song was written, and he rehearsed the girls at Frau Schumann's house. Early on the morning of Mme Garcia's birthday, Brahms and her group of satellites slipped into the garden and hid themselves behind a clump of lilac bushes underneath the lady's window. Soon a chorus of girls' voices, directed by a serious-faced young man in a black frock-coat, arose in competition with the singing birds.

Presently the window opened. Mme Garcia, in frilled mob-cap and lace-trimmed negligee, smiled down from above. With an incredibly high obbligato she began to accompany them.

Soon after his arrival in Lichtenthal, Brahms heard the family speak of Princess Anna of Hesse, who was spending the summer there.

"Mother has promised to play for her," Julie Schumann informed him. "Her Highness is very fond of music."

Clara was always looking for ways to further the fortunes of Johannes. "It would be a good thing for you to know the Princess. She does a great deal to encourage music and musicians." Frau Schumann thought a moment, then suggested: "Why don't you come with me when I go to play for her, and together we will perform your sonata for two pianos."

For some time Brahms had been working on this composition. Originally it had been a string quintet; recently he had rewritten it as a sonata for two pianos; and even now he was thinking of making it into a piano quintet—in which final form it became one of his most popular chamber-music works.

When Frau Schumann and Brahms played the two-piano version for Princess Anna the latter was so cordial in her appreciation that Brahms took courage and asked if she would allow him to dedicate the work to her.

"I should be honored!" exclaimed Her Royal Highness warmly.

Brahms immediately made a copy with the Princess' name on the title page, and left it at her villa. Soon after this a lackey from the royal household appeared at Frau Schumann's door.

"I have a package for Herr Johannes Brahms," the man announced.

Brahms opened it in surprise. "No—not really!" he exclaimed in amazed delight. "Look, Clara—Marie—Julie, only see what Princess Anna has sent me. Nothing could have pleased me more!"

Frau Schumann and her daughters bent over the gift. It was the original score of Mozart's G Minor Symphony.

Brahms was just about to leave Lichtenthal for Vienna when he received a letter from Joachim. In high excitement he hurried over to the Schumanns'.

"News from Hanover. Can you guess what?" he cried.

"Hanover? Is it from Joachim? Can it be—already . . . ?"

"Yes, our Yussuf has become a father. A fine son. And what do you think? They want me to be godfather!"

"I think that is very natural," Frau Clara said, smiling. "After all, you are his closest friend."

Johannes' face clouded over. "But I don't see how I can possibly get to the christening." He had just enough money left to pay his way back to Vienna. Then his expression brightened. "I'll send a cradle song instead for young Johannes Joachim."

A charming lullaby was speedily forwarded to the proud parents. Founded on an old melody entitled *The Virgin's Cradle Song,* it was written for voice and piano with viola accompaniment, and began:

> Joseph dearest, Joseph mine,
> Help me rock the babe divine.
> Heaven's blessing shall be thine.

There was rejoicing among the friends in Lichtenthal over the birth of Joseph and Amalie's son. Clara wrote to congratulate the couple:

> We had a very happy day with Johannes on the 13th, and drank dear Joachim's health so heartily that he must have heard it; but it was meant for two of them.

Brahms did not believe that anything could ever come between him and Joachim. But some years later there was a misunderstanding that threatened a permanent rupture. Joachim's great fault was jealousy; and ultimately his wife sued for divorce. Johannes recognized that his friend was in the wrong, and sided with Amalie. This so wounded Joachim that for several years he would not speak to Brahms. Eventually, however, through the composer's efforts, they were reconciled.

In the fall of 1864 Brahms returned to Vienna with the intention of establishing himself permanently. But he had not been there long when a sad message called him back to Hamburg.

A friend, coming to his rooms, was surprised to see the composer seated at the piano, playing Bach's *Goldberg Variations,* while tears streamed down his cheeks.

"What has happened?" he cried.

Brahms nodded his head towards a telegram that stood open on the table. It announced that his mother was seriously ill, and not expected to live. The other stood silent, while Johannes, paying no further attention to the visitor, played on. Gradually his tears ceased flowing.

Finally he said, with a great sigh: "What music that is! Like oil. . . . Bach has power to soothe troubled hearts!"

Brahms took the first train for Hamburg, but his mother died before he could get there. Now he began to realize how much she had meant in his life. "I have no mother now," he cried brokenheartedly. Then he muttered to himself, "I shall have to marry!"

He went over to Jakob's lodgings and took his father by the arm. "Come," he said simply. Together the two returned to the little apartment which Elise shared with her mother. They went into the room where Frau Brahms lay, and stood silently beside her bed. Gently Johannes took his father's hand and placed it over the cold hand of Johanna Brahms. "Say you forgive her," he whispered. "She will know, and it will comfort her!"

After her mother's death Elise went to live with an uncle. Some years later (at almost the same advanced age at which Frau Brahms had married) she became the wife of a widowed watchmaker with several children. Johannes continued to send her financial support until, in 1891, she died.

Brahms felt the loss of his mother very deeply. It was inevitable that his grief should find expression in music —that natural release for emotional stress; and from this tragic experience came one of his greatest inspirations, the lovely soprano solo which forms Part Five of

A German Requiem. It begins: "I will comfort you as a mother comforts. . . ."

Already at Schumann's death the idea of this mighty work had occurred to him, and for years it had been uppermost in his mind. At Lichtenthal, that summer following his mother's death, he spent a good part of his time working on it. But it was not entirely completed until more than two years later.

During this period Brahms also composed a trio for French horn, violin, and piano. The adagio has a mournful, dirgelike quality of profound sadness, and many believe it was written in memory of his mother. This "Horn Trio" was one of Brahms' favorite works. The inspiration, he said, came to him as he was climbing through the pine-clad hills surrounding Lichtenthal. Some time later he showed the exact place to his friend Dietrich: "I was walking along here one morning," he said, "and as I came to this spot the sun shone out—and so did the idea for my trio."

Brahms' father was not long in taking advantage of his freedom. While still in Lichtenthal that summer, Johannes received an urgent summons from Jakob, who wanted to see him on important business. Putting together this and that, he suspected the old man of wanting to marry again.

When Brahms reached Hamburg, his father met him with a beaming face. "*Ach,* Hannes!" he cried. "You don't know what happiness I have!"

Johannes had a very great affection for his lovable old parent. Though at first the idea of another woman taking his mother's place shocked him, he came to realize that Jakob's happiness was the only thing that mattered.

"Well now—" laughed the older man a trifle self-consciously. One could see that he hardly knew where to begin. "You know I wrote you about the fine cooking at the widow Schnack's, where I've been taking my meals?"

Johannes smiled. "The way to a man's heart . . ." he murmured.

"What a woman that is, Frau Caroline Schnack!" Jakob continued enthusiastically. *"Ach,* you should see her—beautiful, shapely," his hands outlined a generous figure, "a pearl without price. And—believe it or not," Jakob paused to let the portentous announcement take full effect, "she has consented to marry me!"

"I'm not surprised," said Johannes, smiling. "In fact, I think she is a lucky woman."

Jakob's moon-face was quite solemn. "No, no!" he cried. *"I* am the lucky one. Why, do you know, she is full eighteen years younger than me. Eighteen years! About as much as your mother was *older."*

Jakob suddenly looked very pleased with himself. "This is the way I worked it. 'Frau Schnack,' I says to her one day—not daring to hope she would have me, 'Frau Schnack, you are a sensible woman. Perhaps you could give this old muddlehead a bit of advice.' " Father Brahms leaned forward and waggled his finger at Johannes. " 'You know,' I says to her, 'I've a mind to take me another wife.' And I hands her a slip of paper. 'Here's a list of the women I'd thought of—which one should I choose?' "

The old man watched Johannes' expression carefully. "And what do you think?" he went on. "She knew very well what I was after, the minx (been married twice before, she had). She looked up at me, coy-like, with a laugh, and marked a cross after her own name!"

"Has she any children?" asked the practical Johannes.

"Just one—a nice boy, too. Thirteen. Fritz is his name." Jakob chuckled. "Just the same as your brother. That's a good one—there'll be two Fritzes in one family!"

At first Johannes was a little skeptical of the widow Schnack's intentions. But after he met her, and saw how practical and goodhumored she was, he changed his opinion. A few weeks later Jakob and "Line," as he called her, were married. Brahms could not stay for the wedding, but he sent a generous sum of money as a present.

Frau Caroline proved a cheerful and devoted wife, and an excellent cook and housekeeper as well. The newly-weds moved into a large apartment and took in boarders to help pay expenses. A sunny room was reserved for Johannes' special use. He moved some books and personal belongings to his father's new home, and whenever he visited Hamburg he stayed with Jakob and Frau Line.

Johannes became sincerely attached to his stepmother and "the other Fritz," as he always called her son. He could not help contrasting the cheer and contentment that reigned in the present home with the quarreling, complaining atmosphere of his earlier environment. Jakob, he decided, had chosen wisely.

CHAPTER XV

ON THE HEIGHTS

THE CHIMES on Zürich's cathedral tower struck twelve. It was flower-market day in late May of 1866. Around the steps of the library building a crowd of peasant women had spread out their baskets of spring blossoms, and the air was spiced with the scent of lilacs, starlike narcissus from Alpine meadows, violets, and tight bunches of lilies-of-the-valley.

A short, stocky man in his early thirties came towards the library. He was clean-shaven, with a protruding underlip which would have given his face a rather scornful expression if the friendly radiance of his blue eyes had not belied it. There was in his bearing a force and vigor impressive even to the casual passer-by. He walked slowly, in complete abstraction, head thrust forward, and hands clasped behind his back. But when the chimes of the cathedral began to ring, he looked up and stood silently until the last note had died away. For a moment he stopped to admire the peasant women's flowers, then went inside the building.

Each noon Johannes Brahms came to the Zürich Museum-Library to read the daily newspapers and consult the great *Concordance.* In this alphabetical classification of all the important passages in the Bible he found the texts for his *German Requiem,* on which he was then at work.

Usually some of Johannes' friends met him at the library, and they would all go off and have dinner together. He had been in Zürich for some weeks already. Early that spring he decided to spend several months in Switzerland. He had taken rooms in a chalet on the Zürichberg, with a beautiful view over the lake and mountains.

Brahms was now a composer of considerable renown, whose works were being played in many countries. The musical circles of Zürich gave him a warm welcome. There he met Wagner's intimate friends, the Wesendoncks, Kapellmeister Hegar, and a number of others, including a Dr. Theodor Billroth. This latter, a surgeon by profession, was also an excellent amateur musician, and when, the following year, he moved from Switzerland to Vienna, he became one of Brahms' most intimate friends. To Billroth were dedicated the first two string quartets, the C minor and the A minor.

On this May day of 1866, Dr. Billroth reached the library just a few moments after Brahms.

"It is all arranged," he called. "Kirchner and Hegar will meet us at Grütli's for dinner."

"On the terrace by the water?" broke in Johannes.

"But, of course—where we always eat on fine days. Then after dinner the others will join us for that excursion we planned to the end of the lake."

"Good!" exclaimed Brahms with satisfaction. Nothing pleased him more than a trip into the country with a group of congenial friends. These expeditions, however, were sometimes a little hard on those who accompanied him. The composer's amazing vitality, and the intense enthusiasm he put into everything he did, set a pace which was often difficult for others to follow.

By the time the party got back to Zürich, late that afternoon, everyone was pretty well exhausted; everyone, that is, but Johannes Brahms—*he* was still fresh and full of energy. "Let's stop at Hegar's house and rest ourselves with some music," he cried. "Kirchner, you shall play me that sonata of yours that you were telling me about. . . ."

To have his work criticized by the celebrated Herr Brahms was no small privilege; so, in spite of his fatigue, Kirchner pulled himself together, and though he had no music with him managed to get through his sonata.

When he had finished, Brahms sat down at the piano and himself played through several parts of the composition, note for note, just as he had heard it, making suggestions as he went along and pointing out the weak places. The other men whispered among themselves. It seemed incredible that anyone could have such a memory as that!

Then he played some of his own compositions for them. The Swiss poet, Widmann, who heard Brahms in concert that same spring, wrote a vivid word-picture of the composer at the piano:

> The broad leonine chest, the Herculean shoulders, the mighty head which the player sometimes threw back with an energetic jerk, the pensive, handsome brow that seemed to radiate an inner illumination, and the Germanic eyes which scintillated with a wondrous fire between their fair lashes—all this betrayed an artistic personality that seemed charged to the very finger tips with the fluid of genius. There was, too, something confidently victorious in the countenance, the radiant serenity of a mind that is happy in the exercise of its art.

Next, Brahms suggested chamber music. Kapellmeister Hegar had recently bought a copy of the newly printed F minor quintet, elaborated from the two-piano sonata which had been dedicated to Princess Anna. With the composer at the piano they began. But when they reached the *Andante,* the strings played too fast to suit Brahms.

This had happened once before in an early rehearsal of the same work, and the composer had discovered a tactful way of handling the situation. Instead of criticizing, he called: "Just a moment, please. Something seems to be a little wrong here!" He made a great pretense of putting on his glasses and examining the score. "H'm, h'm," he grunted. "I see I've marked that passage wrong!" Taking out his pencil he carefully wrote in *"Meno mosso"*—less fast. The others took the hint and finished the movement in correct tempo.

When the quintet was finished they started on the G major sextet—the famous "A G A D E" sextet, which had been published that spring. By now the musicians were so absorbed that they were no longer conscious of time or fatigue. Hegar's servant-girl brought in platters of cold meat and rye bread, with chunks of rich Swiss cheese and steins of local beer. Absent-mindedly the men reached for food and continued with their playing, stopping only occasionally to call for more beer.

Brahms suddenly looked at his watch. "Heavens!" he cried. "It's past midnight. And my lodgings are far away from here, on the other side of town."

"You must stay with me for the rest of the night," Hegar insisted. "And you, Dr. Billroth, your home is a long way off too—" He stopped short in dismay. "Only —well, as a matter of fact I have nothing but one sofa to offer the two of you!"

Brahms laughed. "That doesn't matter a bit. I can sleep perfectly on the floor. Here—" he pulled a cover from the couch, rolled himself in it, and slid under the grand piano.

Nothing would budge him from the spot. In fact.

while the others were still arguing, he began to snore peacefully.

The next morning he insisted that he had never had a better sleep!

In late August, Clara Schumann was just leaving her house for a walk into town when a strange, bearded man approached her. He took off his hat and swept it to the ground with an elaborate bow.

"Gracious lady—" he began, in a high, cracked voice.

"What do you wish?" asked Frau Schumann coldly, suspecting that the man wanted money.

Suddenly the stranger burst into laughter and seized her by both shoulders. *"Ach,* Clara! Now really—don't you recognize your Hannes? Don't you like my beautiful beard?"

Frau Schumann stared at him in amazement. The good Clara was not born with a lively sense of humor. Finally she remarked dryly, "No, I do *not* like that awful beard."

Johannes sighed, crestfallen. "Very well, then, dearest Clara, I shall have to shave it off."

He was true to his word. Not until twelve years later did the famous beard, which appears in all of Brahms' most familiar portraits, return to stay.

That same fall of 1866 Brahms and Joachim decided to go on a concert tour through Switzerland. In the future the two were to make many concert trips together. This season they played first in Schaffhausen, and later in the little city of Aarau.

After the program, Brahms and Joachim went to a tavern, where they opened several bottles of the best vintage Swiss wine, including the popular *vin mousseux* of Lausanne. Brahms felt decidedly genial.

"How did we do this evening, my friend?" he asked the concert manager.

"Very well, very well!" the small, meek-looking manager replied, rubbing his hands together. "I have all the receipts in here," he whispered, pointing to a small sack which he held close to his side.

"Give it to us!" exclaimed Joachim, seizing the bag. "Here, Hannes, we'll divvy up the swag."

"Gentlemen—but please, I haven't yet made up my accounts," the little man cried anxiously.

"No matter—we'll divide it anyhow. Here, Hannes—a five-franc piece for you." He tossed a silver coin to Brahms.

By this time a crowd had gathered round to watch the fun. Piece by piece the "swag" was doled out—one to Yussuf, one to Johannes. Finally nothing was left but a twenty-franc note. "I'll take that," said Joachim, nonchalantly putting the bill in his pocket.

"Hold on—that's mine!" Brahms shouted in an outraged voice.

"And how do you figure that out?"

"Why, I played the best part of the program—all my own solos, and your accompaniments besides."

"Listen—" Joachim addressed the company. "That fellow is a complete egotist." He fixed Johannes with an accusing eye. "Didn't you insist that your name should be printed first on the programs?"

"Correct alphabetical order," grumbled Johannes.

"Alphabetical order? *Musical* sequence is more important than anything else. It should be:

"Why," he went on, "I was playing in concerts—a big artist—when you were still in the nursery." (Nursery! thought Brahms, remembering the Hamburg dance-halls.) "Yes," Joachim insisted, "this money rightfully belongs to me."

"On guard!" shouted Johannes in mock fury, seizing a tall alpenstock that stood near, and thrusting another into Yussuf's hands. "We'll fight for it."

"Gentlemen! Gentlemen!" begged the anguished manager; but no one paid any attention to him. Then suddenly he left the room. Just as the two friends were about to attack each other, the little man returned, waving two ten-franc notes.

"Stop!" he cried. "See—here is change—!"

Brahms returned frequently to Hamburg to see his family. During these visits he was often invited to conduct the orchestra there. On one such occasion, at a rehearsal, he suddenly stopped short in the middle of a phrase.

"Who played that wrong note?"

There was complete silence. Brahms looked accusingly in the direction of the bass viols at the rear. All at once he caught sight of his father, whose face wore an agonized look. The truth suddenly dawned on Johannes—Father Brahms was the guilty party!

His expression was so droll that Johannes wanted to burst out laughing. Instead, he rapped sharply with his baton.

"We will begin again, gentlemen. . . ."

One morning in the early summer of 1867, a friend of the Brahms family named Carl Bade went over to call on Jakob.

The door opened cautiously to his knock. There stood Father Brahms, his finger on his lips.

"Sh-h-h!" he whispered mysteriously.

Bade was alarmed. "Is the good wife sick?" he asked.

Jakob shook his head. *"Nein, nein,* no one is sick. But"—he pointed impressively towards the corner room, with the air of one who shelters royalty—"*he* is there! And he has brought a friend, a great man from Vienna, Herr Doktor Gänsbacher, who is to go with us."

Carl Bade suddenly noticed that Jakob was dressed in his very best clothes, and looked strangely elated and keyed up. "What's doing?" he asked inquisitively.

Jakob drew himself to his full height and adjusted his

new tie with dignity. "You could never guess." He stood there, bristling with pompous importance, while Bade became more and more curious. Finally the old man spoke:

"My Hannes has invited me!" he announced solemnly. "*Ja, ja,* believe it or not. He has come to take me on a trip."

Jakob stood in great awe of his famous son. When Johannes asked him to go on a tour through Austria, he was quite overwhelmed at the honor of traveling in such distinguished company. Father Brahms had never been very far from Hamburg, nor had he ever seen a real mountain, except in pictures.

Johannes was always trying to find ways to please and surprise his old father. Before they set out on their journey, he asked his friend Gänsbacher to sing for him. The two beautiful songs "*Mainacht*" and "*Von ewiger Liebe*" had recently been completed, and Jakob was vastly pleased to be the first to hear them.

Brahms had met Josef Gänsbacher when he first went to Vienna. Gänsbacher was professor of singing at the Conservatory there, and an amateur 'cellist. He had been instrumental in procuring Brahms' appointment as director of the Vienna *Singakademie,* and the two were close friends.

The trip through Austria was full of wonders for Jakob. But it proved a little more strenuous than the old man had bargained for. They visited Vienna and Salzburg, then traveled by stage and mountain railway through picturesque Styria and Carinthia. There were frequent side excursions on foot. Johannes was putting on weight these days, but he still seemed to have energy enough for four. Even Herr Gänsbacher had difficulty in keeping up with him, while poor Jakob trailed far in the rear.

As the *pièce de résistance* of the journey, Brahms took his father on a climb to the top of the Schafberg, above the Wolfgang See. It was a stiff pull, and the old man could hardly make the grade.

When they reached the summit, Johannes, still fresh as a daisy, drew in great breaths of the stimulating air. "Now then—isn't that a magnificent view!" he cried. "I'll wager you never saw anything like that around Hamburg."

But at that moment poor Jakob was more interested in finding a place to sit down than in all the mountain views in Austria.

"Look here, my boy," he wheezed. "Promise never to do this to me again!"

A few days later they visited the charming lake of Grundlsee, one of the loveliest, most romantic spots in Austria. Father Brahms, however, only looked at the water in mournful silence. Finally he heaved a deep sigh and said: "Just like the Alster Basin at home!"

By now Jakob was surfeited with foreign scenes. He longed to be at home in his comfortable armchair, with his Line beside him. "See, Hannes," he said wistfully, pointing to a small plant at their feet. "Here is a little blue flower just like the ones we have near Hamburg!"

Brahms took his father home by way of Heidelberg and showed him the University and the fine old castle on the hill. After he got back to Vienna he sent Jakob a collection of maps of the districts they had visited, with blue lines drawn to show the route that had been followed.

The old man was tremendously proud of this souvenir of his travels. Now that he was safely home he forgot the hardships. He never tired of telling his cronies about the marvelous journey that "me and mine Hannes" went on together.

The next summer Brahms again invited his father to travel with him. They spent ten days, first on the Rhine, and then in Switzerland. Here there were more mountains. . . . This time Jakob definitely had enough of traveling. When he returned to Hamburg he settled down in his chair with a sigh of relief. "*Na,* Line," he said to his wife. "Mine Hannes will not get around me again!"

Josef Gänsbacher's name has become familiar to music-lovers because it appears on the title page of Brahms' first 'cello sonata.

"Do not be alarmed or annoyed if I put your name on the violoncello sonata that I'm about to send you," wrote the mischievous composer, knowing well how delighted his friend would be. Gänsbacher admired Brahms' music extravagantly, and he was quite overwhelmed by the honor of the dedication. As soon as Johannes came to see him, he begged him to try the new work over with him.

Brahms raised his eyebrows a little, but sat down at the piano. He began his part *fortissimo.*

Gänsbacher, wrestling with the 'cello part (he was more enthusiastic than proficient), finally stopped playing. "But, Johannes—you play so loud I cannot hear myself."

Brahms looked over his shoulder quizzically. "Lucky chap!" he remarked dryly.

CHAPTER XVI

THE GERMAN REQUIEM

PROMPTLY at six o'clock on the evening of Good Friday, 1868, the doors of St. Peter's in Bremen were thrown open. Soon the cathedral filled with an expectant audience of musicians, critics, and distinguished visitors from all over Europe. They had come for an important event—the first full * performance of Johannes Brahms' *German Requiem*.

An air of subdued excitement filled the church. This new work was said to be the greatest masterpiece Brahms had so far written. It had certainly attracted an exceptional audience! As one celebrity after another walked up the aisle to seats reserved at the front, the citizens of Bremen nudged each other. "Look over there

* Full, that is, but for Part V, which had not yet been written.

near the choir," they whispered. "That's Herr Joachim, the great violinist; he's director now of the Berlin Conservatory of Music."

"He and his wife are both to take part in the program this evening," said another.

"Stockhausen is singing the main part, I understand."

"You mean the Conductor of the Hamburg Philharmonic?"

"That's right—and more shame to Hamburg that Johannes Brahms wasn't nominated to the post!"

"Perhaps it's just as well," interposed a philosophically-minded listener. "If Brahms had taken that position he probably would never have found time to write a mighty work like this *German Requiem*."

"I wonder if it is really as fine as they've been saying," whispered a long-faced gentleman who had relatives in Austria. "Last November three movements of this Requiem were played in Vienna, and the performance was a regular fiasco. They said there were even hisses at the conclusion."

"I heard about that," answered the man sitting beside him. "It was because they didn't have enough rehearsals. A very sloppy performance. Just wait until you hear it tonight. My daughter sings in the chorus, and she says it's magnificent."

Another listener took up the defense. "Hanslick praised the work! He insisted that only a few old 'bald-headed fanatics' didn't like it. He got off a good one in his review—said the hissing was 'a requiem on the decorum and good manners of a Vienna concert-room.' "

The first speaker had a word to add to that. "Yes, but didn't he say too that part of the work made him feel 'like a passenger rattling through a tunnel in an express train'? What do you make of that?"

"All the drummer's fault. He suddenly went mad in the fugue, and drowned everybody out."

Just then a group of people from Hamburg came in. For sentimental as well as musical reasons, Brahms had invited four members of his "Ladies' Choir" to sing with the Bremen chorus. Fräulein Marie Wölckers was a member of this quartet; her father and sister accompanied the group to Bremen.

With them came a stout, elderly man, tightly buttoned into a well-brushed frock-coat. His round, good-natured face was flushed with excitement and beaming with pride. In the whole audience no one felt himself so important! It was old Jakob Brahms.

Johannes smiled at his father with affection. As he watched the crowds fill the cathedral, he was deeply moved to see how many of his old friends had gathered to do him honor. There, across the aisle, sat Dietrich, and with him Julius Grimm (the famous "Ise"). Nearly all his intimates were there—only the Schumanns were missing.

Johannes was disappointed to think that none of this dear family had come to hear the first performance of what he knew was, so far, his greatest work. Robert

Schumann, in a sense, he felt to be present, for had his death not inspired the first beginning of the *Requiem?* But Clara—why had she not come?

"Someone is asking for you at the door," a voice whispered at his elbow. Brahms looked around impatiently. It was almost time to begin. Should he go? Perhaps it was something important. . . . He left his seat and hurried back to the cathedral entrance.

There stood two ladies, one dressed in black and wearing a veil over her bonnet, the other younger. Both were wreathed in smiles.

"Clara!" cried Brahms in joyous surprise. "Is it really you? And Marie too! I thought you weren't coming."

"We wanted to surprise you," Frau Schumann said, laughing at his expression. "Of course we couldn't miss such an important occasion."

A few moments later Brahms—beaming with delight—led the two ladies down the aisle and seated them in the front row. Then he took his place before the massed orchestra and chorus, and gave the signal to begin.

"Blessed are they that mourn, for they shall be comforted."

In the audience that evening were many with sad hearts, who had lost dear ones and could not forget their grief. To these the mighty harmonies of Brahms' moving work brought consolation. For one of music's most important functions is to release emotion—to liberate the pent-up anguish of the suffering. Down through the ages Brahms' music, and especially his great *Requiem,* will speak to all who can understand—to all who are "weary and heavy-laden." "They that sow in tears shall reap in joy." And who that has once heard it can forget the tremendous climax of the work? After one of the most exciting and overpowering passages in all oratorio literature, death is swallowed up in victory, and the exultant chorus bursts into the Master's greatest fugue:

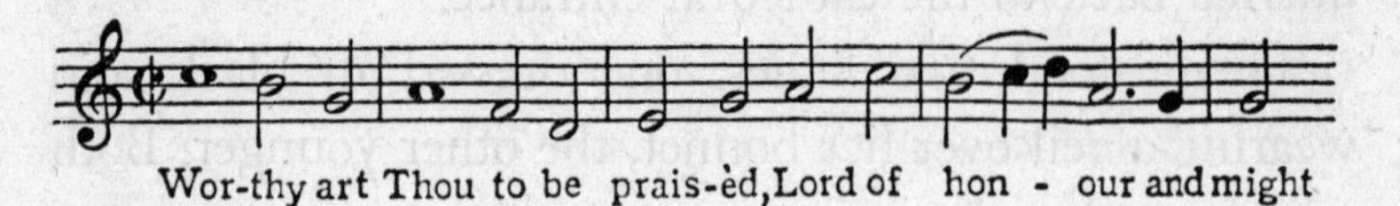

This performance of Brahms' *German Requiem* was the greatest event in the composer's career so far. He had written the work with deep feeling, in memory of Robert Schumann and of his mother, and it was closer to his heart than anything he had yet composed.

The concert produced a powerful effect on everyone. It was agreed that the *German Requiem* was one of the mightiest compositions that had ever been heard—worthy to take its place beside Beethoven's *Missa Solemnis.*

In a review Dietrich wrote:

> The impression made by the wonderful, splendidly performed work was quite overpowering. It immediately became clear to the listeners that the *German Requiem* would live as one of the most exalted creations of musical art.

The performance at St. Peter's Cathedral made such a stir that a few weeks later a repetition was necessary.

During the year that followed, the *Requiem* was given twenty-one times in different cities of Europe. Johannes Brahms, now aged thirty-five, was acknowledged one of the greatest composers of his day.

At the conclusion of the Good Friday concert, a gay celebration was held at the *Rathskeller,* across the square from the cathedral in Bremen. Those who had taken part in the *Requiem* gathered there, together with Brahms' friends and a number of out-of-town visitors—over a hundred in all. After the banquet there were speeches and toasts to the composer.

Brahms, who was never able to overcome his natural shyness and dislike of public attention, listened to all the eulogies with increasing embarrassment. He always felt ill at ease when anyone praised him. Finally the moment he had been dreading arrived.

"Speech from Herr Brahms now!" they cried.

"I'd rather write a dozen Requiems than make a speech," Brahms muttered to Clara Schumann, who was sitting at his right.

Clara laughed a little maliciously. "This time you'll have to do it!" she said, remembering how often she had tried to bring Johannes out in public.

Brahms rose slowly to his feet. "I—I do not have the gift of oratory . . ." he began. In his nervousness he couldn't think of a thing to say. Then, as he looked out over the sea of familiar faces that filled the oak-raftered banquet hall of the *Rathskeller,* he was seized with an emotion that made him forget his self-consciousness. "I only want to thank all the good, kind friends who have gathered here tonight," he stammered in a voice filled with feeling, "and those who made the *Requiem* such a success. . . ." He raised his glass unsteadily. "To Herr Reinthaler!" he cried. "Let's give three cheers for the music-director of St. Peter's!"

While in Bremen, Brahms stayed with the Reinthalers. There were several little ones in the family, and Johannes, who was passionately fond of children, soon became a great favorite with them.

Little Misi, only six, had already started her musical education. Her father had been teaching her a duet. "We shall play it for Herr Brahms," he told the child shortly before the composer's arrival.

Misi was a little frightened at the thought, but when she saw what a jolly companion the blue-eyed musician from Vienna proved to be, she could hardly wait to show him that she too could play the piano.

But now her father was too busy with rehearsals of the *Requiem* to think of such trivial things as piano duets. . . . Misi waited patiently, and continued with her practicing.

One day, as Brahms came in the house, he heard a tinkling of the piano in the parlor. Opening the door a crack he saw Fräulein Misi perched on the piano bench, her small feet miles above the pedals, her face puckered with intense concentration.

"What are you playing there, little Misi?" asked the visitor, a twinkle in his eyes.

The child stopped short. Tears gathered. "It was to be a surprise," she said in a low voice. "We were going to play it together for you, Papa and I. But he never has time. . . ."

"H'm-m," exclaimed Brahms, looking over Misi's shoulder. "A duet! Well now, perhaps *I* could manage the bass, and we could play it together, you and I."

"Do you know how to play the piano?" asked the child a little doubtfully. She knew that Brahms composed music. But piano-playing—now that was something different!

"Yes, I play a little," answered the man who was considered one of the best performers of his day.

Misi moved the big book she was sitting on and made a place for her friend on the bench beside her. They began. "Oh!" cried the little girl, stopping short. "You have played a wrong note!"

Brahms pretended great amazement. "No—not really? *Ach,* so I have," he exclaimed, looking at the music with great care. "We must start once more."

But a second time the wrong note sounded. "No, no!" Misi was indignant. "You are wrong again!"

"Again?" Brahms chuckled. "Well, I see I cannot keep up with you, Fräulein Misi. I shall have to practice this part by myself first."

Brahms loved to play jokes on his unsuspecting friends. Some years later he was visiting in Grundlsee.

Coming into the house unannounced, and finding no one in the music-room, he sauntered over to the piano. There stood an open copy of Czerny's *School of Velocity*. He sat down at the piano and began to play the exercise, stumbling over the notes as a young child might do.

All at once, from the next room, an irate voice called. "That's *wrong,* Hans! There you go—playing C for C sharp again." Brahms shook with silent laughter, and continued to play, making more and more mistakes.

"No, *no*—you miserable boy!" came the voice again. "Why, only yesterday you played *much* better."

Brahms tried hard not to let his laughter get the best of him. He went on, playing steadily worse.

Suddenly there was an indignant rustle of skirts, and Hans' mother threw the door violently open. "Enough, you wretch! Just wait till I teach you—" she cried—then stopped in confusion. *"Mein Gott.* Herr Brahms, was that *you!"*

The "wretch" leaned back and shook with laughter. *"Ja, ja,* dear lady, I am the guilty one. Of course you can't expect me to play as well as Hans!"

Although Brahms loved children dearly, he also teased them unmercifully. He liked to take little boys on his lap and threaten to snip off their noses with his cigar-cutter. Or he would suggest a drink, and then, when a small mouth was trustingly opened, pour the water down their necks. Little girls would have their apron strings untied, or pigtails pulled. And Brahms would laugh heartily at their consternation.

When he was in his early twenties he composed a song (later destroyed) for the Schumann children, and wrote their mother: "I send you herewith a fear-inspiring sermon for naughty children . . . to be sung with much pathos!"

Shortly after the lovely *Cradle Song* appeared, Brahms suggested to his publishers that there should be a special edition "printed in a minor key for naughty or ailing children!"

The "AGADE" sextet was composed to express Brahms' love for Agathe von Siebold; the *Cradle Song,* for Bertha Porubszky. Now, in the year after the *Requiem's* first performance, another love—or rather, lost love—inspired one of his important compositions.

For years Brahms had been attracted to Julie Schumann. She reminded him of her mother when he first knew Clara in Düsseldorf. Each summer when he went to Lichtenthal he would think: "This year I shall ask Julie to marry me." Yet he could never quite make up his mind. . . .

Then suddenly, in 1869, he had news of her engagement to an Italian count. He was overwhelmed by the realization of what he had lost. "Now," he exclaimed bitterly, "it merely remains for me to compose a bridal song." "I do this sort of thing with concealed wrath—with rage!" he wrote to Simrock.

Once again Brahms' frustrated emotions found expression in music. He wrote for Julie's wedding a "Rhapsody" for contralto solo with men's chorus and orchestra. The revealing words were from Goethe:

> Ah, shall any heal his anguish whose balsam has turned to poison—who has drunk hatred for men from the plenitude of love?

Brahms composed a large number of songs. Of these, the *Magelone Romances* alone (written over a considerable period of time) fill five slim volumes. Almost every year of his creative life, until the very end, saw the publication of one or several collections of songs. Some of these were for voices alone, others with piano or orchestral accompaniment. There were duets, quartets, part-songs for chorus and groups of voices together. Two choral works in larger form are almost as much orchestral as vocal—the *Song of Destiny* and the *Song of Triumph.*

Acknowledging the money sent him for the *Song of Destiny,* he wrote, half in earnest, half in jest: "Here is the receipt for my heart's blood. Also my thanks for the purchase price of the poor little piece of soul."

The noisy *Song of Triumph* is definitely dated and seldom performed. But when it first appeared it was tremendously popular, and added new laurels to the composer's fame.

In 1870 Brahms, now aged thirty-seven, was not only internationally acclaimed, but financially independent.

The royalties from his printed compositions and the proceeds from his concert tours brought him a comfortable income—in happy contrast to the poverty of many of the world's greatest musicians. Unhappily Bach, Mozart, Schubert, all lived and died in bitter want. Johannes Brahms was fortunate in living in an age in which genius was both recognized—and rewarded.

Jakob Brahms had been ailing for nearly a year. He did not complain, but he seemed to have no strength, and was obliged to give up his position with the Philharmonic orchestra. He appeared quite content to sit at home in his comfortable armchair, and watch Frau Line as she went about her housework. Sometimes she would see him look wistfully at his double-bass standing silent in the corner.

The two Fritzes had been away for some time, one in Venezuela and the other in Russia; but both had recently come back to Hamburg. Frau Line's son returned because of poor health, and as soon as he arrived she sent for a doctor. The latter found nothing much the matter with the "second Fritz," but when he saw Jakob, who rose with difficulty to greet him, he stopped short.

"Herr Brahms, I do not like your color!" exclaimed the doctor with genuine concern. "You had better let me examine you while I am here."

A few days later (it was in January 1872), Johannes received an alarming letter from home. The doctor had discovered that Jakob was seriously ill. Brahms went to

Hamburg as quickly as he could get there. He found his father in the last stages of cancer of the liver. Two weeks later the old man died.

Johannes grieved like a child. Now he was more than ever grateful to Frau Line for all she had done to make his father's last years happy. Although Jakob's widow would not let her stepson support her (she managed to earn all she needed by taking in boarders), he often sent her presents and gifts of money, and scolded her because she did not ask for more.

> I beg you always to remember that I have more money than I need and that it gives me the greatest joy if you make use of it for yourself and yours. [And again:] Have you a great deal too much money, or may I send some? I should like Fritz to spend plenty in traveling, and he can afterwards entertain you and himself again with his sufferings.

Frau Line's son, the "second Fritz," was sent by Brahms to Holstein for his health, and later set up in business as a watch- and clockmaker.

The day before Johannes left Hamburg to go back to Vienna, Frau Line found him standing before a small oil-portrait of his father.

"This must stay with you as long as you live," he said, adding with emotion, "but promise me that I shall have it when you are gone!"

"But of course," she answered. The good soul always regretted that she was unable to fulfill this promise. Johannes Brahms was to die six years before his stepmother—of the same disease that ended his father's life.

FROM DRAWINGS BY PROF. W. VON BECKERATH

CHAPTER XVII

"FLYING MELODIES"

I AM LOOKING for rooms," said Brahms to the Ischl landlady, who promptly replied: "Yes, yes, *mein Herr,* I have charming rooms for a single gentleman." Brahms cocked a suspicious eyebrow, and watched the woman closely. "I have quite an ear for music—like to hear it going on around me. Perhaps," he continued in an offhand way, "you have someone here who plays, or practices?"

The landlady beamed. "But certainly, *mein Herr*. May the gentleman rest quite content. The lady just below here keeps her piano going all day. My daughter sings, and there is another boarder who plays the cornet. Yes, we are a very musical neighborhood. Even the hand-organs seem to know how we love to hear them. Nearly every day they play under our windows."

Having found out exactly what he wanted to know, the gentleman beat a hasty retreat. Quiet was indispensable to Johannes Brahms for his work. He had had so many unfortunate experiences that he no longer trusted people's word—not even if they insisted that their neighborhood was as still as the tomb.

During his summers he was sometimes obliged to change his lodgings because of officious celebrity-seekers. "Female lion-hunters" he called the women who threatened his peace. Once, having established himself at a small inn on Lake Starnberg, on the very evening of his arrival he was presented with a written invitation to join a group of artists and musicians who met there. The following morning when they called for an answer, they found only an empty room, with torn bits of the invitation scattered over the floor. Brahms had again taken flight.

In the fall of 1871, when the composer decided to change his Vienna lodgings, he made up his mind to find a quiet apartment, no matter how long it took him. He finally settled down at No. 4 Karlsgasse, and this remained his home until he died, a quarter of a century later.

The flat in the Karlsgasse consisted of three small rooms: parlor, bedroom, and study or workroom. In the parlor stood Brahms' piano, his writing-table, and a sofa. Beyond this was the smaller workroom. It was furnished with rows of bookshelves, where he kept his library, and a high desk, at which he always stood when writing his compositions. There were several cupboards for music, but he never seemed to find enough space to stow away his scores and manuscripts. Chairs and tables, and even the floor, were usually stacked with piles of music.

The composer's lodgings were far from elegant. To reach the parlor it was necessary to go through the bedroom. There was no bath (although this was not unusual in the Vienna of 1871), and it was difficult to heat the place in winter. Nevertheless these rooms were luxurious compared with those in which Brahms had lived before. He was quite satisfied. From his early days he had been accustomed to the plainest surroundings, and felt more at ease in simple quarters than in the elaborate homes he often visited.

Someone once inquired about his "studio." "My studio?" he answered. "Good God! I've never pretended to belong among those enviable beings who possess a 'studio'!"

The furniture in the new apartment was neither new nor beautiful; but it suited the composer. One strange-looking chair had a tricky set of rockers. Brahms, who loved to play practical jokes, delighted in inviting his visitors to sit in this chair—especially if they were women, and pretty! If they sat on the edge, plump they would fall forward onto the floor. If, on the other hand, they leaned back, their feet would fly high into the air. Then Brahms would laugh heartily to himself.

Remembering how he disliked hearing others play, he covered his piano with a thick rug, and even had a special mute made so that his music should not disturb anyone else.

His neighbors, however, were not always so considerate. Some years after he moved into the apartment in the Karlsgasse he heard a piano pounding incessantly beneath his room.

"Who is making that infernal noise?" he asked his landlady.

"A lady musician has taken the apartment beneath you."

"Female piano-beast!" he grumbled. "She is driving me mad. She insists on playing *my* compositions—it's *terrible!"*

Brahms was very blunt in his manner, and the next time he met his neighbor on the stairway, he informed her in no uncertain terms that her music disturbed him. This made the lady so furious that she hired a pupil from the Conservatory to come every day and play *Brahms, fortissimo,* in the room under his study.

It was more than Brahms could stand. "What on earth shall I do?" he groaned.

His housekeeper was a resourceful soul, and she finally thought of a plan. She went down to the apartment below, and called on the newcomer. "It really is a pity," she cooed, "that you confine your great gifts to one instrument alone. Have you ever tried the zither?"

The lady swallowed the bait. "The zither! Is it difficult? Do you think I could learn to play it?"

"Oh, but certainly. I play it myself. I should be glad to give you lessons."

The "female piano-beast" took to the zither with enthusiasm. Presently she sent the piano student away and devoted all her time to the new instrument. The tones of the zither were so weak that the composer was no longer disturbed.

Brahms could be more than considerate on occasion, however. When, in the spring of 1883 he learned that an elderly lady who was an invalid had moved into the apartment below, he spared no pains to be as quiet as possible. He even took his boots off when he came in late at night, and went upstairs in his socks, so that the delicate old lady would not be disturbed.

Like most musicians Brahms was terribly sensitive to harsh or inharmonious sounds. Once, seated between two charming ladies at a dinner-party, he grew more and more exasperated, and finally refused to speak to either of them. Later a friend asked him what on earth had been the trouble. "How could I help being cross?" answered the composer, his blue eyes round and guileless. "Why, the lady on my right talked in E major, while the one on my left had an E minor voice!"

The temperamental Master was not always silent. Sometimes he exploded. "Sitting next to Brahms is like sitting next to a barrel of gunpowder," the long-suffering Joachim once exclaimed.

In 1872 Brahms was appointed "artistic director" of Vienna's leading choral group, the Friends of Music Society. Ten years before, when—an unknown composer—he had for a season directed the Singing Academy chorus, he had been criticized for choosing music that was too somber and heavy. Now the same complaint was lodged against him.

"When Brahms is feeling particularly genial and jolly, he sets to music 'Halli, Hallo, the Tomb Is My Joy!'," wrote one critic following a program which included Cherubini's *Requiem* and Bach's *Dearest Lord, When Shall I Die?* Even Hanslick, now Johannes' stoutest champion, rebelled. "The Viennese object," he said, "to being buried twice in one evening—once as Catholics, and a second time as Protestants."

Brahms heard of these criticisms, and at the next rehearsal he announced to his singers: "Ladies and gentlemen, I understand you have been criticizing the sad tone of the programs. I have therefore prepared for you an agreeable surprise. Our next concert will begin with 'Death is my Delight.' "

Everyone laughed tremendously, and Brahms continued to choose the music that he preferred. But the regular work soon irked him. He resigned from the Friends of Music Society at the end of the third season, and never again accepted a steady position.

Early in 1877 Brahms was offered the degree of Doctor of Music at Cambridge University. Joachim was to receive a musical doctorate at the same time. He urged Johannes to join him in England, for they were required to accept the honor in person.

Brahms had often wished to visit England. This seemed a good opportunity—until he began to think of the drawbacks to such a journey. In the first place he knew neither the language nor the customs of the country. He hated ceremonies and strange people. And worst of all, he would have to cross that terrible English Channel. Johannes had only been on the ocean once, years before. The boat was very small—he had never forgotten how terrified he had been—and seasick.

The Cambridge honor was declined with thanks.

Three years later, however, when the University of Breslau invited him to become a Doctor of Music, he did not refuse. (There were no Channels to cross!)

The diploma described him as "*princeps artis musicae severioris*" (foremost exponent of musical art in the severer style). It would have been quite appropriate if he had submitted the somber *Tragic Overture,* composed that same year, for his doctor's thesis. But Brahms' mischievous spirit of contradiction moved him to offer, instead of music in the "severer style," which he knew was what the University expected, a rollicking *tour de force* studded with gay college melodies. "A very jolly potpourri of students' songs à la Suppé," he called it, humorously belittling his own work as was his custom.

The *Academic Festival Overture* is one of the merriest, most vigorous and brilliant compositions that ever came from the pen of Johannes Brahms. The best of the themes are original. Others were frankly taken from actual student songs (one of these drolly scored for two staccato bassoons), and all woven together with consummate skill to culminate in the smashing climax of *Gaudeamus Igitur:*

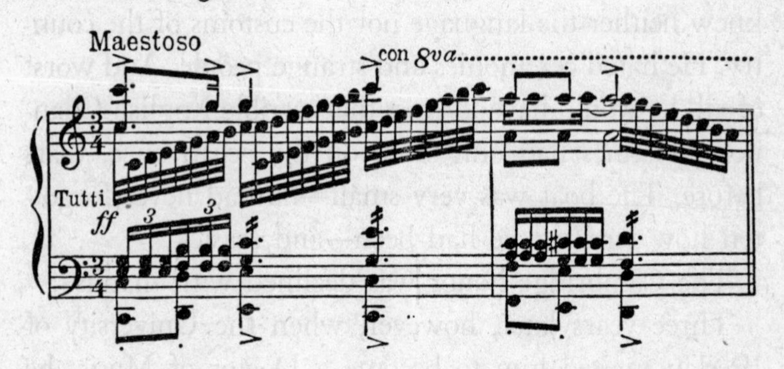

At heart Brahms was one of the most modest and unassuming men that ever lived. Yet in a naïve way he was vastly proud of his doctor's degree. Hanslick reminded a friend of this: "Don't forget the 'doctor' title, of which Brahms is very vain!"

As he had had little or no formal education in his youth, a university degree held for him an exaggerated significance. He now became "Herr Doktor" to everyone.

During this period Brahms was often asked why he had never written a symphony.

"A symphony?" he would reply. "Ah, my friends,

that is not so simple. Only a great artist should attempt this highest form of music-writing."

"But who better qualified than yourself?"

Brahms would shake his head solemnly. "Some day, perhaps. But not yet."

He never told them how much time and thought he had already given to the preparation of a symphony. As early as 1855, a few months before Schumann's death, when Johannes was only twenty-two years old, a theme had suggested itself to him. He had at various times outlined ideas for a symphony, but none of them satisfied him, and they were all abandoned. Brahms was tremendously stern with himself. Most of us spend our lives persuading ourselves that our poorer efforts are really not so bad. The psychologists call this sort of thing "rationalization." Brahms would have none of it.

In middle age he grew dissatisfied with his first work of chamber music, the B major Trio. So he rewrote it assiduously, cutting out 533 measures, and vastly improving it. Whereupon Popper, the witty Hungarian 'cellist and composer, exclaimed, "I wish Brahms would do that to all the works of Popper!"

"It is not hard to compose," he told an ambitious young musician; "but it is wonderfully hard to let the superfluous notes fall under the table." By the time his first song appeared, he had already "let fall under the table" hundreds of others.

Before the year 1876 Brahms had composed comparatively little for full orchestra. There were, besides the

First Piano Concerto (1854), several works for voice with orchestral accompaniment, including the *Requiem,* the *Alto Rhapsody* (dedicated to Julie Schumann), the *Song of Triumph,* and the *Song of Destiny*. For orchestra alone he had written but three compositions: the two Serenades, begun in Detmold in 1857, and the *Variations on a Theme of Haydn* (1873).

Brahms spent the summer of 1876 on the island of Rügen, in the Baltic, with a highly congenial friend, George Henschel. This remarkable singer was the first conductor of our Boston Symphony Orchestra and of the London Symphony Concerts, after which he became a British subject and was knighted.

Brahms was in high spirits at this time, happy as always to be close to the outdoor world he loved so well. Henschel records lazy, carefree hours which the two spent lying in the grass by a stream, catching tiny frogs. Johannes, once more the boy of Winsen days, would pick up the frogs in his hands, then let them jump into the water. Just as the little animals imagined themselves free and started to swim vigorously away, he would seize them again—very gently, so as not to hurt them—and then laugh enormously.

One day Henschel began to whistle the Andante from Brahms' C minor piano quartet. The composer beamed with delight, and beat a rocking accompaniment with his hands. "It is a great joy to me if I succeed—or seem to succeed—in a composition," he exclaimed. "I'm not ashamed to confess it." He was silent a moment.

"Just imagine how those gods Mozart, Beethoven, and the other great ones must have felt when they put the finishing touch to masterpieces like *The Marriage of Figaro* and the Ninth Symphony! What I don't understand is how men like myself can be vain." Brahms looked down at the little frogs they were playing with. "Why, there are gods above us who are as much higher than ourselves as we are greater than these little creatures. To tell you the truth—when people praise me to the skies, I should be disgusted if it weren't so ridiculous."

Brahms considered Bach, Mozart, and Beethoven as "gods above him," but he was at that very time working on a masterpiece which would make the world acknowledge him nearly, if not entirely, their equal. This was the tremendous C minor symphony, first of four great orchestral works which, even if he had written nothing else, would have made the name of Johannes Brahms immortal.

No one suspected what he was up to, that summer in Rügen. He was always secretive about his work. He never let anyone know what he was composing. The tall writing-desk in his Karlsgasse study in Vienna had a hinged lid which was hastily closed if anyone came in unexpectedly, and he always kept it locked when he went out. Sometimes—but only occasionally—he would let a hint drop. From Rügen he wrote to his publisher Simrock that a "lovely symphony" had remained hanging to the tree-tops and chalk-cliffs there. Simrock did not guess what was in the air until a second letter came, some weeks later.

> Too bad you are not a music-director, otherwise you could have a symphony. It will be performed on the 4th in Karlsruhe. I expect from you and other friendly publishers a present of honor in recognition of my not importuning them with such things.

"Importune!" thought Simrock in high excitement. Why, this was the most important musical event in years. A symphony, at last, from Johannes Brahms! Naturally the importuning was all on the part of the eager publisher.

The C minor created a sensation. It was hailed as the greatest orchestral work since Beethoven's Ninth—indeed, Bülow started the fashion of calling it the "Tenth Symphony." And there was another reason for this. The opening theme of Brahms' last movement has two identical measures (marked by a bracket in the example given below) which are like one out of Beethoven's *Hymn to Joy* in his Ninth Symphony.

Brahms never stated whether his use of this theme was intentional or not. But he remarked impatiently to someone who commented on the resemblance, "Every donkey hears that!"

Hanslick wrote of the First Symphony:

> Brahms' close affinity with Beethoven must become clear to every musician who has not already perceived it. The new symphony displays an energy of will, a logic of musical thought, a greatness of structural power, and a mastery of technique such as are not possessed by any other living composer.

Nor, one might add, by any composer since that day! Brahms' C minor is one of music's masterpieces. It is filled with a nobility, grandeur, and tenderness which raise the listener to special planes of musical enjoyment that are known only to lovers of Brahms.

The Second Symphony, composed the following summer at Pörtschach on the Wörthersee, was written in a very different mood.

The country around this largest and loveliest of southern Austria's lakes is mellow and charming. Brahms, always sensitive to his environment, reflected the smiling countryside in his music. To Hanslick he wrote: "The Wörthersee is virgin soil. The air is so full of flying melodies that one must take good care not to tread on them."

But in writing to Simrock, with his usual delight in mischief he declared:

> The new symphony is so melancholy that you will not be able to put up with it. Never before have I penned anything so sorrowful, so minor-y. The score must be published with a black border. Don't say I haven't sufficiently warned you. Do you really consider investing in such a thing?

Simrock had a shock in store for him. That supposedly "minor-y," lachrymose affair, the D major symphony, far from being melancholy, turned out to be one of the gayest, happiest works ever written by Brahms, and its success was immediate.

At Pörtschach during the summer of 1878, another great composition was written—the Violin Concerto, dedicated to Joachim. The slow movement of this is based on an old Czech folk theme, which is first announced in a lengthy orchestral passage. Once a haughty violin virtuoso refused to play this concerto because he had to stand silent so long while the orchestra had the floor.

An amusing incident occurred when the Violin Concerto had its première in Leipzig, with Joachim as soloist and the composer conducting. Brahms was always indifferent about his personal appearance—not to say absent-minded as to details. When dressing for this concert he kept on his gray street trousers, and forgot his suspenders.

Suddenly, in the middle of the performance those trousers—usually inches above the tops of his shoes—began to slip. He continued serenely to conduct, while the audience watched, fascinated. Lower—lower came the nether garments. Modest ladies averted their eyes. Then fortunately the music came to an end. The listeners shuddered to think what might have happened if the concerto had been one movement longer!

Brahms wrote four symphonies in all. The Third, in F major, appeared six years later, in 1884; the Fourth, in E minor, in 1886.

To Kalbeck (later to become his biographer) Brahms said, in September 1885: "You evidently want to know if I've been careless about composition [this summer]. . . . Once more I've just chucked together a set of waltzes and polkas." The "set of waltzes and polkas" turned out to be the Fourth, perhaps the most austere, but by some considered the greatest, of all the Master's symphonies.

However, this business of setting one Brahms symphony over another is dangerous. When asked which is the best of the four, many excellent musicians declare that it is the one which they happen to be playing or hearing. And some feel the same about the concertos, trios, quartets, quintets, and sextets.

Brahms' level of excellence was higher than that of any other composer, although Bach, Mozart, Beethoven, and Schubert sometimes wrote greater music than Brahms' greatest. But Brahms had more severely self-critical standards. What other composer, for instance, would have burned twenty string quartets before publishing one? The others printed plenty of uninspired stuff mixed in with their masterpieces. Brahms printed almost none.

And that is why the *average* quality of Brahms' music surpasses the *average* quality of every other composer's; and why so many of us are inclined to feel that the symphonic or chamber work which we are just now hearing or playing is Brahms' best one.

CHAPTER XVIII

"ONKEL BAHMS"

TWO RAGGED urchins stood with their noses flattened against the window of a fashionable bakeshop near the Stephan's Platz. There gleamed a large, proud wedding-cake, glistening with scrolls of white icing; and on either side were equally luscious-looking coffee-breads, pies, gingerbread-men, and a whole assortment of miniature fruits and animals made of the famous Viennese *Marzipan,* or almond-paste.

For some time the little boys had been mutely eyeing the tempting collection. The smaller one heaved a deep sigh. "Hansl," he said wistfully, "what would you buy if you had a *Kreutzer?*"

A sudden shadow fell across the sheet of plate-glass (a shadow almost as broad as it was tall!), and a gruff voice broke in: "Well, well, now, isn't that a fine display. Makes me think. . . ." The man reached into the ample pocket of his coffee-colored greatcoat. "I wasn't very hungry at dinner today." He pulled out a piece of cake, wrapped in a bit of newspaper. Before the astonished boys knew what he was about, he had slipped the parcel into their hands, and then—like manna from the skies—two *Kreutzer* pieces jingled at their feet.

By the time the youngsters had scrambled for the coins, the stranger was already disappearing into the distance. The smaller boy danced up and down. "That was *Onkel Bahms!*" he cried gleefully.

Children were always on the lookout for Brahms as he walked by each day, puffing at his perpetual cigar. From the back he appeared a funny, fat little man, with "ground-shy" trousers and hands clasped behind him—usually holding an umbrella and often his hat. But when they met him face to face, his fine head and patriarchal beard, and most of all the friendly smile that lit up his face whenever he saw any of his "little ones," gave him an expression that endeared him to all of them.

Next to music, Brahms loved children better than anything in the world. To Clara Schumann from Ischl he wrote:

You ought to see me here in the role of the children's friend! There are no more lovable and agreeable folks and little folks anywhere than in this neighborhood. I cannot go for a walk without my heart laughing; and when I caress a couple of these adorable children, I feel as though I'd taken a cooling drink.

Brahms was sometimes a little rough with the small boys and girls of rich families. "His teasings were awkward expressions of tenderness," writes Kalbeck, "or more often well-meant attempts at education, if he thought the little ones were being made too soft or were spoiled by their parents."

But with the children of the poor—perhaps in memory of his own unfortunate youth—he was gentle and considerate. He always carried a bag of candy for them, or a bit of his dessert.

When, on his walks through the city, he would sight some of his young friends, he would pretend to be deeply absorbed in his own reflections. Pacing along with head down and hands behind his back, he would seem completely unaware of everything around him.

But the children knew what to expect. They would troop along behind, watching closely those austerely clasped hands. And soon they would be rewarded. Presently a sugarplum, a chocolate drop, even a dribble of *Kreutzers* would fall miraculously to the ground. A few moments later the Master would be installed on the nearest bench, with youngsters swarming over his ample knees.

One day he pulled from his pocket an innocent-looking pebble. "Did you know that stones are good to eat?"

he asked, chuckling at the incredulous look on the small faces. "You don't believe me?—look!" He tossed it into his mouth and made a great show of chewing and swallowing, while cries of amazement greeted the performance. "Want to try a stone?" he offered, holding out another pebble. One youngster finally opened his mouth, and in Brahms popped the "pebble." Suddenly the child's expression changed to one of surprised delight. What *Onkel Bahms* had given him wasn't hard and tasteless at all; but candy made to resemble a stone!

Sometimes the composer tossed what looked like golden coins to his small friends—flat chocolates wrapped to represent money. Once he was overjoyed by a friend's gift of a box of "mineral specimens."

> Your mineral collection [he wrote, thanking the friend] is something too superb for words. It's a thing I've long known. I used to notice it with pleasure every day in the Stephan's Platz on the way to the Hedgehog. But I never dreamed that such magnificence could be anything for me and "my little ones." So many thanks for all the fun it will bring me and others!

Brahms usually went out each day at 12:30 for his dinner. The "Red Hedgehog" was his favorite tavern. If he was to eat with friends, he would pass through the main part of the restaurant, where the more fashionable patrons sat, and go to the small, low-ceilinged room at the back, reserved for workingmen and people of the poorer classes. If he was alone, his place was on a bench behind the door, separated from the taproom by no more than a red curtain. In the few days of Indian Summer after his return from the country, he would eat in the so-called *Schonny Garten*. This consisted of two or three tables out on the sidewalk, screened by a few large pots of evergreens. "Schonny," the Viennese way of saying "Johnny," was the traditional name for the small boy who set these plants out, and took them in for the night. Hence the *Schonny Garten* meant the Johnny Garden.

Brahms was a hearty eater. From his humble parents he had inherited simple tastes, and he liked plain, solid food, washed down with a glass or two of wine or beer. Each year his figure grew a little rounder. The "Red Hedgehog" he liked because he thought it one of the best for the money, and—still more important—one of the least expensive restaurants in Vienna.

The Master was extremely frugal in his personal habits. Although no one could be more generous with others, he never liked to spend money on himself. One winter day a friend noticed that his hands, always rough to the touch, were unusually chapped and cracked. The Master confessed, "I've lost my gloves—and I can't make up my mind to get another pair!"

He even hated to have others spend money on him. When Clara Schumann wanted to give him a new portmanteau, he wrote:

> My best thanks for your friendly idea of buying me a traveling bag. What I have in that line ought to do me. Truly I am

a person so far from spoiled and sophisticated that such a gift would be sheer waste.

Brahms usually traveled third-class on the train. Once he was returning from a trip abroad, when, at the border, a Customs official came through the cars.

"Anything to declare?" asked the man, looking inquiringly at the passengers. "Any tobacco?"

Brahms turned a guileless blue eye in his direction and then looked quickly out of the window.

"Open up!" said the official, pointing to a battered valise on the rack above.

The composer hesitated for a moment, then with an air of innocent casualness he lifted down his portmanteau for inspection.

"What's this?" cried the man, pulling out an object that looked like an amputated leg.

Brahms shook with silent rage. He had thought himself so clever, hiding all that Turkish tobacco in an old stocking so that he wouldn't have to pay duty!

But Customs officials are used to all kinds of ruses. To his anguish, not only did Brahms have to pay a fine of seventy gulden, but the "leg" was permanently amputated, and he lost his precious tobacco as well.

Brahms had always wanted to visit Italy. In April of 1878 his Swiss friend, Dr. Billroth, suggested a trip to the south. They went together, and this started a whole series of pilgrimages which Brahms made during the following years into Italy.

On one occasion he was accompanied by the poet Widmann. Another time he invited the old musicologist Nottebohm to go with him. Herr Nottebohm, however, got no farther than Venice. There he discovered some rare old wine. . . .

Later, at Gause's Beer Hall in Vienna, a song was dedicated to the incident:

> At Gause's, too, drank Nottebohm,
> Who started once to get to Rome
> But got to Venice merely.
> Old wine of Cyprus made the man
> Scorn wandering sincerely.

Everything about Italy enchanted Brahms: the brilliant sunshine; the beautiful vistas, which were like the landscapes in the old Italian paintings he loved so well; the picturesque towns and wonderful cathedrals; the gay, light-hearted people who seemed born with music in their hearts, and on their lips. All of these moved him to equal enthusiasm. In matters of art he was not over-discriminating.

In Siena the jewellike church of many-colored marbles inspired him to rhapsody. He wrote to Clara Schumann:

> If you stood only an hour before the cathedral of Siena, you would be blessedly happy and feel that was enough to repay the whole journey. And now you would enter; but there, on the pavement and in the whole church, there would be not an inch that would not enrapture you equally.

In Milan Brahms marveled at the thousands of elaborately carved statues which crowd the roof of the cathedral there. He, who spared no pains with the smallest details of his music, could understand the loving, patient labor of the old sculptors who had given a lifetime of work to the obscure corners of that vast edifice.

When he visited Cremona, where great violins were made, he discovered a statue of St. Joachim which pleased him mightily. "Now that is right fitting," he remarked. "I shall have to tell friend Yussuf how, in this city sacred to the fiddle, his patron saint is placed upon a pedestal."

It was during his first visit to Italy that Brahms finally decided to let his beard grow—that familiar and luxuriant beard which appears in all of his later photographs. There were several reasons for this decision. For one thing, the beard saved a lot of time and bother in shaving. For another he could, without its being too apparent, dispense with a tie, or—even at a pinch—with a collar! Brahms was notoriously indifferent to the fine points of personal attire.

Most important, however, the beard gave him a venerable and dignified expression which helped to counteract his short, now rotund and unimpressive figure. To Widmann the Master said, "With a smooth chin one is taken for either an actor or a priest."

When Brahms' head, with its patriarchal beard, was chosen to illustrate the perfect "Caucasian type" in a German schoolbook, he was naïvely flattered. Even strangers were impressed by the finely modeled nose and clear, wide-set eyes with their expression of keen intelligence, and, of course, by the beard! Once in a railway carriage in Italy, when he was asleep in a corner, his companion overheard two Italians whispering about him. "That must be a man of genius!" they said admiringly.

When Brahms returned to Vienna with his new beard, his friends hardly recognized him. One day as old Nottebohm and some others were dining together at the "Red Hedgehog", Dr. Billroth and a bearded stranger came in together. They both seemed in hilarious spirits.

"Gentlemen, let me present to you Herr Kapellmeister Müller from Brunswick," said Billroth, advancing.

The stranger bowed. He had a curious, high-pitched voice, and spoke in abrupt, short phrases. Nottebohm questioned him extensively about music in Brunswick. Billroth sat with his hand over his mouth. He seemed to have trouble stifling a cough.

Suddenly the "stranger" could stand it no longer. He burst into gales of laughter. "So—o—o!! It *is* a good disguise!" shouted Johannes, hugely pleased at his successful hoax.

Nottebohm was somewhat disgruntled at having been so completely taken in. But he had had occasion to know the genuine kindness of Brahms' heart. And when, some years later, the old Beethoven scholar died, it was

Brahms who closed his eyes and paid the funeral expenses.

Fritz, "the wrong Brahms," called on his stepmother one afternoon in the summer of 1878. He did not often find time to see Frau Line. She wondered what had brought him.

"Have you heard about the big music festival which is to be given in September to celebrate the Hamburg Philharmonic's fiftieth anniversary?" he asked. "All the leading musicians will be invited. Frau Schumann is coming, Joachim, and dozens of others. I understand our Hannes is to be specially honored."

Frau Caroline shook her head doubtfully. "I doubt if he will come. You know how he feels about the Philharmonic here—their not asking him to be conductor, and all that."

"But Hannes *must* come!" insisted Fritz, who was always glad of a chance to bask in the reflected glory of his brother's fame. "Do you write, Mamma, and urge him. Tell him we are counting on it."

Frau Line was right in saying that Brahms had not forgotten the slights he had received in the past. He was not at all sure that he cared to accept his native city's belated acknowledgment. It took considerable persuasion before he finally agreed to attend the music festival.

Now, at last, the people of Hamburg realized what a "man of genius" had been reared in—and driven away from—their city. They tried to make amends for past injustice. The Philharmonic anniversary celebration turned into a Brahmsian triumph.

The festival lasted for several days. There were three concerts, a banquet, and an excursion down the river and back. The leading citizens of Hamburg vied with each other in honoring their distinguished native son. Said one speaker, following the banquet: "The old saying about a prophet's being without honor in his own country can hardly apply here!"

Johannes nudged his neighbor at the table. "Is that so?" he whispered. "Has the gentleman forgotten that twice the conductor's post of Hamburg's Philharmonic was given to someone else? If they had offered it to me," he continued, muttering into his beard, "I could have married and become a good citizen. Now I'm no better than a vagabond!" He had never been able to outgrow the conservative peasant feeling that it is not respectable to be a free-lance artist!

The excursion down the river pleased Brahms most of all. As the boat started back for Hamburg that evening, three rockets were sent into the air, and three shots fired. Suddenly, at this signal all the villas along the river illuminated their houses and gardens. "Ah-h-h!" cried Johannes ecstatically.

Late that evening the boat docked at the St. Pauli landing. As Brahms made his way through the unsavory quarter, he thought with pity of the delicate, blue-eyed boy who had spent so many hours of his youth banging out dance-tunes in the taverns of this district.

What a contrast, the life of that child, to the ease and honors of his present existence!

At the final concert (Joachim was concertmaster) a real ovation was given to Johannes Brahms. When he mounted the platform to conduct his Second Symphony (the D major), they presented him with a large laurel wreath. Brahms, who was inclined to toss wreaths unceremoniously to one side, restrained himself and bowed gravely, while the audience burst into a storm of applause.

After each movement they cheered and clapped with mad enthusiasm, and at the end of the concert the ladies in the audience rose in their seats and threw their bouquets at the composer's feet. He found himself the center of a rain of roses.

Elise begged her brother to give her the wreaths which had been presented to him. But Johannes did not care to have her make a show of his triumph.

"So you want to brag to others with them?" he said. "No—come with me early tomorrow morning. We will go together and lay the wreaths on Father's grave."

Some years later Hamburg presented Brahms with the freedom of the city—an honor accorded to only two other "native sons": Moltke and Bismarck. The Master was touched. "This is the best that could come to me from mankind," he said with emotion. "And yet," he added thoughtfully, "to write a beautiful melody is better than any decoration, and to compose a good symphony, than an honorary citizenship."

CHAPTER XIX

HALF A CENTURY OLD

"BAH!" snorted Brahms in disgust. "Another morning wasted." For hours he had been working at his high desk (he always stood when writing music); but nothing would come right. For the twentieth time he had rewritten the opening pages of a new symphony. Now he quickly tore the sheets across, crumpled them up and threw them into the wastebasket.

Brahms was never satisfied with anything but the best in his music. No expenditure of time or effort was too much. He believed that only by taking infinite pains could anything really worth while be accomplished. "To do one's level best is never in vain," he wrote Kalbeck. "The benefits of this need not necessarily show in the place one intended." He did not, however, minimize the necessity for "inspiration," in addition to hard work. "My themes come to me in a flash," he said. "They are intuitive. Long after their arrival I take them up and work very hard over them."

An American violinist, Arthur M. Abell, once questioned the Master about his method of writing music. "Do you ever have, when composing, sensations such as those described by Mozart in a letter to a friend? He wrote: 'The process with me is like a vivid dream.' "

"Yes, I do," replied Brahms. "Mozart is right. When at my best it is a dreamlike state, and in that condition the ideas flow much more easily."

"Are you conscious when in this state?"

"Certainly, fully conscious; otherwise I should not be able to write the ideas down as they come. It is important to get them on paper immediately."

"Do you ever lose consciousness when in this mental condition?"

"Yes, sometimes I become so drowsy that I fall asleep, and then I lose the ideas."

"Can you do anything to induce this dreamlike state?"

"Yes, I early discovered that to obtain good results certain conditions had to be met. First of all, I have to be absolutely alone and undisturbed. Without these two requisites I cannot even think of trying to compose."

"Do you mean that you always have to be locked up in your rooms?"

"By no means. If I am alone and free from intrusion, I often get themes when out walking, especially in the country. But I always have to jot them down immediately; otherwise they quickly fade."

"Do you work these ideas out on paper as soon as you return home?"

"Not always. I let them germinate, sometimes for years; but I occasionally look at them again. This habit is important, for it engenders the same state of mind that gave birth to them, and in this way the original thoughts expand."

"Are there any requirements for entering this mysterious realm, aside from isolation and freedom from disturbance?"

"Yes, once I have these requisites, concentration to the point of complete absorption seems to be the key that unlocks the door to the soul-realm."

"Then you do not believe that composing is purely an intellectual process?"

"So far as the mechanics of composition are concerned, it is an intellectual process. Patience and much hard work are needed to acquire technical skill; but that has nothing to do with inspiration, which is a spiritual process."

"Then you would not endorse Carlyle's famous definition of genius as 'an infinite capacity for taking pains'?"

"Certainly not. I consider it very faulty. If taking great pains were all there is to genius, any patient plodder could become a Mozart or a Beethoven. I never could understand how so keen an observer as Carlyle could fall into such an error."

"Who, in your opinion, was a perfect type of the creative genius?"

"Beethoven. He had lofty aspirations, and at the same time he was an indefatigable worker. We all have to work hard."

For his own music the Master had little regard. "I never believe that a new composition of mine can please anybody," he once wrote to Frau Schumann. And again:

> Do not wonder, dear Clara, that I write you nothing about my work. I do not want to do it and cannot do it. I have . . . so little disposition and desire to lament to others about my lack of genius and skill.

To Simrock, his publisher, Brahms was always running down his own compositions. "I cannot imagine why anyone would want to invest in such a thing," he would say. "I have been ashamed," he wrote when sending some songs,

> not that anyone can write this sort of thing—what nonsense can a man not devise, the livelong day?—but that anyone prints such stuff and sells it for dear money! Is there, then, no government examination for publishers, so that one can be satisfied that they are able to distinguish garbage from salad and vegetables?

"I have always thought it an exaggeration to believe the half of what people say," he told another friend.

To Widmann he confessed that he usually slept badly after a performance of his own music, because (he said) he was too excited—not from pleasure, but from the distress of realizing how far inferior his finished work was to what had been his intention.

When Brahms sent Simrock his *51 Technical Exercises for the Pianoforte,* he wrote:

> Not that you will want to buy and print them, but merely that your connoisseur's eye may linger on them a moment. Apart from the melodies the only things capable of attracting you are their bulk (?!) and the title-page, which must be very beautiful and loud in color. I have in mind that all possible instruments of torture should be represented, from the thumbscrews to the Iron Maiden; perhaps some anatomical designs as well, and all in lovely blood-red and fiery gold.

Now, as the composer stared at his empty writing-desk, he was seized with a feeling of futility. Lately nothing had succeeded. Perhaps he was getting too old to write music. . . . Soon he would be fifty. Soon? He pulled himself up short—why, this very day! He had always felt that after fifty all poetry would be gone from life, and it would be high time to stop working and retire.

What had he accomplished? he asked himself. Nothing that really pleased him! He had been quite right to send that letter to Simrock saying that he was through with music and would probably publish no more.

Brahms stood for a moment frowning. What he needed was a good long walk in the country. It was such a fine May morning! He decided he would go to the woods. Then he remembered—he had promised to have lunch with the Ehrbars. Just because he had happened to mention his passion for asparagus! They said they would send out to the country for some.

Funny, he thought to himself, how people run after a man if he makes any kind of name for himself! Perfect strangers would come up and speak to him—ask him for his signature. Johannes disliked autograph-hunters. And usually he was too smart for them! That woman, for instance, who year after year used to order from him one of his "world-renowned, excellent Viennese pianos," or the people who wrote to say that "ten dozen Solingen knives have been forwarded as per your request." After a few such experiences he came to understand that all they wanted was a letter from him with his signature. And so he did not answer.

But the luncheon party! How could he possibly go, feeling in such a depressed mood? Would he have to dress up? He looked down at his faded black alpaca jacket. It was turning green in spots, and there were several patches. Suddenly a smile broke over his face.

"The new suit!" he murmured. To be sure—he had almost forgotten that the tailor had delivered it over a week ago. "Won't it give Billroth and Hanslick a shock! They're always after me to pay more attention to my clothes."

As he put on the new suit, Johannes felt quite virtuous and pleased with himself. But a tie now—surely it wasn't necessary to go *that* far! No one would notice, under his beard, and it was such a nuisance tying the beastly affair. Then his eye fell on the open drawer of his bureau. There was that newfangled, ready-made bow—just the thing!

As Brahms adjusted the tie he suddenly became conscious of a flapping around his ankles. *"Donnerwetter!"* he cried, looking angrily down. "I knew that fool of a tailor wouldn't listen to me. I knew he'd make those trousers too long. What if it *is* the style? *Silly* style!" He reached for a large pair of scissors on the table.

Snip—snip—off went three inches of trouser from the left leg. Snip again on the right, and Brahms triumphantly fired two trouser cuffs at the wastebasket. He adjusted the mirror over his washstand so he could see the effect. "Heavens!—the right one is a good two inches shorter. But what does it matter?" With a certain naïve satisfaction he studied the impressive head in the mirror before him. *"Ja, ja*—the perfect Caucasian type," he chuckled. "People will look at my head and not at my feet!"

It was really too warm for his topcoat—that famous coffee-colored overcoat that his friends made so much fun of because he had worn it so many years. But the air was still a little cool. . . . He reached for his old plaid shawl, folded it across his shoulders, fastened it with a large safety-pin and, with his umbrella under his arm, sallied forth.

The Ehrbars had invited nearly a dozen of his best

friends, and the luncheon turned out to be a real banquet. First there were oysters (how Brahms loved them!) and caviar. Then all kinds of cold meats, and, best of all, asparagus fresh from the country—two fat bunches for each guest. This was followed by cheese and dessert. With the dessert came several bottles of champagne. Now the Master was really suspicious. "Did you guess—" he began.

"Ja, ja, Herr Doktor," they laughed. "To be sure we knew it was your birthday! And since you have enjoyed this so much, we shall repeat it every year on May the seventh." True to their promise, on each succeeding birthday the Ehrbars gave a luncheon for Brahms with exactly the same menu.

By the time everyone had finished toasting the composer he had forgotten his earlier depression. Looking about at his assembled friends, he decided that there were compensations, after all, in reaching the ripe age of fifty years. And what was more—in the back of his head a new idea was stirring. If only he could get away by himself for a while. . . .

Brahms excused himself and went out to the Prater—Vienna's loveliest park. The main drive, with its overarching trees and fashionable restaurants, was thronged with elegantly dressed people, out to enjoy the sunshine of the warm spring day. "Nowhere else does one appreciate the jolly and amiable character of the Viennese so much as in one's strolls in the Prater," Brahms once remarked.

Today, however, the composer hurried along until he reached the wilder part, where the natural forest stretched out for some distance beyond the city, beside the Danube Canal.

And now, as he paced along the deserted path, hands behind his back, completely absorbed in his thoughts, the barriers which had shut him away from that inner flood of inspiration suddenly lifted, and he found himself filled with streams of musical ideas. He was so delighted and overjoyed that he laughed out loud.

"Now I have it!" he cried. "F A F! My own device—that's what I'll use as the motto of the next symphony. And F shall be its key."

Quickly he reached into his pocket for his always present notebook, and began to write. That summer in Wiesbaden, the F major (Third) symphony, with its ineffably lovely *finale,* was completed.

Part of Vienna's Prater was given over to an amusement center. This section, with its gay booths, sideshows and carrousels, had a special fascination for Brahms. For hours he would linger there, watching the crowds, listening to the gypsy orchestras, sometimes even riding on the merry-go-rounds.

Friends often joined him in the Prater, and if the weather was warm they would eat their supper under the trees. Nottebohm, the learned musician who had deserted him in Italy for the "wine of Cyprus," frequently bought sandwiches from a cheese and sausage peddler in the park. Brahms loved to play tricks on the old man.

One evening Herr Nottebohm, opening his package of bread and cheese, gave a gasp. Without saying a word he walked over to the nearest lamp-post and examined the wrapping paper with bulging eyes. It was a piece of manuscript music, old and faded. Was it possible? Yes, he decided with growing excitement, he was almost sure he recognized Beethoven's handwriting. Who should know it better than the man who had edited that Master's notebooks? What a find! Nottebohm smoothed the paper carefully and put it into his pocket without saying a word.

But when he examined it at home, later that evening, he was surprised to find that the crabbed notes, instead of being a forgotten masterpiece, were only variations on the latest popular Viennese song-hit. And now that he looked more closely, the writing had a vaguely familiar and modern air. . . .

"That rascal, Johannes!" muttered the disappointed Nottebohm, shaking his head ruefully.

Brahms played a different sort of trick on the friend who was later to become his most voluminous biographer. One day he presented Kalbeck with a roll of music. When the latter eagerly opened it, he found, to his disgust, only a cheap piece by a comparatively unknown composer.

"No, thanks!" he cried, tossing the manuscript back to Johannes.

"Now wait a minute," insisted Brahms. "I give you my word it's not so bad. . . ."

"Well—" Kalbeck growled, "if you insist, I'll keep it, but it looks like dreadful trash to me."

"Why don't you try it over?" urged the composer, chuckling in his beard.

Kalbeck stared at him with sudden suspicion. Then he pounced on the roll, opened it quickly, and found beneath the outer sheets a real treasure—some original manuscript sketches of Beethoven's C sharp minor quartet!

Brahms laughed heartily. "Well, what did I tell you? Not so bad after all, eh?"

All through his life Johannes Brahms kept a singularly childlike love of fun and mischief. He liked to frighten people by jumping out at them from behind doors and screens. He would dash up the stairs to the apartments of his close friends, bang vigorously on their doors with both fists, and then burst in without waiting for an answer. There was something impetuous, not-to-be-denied in the strong vigor of his personality.

Brahms never lost his youthful passion for lead soldiers. Even after he was grown up he played with them. Setting out miniature battle lines helped to stimulate his musical ideas, he said. His correspondence, too, was often filled with childish fantasy. He liked to illustrate his letters. Sometimes he made sketches of insects. A note to Clara Schumann, decorated with a house-fly, began: "Flies are a nuisance, even when they are pretty.

And so the above indicates that I am about to be a nuisance to you."

Postcards were Brahms' favorite means of correspondence. He used them whenever possible. They were, he felt, such marvelous time-savers! On more than one occasion he answered an invitation by simply writing, on a postcard, the following notes:

He took it for granted that his friends would recognize this as a phrase from the famous minuet in Mozart's *Don Giovanni* where, in response to Leporello's invitation, "To ball and wedding banquet my master bids you come," Ottavio replies, "Who could decline this charming bid?"

To amuse his young friends, the Master invented a system of dividing phrases between two postcards, like these addressed to the Fellingers' two sons:

Magnificent	weather!
Glorious	journey!
Best	greetings
to father	and mother
and everything possi-	ble and impossible
from one who heartily	remembers you all
	J. B.

Brahms was frequently asked to listen to the works of other composers. If these gentlemen were mediocre, or more especially if they had an exaggerated idea of their own importance, then he could be merciless in his comments.

Pointedly omitting all references to the composition, he would remark, "How well you *do* play the piano!" Or, "Look here, where did you buy this splendid music-paper?"

To a musician who angled for compliments he said, in deep sententious tones, "Yes, you have talent." Then, changing his voice to a high falsetto, "But very little!"

Once a Viennese doctor asked Brahms to look over some compositions of a friend. "Beautiful—wonderfully beautiful!" murmured the composer politely. The doctor looked surprised; he had not suspected his friend of so much ability. Kalbeck, who was present, chuckled. "That means," he explained, "that the things aren't even worth the powder to blow them up."

The Master looked up with a reproving twinkle in his eye. "Did I say that?" he bleated, in seriocomic tones. "My God, my God! What sinners men are!"

His spirit of contradiction made it sometimes difficult for others to know just what his reactions were. He had a way of appearing lugubrious when a concert pleased him, and full of enthusiasm if he didn't care for it.

"Oh, that's just my nature," he explained to a young lady who commented on this. "If a piece or a performer impresses me I am serious; but if I seem vivacious and sympathetic, then the music has certainly not appealed to me."

With modest young ladies Herr Doktor Brahms was more genial. One girl pianist confided to him that she was studying the violin.

"I must hear you!" said the Master.

"Oh, but I really haven't got far enough," the bashful girl replied, overcome by such a prospect.

"But if I compose something specially for you, won't you play it for me?"

"Alas—" said the young lady, "I can only do the second violin."

Brahms chuckled. "Well then, I'll write a piece for second violin alone. I've never tried it before!"

CHAPTER XX

FRAU TRUXA

"Now who's there?" grumbled Brahms as he heard a knock at his door. The fourth time this morning that he had been disturbed! Really, it was a nuisance not to have someone in the house who could protect him from interruptions when he was working. Perhaps it had been a mistake trying to take over the whole upper floor and get along without a housekeeper after old Frau Vogel died.

He left his high desk and, shuffling into the hall in his bedroom slippers, impatiently threw open the door.

"I have come to see the flat," said a plainly dressed, respectable-looking woman. "Frau Fellinger told me there was an empty apartment here. But perhaps she was mistaken?" .

Brahms stared at her a moment in suspicion. Was this just a ruse to see his rooms, or perhaps to get an autograph out of him? He was constantly besieged by sentimental women. However, this one seemed a little different.

For some time his good friend Frau Fellinger had been trying to persuade him to engage another housekeeper. He was afraid, however, that he would never find the right person. He needed someone who would be efficient but unobtrusive, tactful but especially not *sentimental!* And this combination was hard to find.

The Fellingers thought they had discovered just the right person in Frau Celestine Truxa. But, knowing the Master's temperament, they coached her well before sending her to see him. "Don't let him suspect that you want him as a lodger, or he'll run away!"

Profiting by this advice Frau Truxa succeeded so well in appearing independent and rather harshly indifferent that Brahms finally let her in and showed her around the place. During the interview he learned that she was a widow with two small sons. Also that she would be willing (she admitted this with well-studied reluctance!) to let him remain in the flat as boarder.

Perhaps it was her independence and forbidding manner that determined him, or it may have been the prospect of having children in the house. At any rate he let her take over the flat, and never, during all the years that followed, had cause to regret his decision. Frau Truxa cared for him with faithful—and tactful!—devotion, and was with him to the last.

The new housekeeper proved delightfully unobtrusive in looking after her eccentric boarder. She developed a rare intuition in discovering his needs. Brahms had a number of curious habits. For instance, when his things needed mending he would leave the garment sticking out of a crack in his bureau drawer. Frau Truxa would then carry it away, make the necessary repairs, and put it back in the same position.

The next day he would exclaim, as if in great surprise: "I found my sock mended last night! I wonder who could have done it?" Equally serious she would reply: "*I* did it, Herr Doktor." Then he would answer: "You? Why, how very kind!"

In his younger days Brahms had had to do his own mending. "When I first set out from home on my adventures," he told his friend Sir George Henschel, "Mother packed a sewing kit in my bag, and showed me how it should be used. But I still recall quite well that when my pants tore I stuck them together with sealing wax. The only trouble was, they didn't hold very long. . . ."

Brahms hated to ask favors. One day Frau Truxa found her maid in tears. "I don't know what I've done," the girl wailed. "Herr Doktor no longer will speak to me."

The landlady examined her lodger's rooms to see if

she could find out what was wrong. She noticed that the lid to the wastebasket was closed. Could it be that? She tried leaving it open.

"Before long," said the good lady, telling about the incident many years later, "the girl came to me, beaming, and exclaimed, 'Herr Brahms greets again!' That had been the whole trouble. He wanted the lid up; but couldn't bring himself to say so."

To Johannes Brahms that open wastebasket was his most important article of furniture. Into it went the countless sheets of music-writing that failed to satisfy his own high standards.

Brahms often went out of his way to show his appreciation of Frau Truxa's efficient care; and when he died he left her a special legacy. Once when she was going on a trip, he bought her everything he could think of to make the journey comfortable. "Two plaid shawls, fur shoes, traveling bags of real leather, a trunk. . . . In order to take them all along I should have had to charter an express van! So I secretly locked them up and made as though I were using them. . . . What a good, kind, thoughtful person he was!"

The Master was devoted to his landlady's two small sons. During her absence he kept close watch to see that they were properly looked after by the servant girl. While they were eating their meals he would come in to be sure they were getting the proper food, and he even slipped in at night after the boys had gone to bed, to see that they were well covered.

But on Frau Truxa's return she was horrified at the dirty and neglected state of his rooms. When she scolded the maid, the girl laughed: "Yes, but the Herr Doktor wouldn't let me clean up for him while you were gone. All he'd allow me was to make the bed and empty the slops. Nothing else whatever. He told me: 'A neglected apartment is easily fixed up. But if one of those children should fall from a chair and break his little leg, that couldn't be so quickly mended!' "

Brahms wouldn't listen to any thanks. "He crept back into his snail-shell," said Frau Truxa, "and I didn't dare say a word."

Brahms spent the summer of 1885 at Mürzzuschlag, a little village in Styria. One day, as he was hard at work on his Fourth (and last) symphony, he was suddenly roused by a commotion in the street below.

"Fire! Fire!" called a dozen excited voices. Smoke began to pour through the open window, and the composer, leaning out, saw flames coming from a small shop just a door or two away.

He knew that a poor carpenter and his family lived there. Quickly he left his work, rushed down in his shirt sleeves, and joined the chain of people who were passing buckets of water from the village fountain. "Come on!" he cried to some listless onlookers. "Everybody help!"

Suddenly a hand touched his shoulder. It was Dr. Fellinger, who, with his wife and two young sons, had also come to spend the summer months at Mürzzuschlag. "Don't you realize," cried the good doctor, "that this fire may reach your own rooms any minute?"

Brahms paid no attention. "But your manuscript!" shouted the distracted friend. "Are you crazy? Don't you know your symphony may be destroyed?"

For just a moment the composer hesitated. Then he went calmly on passing buckets. "This is more important," he answered.

Dr. Fellinger was beside himself. "At least give me your key, and we will do our best to save your things."

When the fire was finally extinguished Brahms found his friends in the garden, back of the house where he lodged—surrounded by his manuscripts and personal effects. In the middle of the pile sat Frau Fellinger, brooding like a mother hen over the precious E minor symphony.

"How could you be so indifferent to your own work?" she asked him reproachfully.

He shook his grizzled head. "Those poor people needed help more than I did. They have lost nearly everything," he added. "I think we should take up a collection to set them up again." Brahms was so active in these efforts, and so generous with his own cash, that the carpenter and his family actually profited by the fire.

Although the Master often proved gruff and intolerant with the fortune-favored "highborn," he was exceptionally indulgent to those less luckily situated. For he knew only too well what poverty meant.

One day his fine gold watch was stolen. He entered no complaint; but the police heard of it and came to make inquiries. He only answered: "Now please—leave me in peace! The watch was probably taken by some poor devil who needs it more than I do."

Each summer Brahms left Vienna to spend several months in the country, usually in Switzerland, Styria, or the Salzkammergut. Ten of the last summers of his life were passed in Ischl.

Mürzzuschlag was not far from Vienna, and while he was there his friends from the city often came to visit him. One day Dr. Gänsbacher, old Epstein, and another pianist named Door arrived to spend the day. All three men rather fancied themselves as musical figures. Brahms decided to have some fun with them.

After they had finished their dinner in a small local restaurant, the proprietor—coached by the mischievous Johannes—reverently approached the table where the visitors were sitting.

"Our humble establishment is greatly honored by your presence," he said, bowing and rubbing his hands.

The three musicians from Vienna tried not to look gratified.

"Please," the man continued, "will the gentlemen consider themselves my guests? It is quite enough reward to have been able to serve such eminent celebrities. I could not think of charging you so much as a *Kreutzer!*"

Brahms, who had already paid the bill, listened with

a properly impressed expression. But inwardly he chuckled. . . .

In 1886, 1887, and 1888 Brahms spent his summers on Lake Thun, in Switzerland. There he had an apartment overlooking the end of the lake, where the glacier-green river Aar flows out on its long voyage to the Mediterranean. "An absolutely fascinating abode," he told Frau Fellinger. To Kalbeck he wrote on a postcard: "The only reason why I do not use a sheet of note-paper is so as not to praise things too highly."

Brahms took a special fancy to his landlord's small son Hans. "Perhaps the boy would like to play the piano—yes?" he asked. "Come and we will try."

But after a few attempts at teaching the boy, he gave it up as a bad job. "Music lessons for you, my dear Hans, would be wasted malt and hops!"

As was his invariable custom, in Thun as elsewhere, Brahms devoted his mornings to work. Then, if the weather was fine he always dined outdoors, and afterwards went to the Casino garden and sat for hours over a cup of black coffee or a glass of beer and his ever-present cigar, listening to the small orchestra which played there every afternoon. During the intermissions he sometimes called the musicians to his table and gave them a franc or two to gamble in the Casino.

Several important chamber music works were written that first summer in Thun: the trio in C minor, and two sonatas—for 'cello and piano (the second, in F), and for violin and piano (in A). This last is often called the *"Prize Song"* sonata, because its opening measure recalls the song by that name in Wagner's *Meistersinger:*

Now as this phrase of three notes is a commonplace that occurs in thousands of other works, and as this composition contains allusions to no fewer than five of Brahms' own songs, the nickname *"Prize Song"* for this sonata might more appropriately be shortened to *"Song."*

Titles, however, are not very important.

> What's in a name? that which we call a rose
> By any other name would smell as sweet.

The music's the thing. This sonata is one of the most melodious of all Brahms' compositions, and one of the most popular, too—even with those who care for little else but the Waltzes and Hungarian Dances. The Swiss poet Widmann wrote a long, fanciful poem about the *"Prize Song,"* or, as it is also sometimes called, the *"Thun"* sonata.

Widmann lived in Berne, not far from Thun, and Brahms frequently went over to spend a week-end with him. There were two special attractions at Herr Widmann's house—his little daughter Johanna (Brahms laughingly called her his "fiancée"), and a small dog named Argos.

The child, the dog, and the gray-bearded musician had many romps together. In the park at Berne were caged pits where lived the brown bears for which the city is named. "Come, Johanna," Brahms would cry, tossing the little girl up to his broad shoulders. "Let's go and visit the bears." And down the streets he would prance, Johanna shrieking with glee, Argos barking violently, and all three equally oblivious of the amused stares of passers-by.

Widmann has left many interesting descriptions of the composer. Of this period he writes:

> His week-end visits were high festivals and times of rejoicing for me and mine; days of rest they certainly were not, for the constantly active mind of our guest demanded similar activity from all his associates; and one had to pull oneself jolly well together to keep fresh enough to satisfy the requirements of his boundless vitality. . . .
>
> I have never seen anyone who took such fresh, genuine, and enduring interest in the surroundings of life as Brahms, whether in nature, art, or even industry. The smallest invention, the improvement of some article for household use, every trace, in short, of practical ingenuity gave him real pleasure. And nothing escaped his observation. . . .
>
> He hated bicycles because the flow of his ideas was so often disturbed by the noiseless rushing past, or the sudden signal, of these machines, and also because he thought the trampling movement of the rider ugly. He was, however, glad to live in the age of great inventions and could not sufficiently admire the electric light, Edison's phonographs, etc.
>
> He was equally interested in the animal world.

One day an excursion to the Grindelwald glacier was proposed. Little Johanna was too young to go, but—"We can take Argos, now, can't we?" begged Johannes.

A gay party set out for the mountain top, and happiest of all was Argos. Then came tragedy. As they were crossing the glacier the dog slipped and fell into a crevasse. Hours were spent trying to rescue the poor animal, but all their efforts were in vain. Night was coming on and they did not dare to linger longer. Finally they had to abandon poor Argos.

Brahms was dreadfully broken up. He blamed himself for urging Widmann to bring the dog, and during the days following the trip to Grindelwald he thought constantly of the small animal, left to freeze in the glacier.

Suddenly, early on the morning of the fourth day after the expedition, when nearly everyone in the house was still asleep, there came an eager scratching and whining at Herr Widmann's door. Brahms, always up at dawn, heard the noise and rushed down. There stood Argos, safe and sound, beside himself with joy. Soon the rest of the family gathered—hardly able to believe the miracle.

Herr Widmann describes the scene: "The most fully dressed was Brahms, the early riser, and I can still see him bending down to Argos and without hesitation abandoning his hands and face to the caresses of the joy-crazed animal. 'So that's what it is!' he cried. 'This is no mere hunter's yarn.'" And in his first letter from Vienna he asked:

How is Argos getting on? Wouldn't he take it as a tender greeting from me if, for a change, instead of dog-biscuit, you gave him a nice piece of meat?

Which—as Widmann concludes—was "naturally done according to his wish."

In the Germany and Austria of those days, Christmas was the great celebration of the year, eagerly looked forward to by grown-ups and children alike. During the weeks before December 25th everyone seemed to catch the holiday spirit. Housewives bustled about, baking dozens of fancy cookies; shops decorated their windows with streamers of red and green paper, and set out their finest merchandise to tempt the gift-seekers. The delicatessen displays were a marvel to see: little pigs, roasted whole with red apples in their mouths, garlands of sausages, pickles, salads—it was enough to make anyone's mouth water!

Usually there was snow at this season, and the frosty air rang with the jingle of sleighbells. In late afternoons, when it was already dark and the stores had turned their lights on, crowds of people filled the streets. The chief attraction was the Christmas fair, with its gay merry-go-rounds and brightly illuminated booths.

Brahms loved the fair best of all. He liked to wander through the crowded lanes and buy gifts for the poor children when he found them gazing longingly at the displays of toys and sweets. With his short, round figure and long flowing beard he could easily have passed for St. Nick himself—if only he had been dressed in Father Christmas' red suit instead of the old coffee-colored overcoat. . . .

One evening shortly before Christmas, Brahms was coming in with his arms filled with gifts for Frau Truxa's children when he discovered the two boys playing together in a corner of the hall. He couldn't resist a little joke.

"Have you heard the sad news?" he cried, pulling a long face. "The Christ Child has influenza and can't bring you anything this year!"

His joke proved more successful than he had expected. The two boys suddenly burst into howls of despair. Impossible to pacify them! Brahms rushed into his room and brought out candy. Even this failed to stop the shrieks. He hurried after Frau Truxa and confessed what he had done. "I don't know which way to turn! Can't you quiet the children? Tell them that the Christ Child has already recovered."

At last the howls were silenced. . . .

Each year Frau Truxa decorated a little tree for her boys, and Brahms always added a generous share to the pile of gifts beneath. He never failed to be on hand at the solemn candle-lighting ceremony on Christmas Eve. Following this he would go to the house of some friend to celebrate—preferably of one who had children, so he could watch their ecstatic delight. The last seven years of his life he chose the Fellingers—on condition that no real presents were to be given him. They knew his love of fun and usually planned some diverting and original surprise.

One Christmas Eve Frau Fellinger escorted him to a charmingly decorated table and, waving her hand, said, "Your gifts." Then she left him to examine them.

Brahms stared down at the display in wonder. Surely there must be some mistake! This was evidently a lady's dressing-table, covered with feminine fripperies. It was fitted with a round, burnished mirror, a pair of candlesticks with lighted candles, a pincushion, some packages done up in delicate pink paper and ribbon and marked "Perfume"—nothing, however, that could possibly appeal to a lone bachelor. Brahms shook his grizzled head in perplexity, clasped his hands behind his back, and sauntered over to look at some of the other gift-covered tables.

"But, Herr Doktor—why don't you open your things?"

"I haven't found them yet," stammered the composer, looking still more bewildered.

Frau Fellinger pretended dismay. "Perhaps you don't like your presents? We thought . . . We understood that you were very fond of perfume. Now please do come over and see."

Brahms eyed her suspiciously. But he allowed himself to be led back to the "lady's dressing-table," and there he found—not perfume, but his favorite unscented soap; not a pincushion, but a sugarbowl; not candlesticks, but two little cream jugs. In addition he discovered a bread-basket filled with the English quills he always used for writing music, and a clothes-brush. Soon nothing was left but the mirror.

The composer was about to pass that by when—"Just examine it carefully," Frau Fellinger insisted, smiling.

The "mirror" turned out to be a highly polished metal coffee-tray.

"Have you looked under the table?" then asked his hostess. There he found the masterpiece of all—a waste-basket decorated with a music staff made of pencils, a clef of gingerbread, and sugar notes. Brahms, delighted as a child at all this masquerade, hummed the "sweet" theme. It proved to be the opening measures of his well-known song, "Oh, sink, oh, sink thy grief."

Brahms was quite overcome. "Now I really must sit down," he cried, his blue eyes shining with joy.

CHAPTER XXI

"CAREFREE OLD AGE"

I HAVE written myself out. Yes, I am already too old. The composing doesn't go." Brahms had been only twenty-three years old when he wrote these words. Now in his late fifties he again felt that he had "written himself out."

"Recently I started various things, symphonies and so on, but nothing would work out well," he confessed to a friend. "Then I thought: I am already too old, and energetically resolved to write no more. I considered that I had all my life been sufficiently industrious and had achieved enough; now I had before me a carefree old age, and could enjoy it in peace."

Fortunately the composer's spirit of contradiction now

came to his rescue. The realization that he didn't *have* to write any more music made him, as he said, "so happy, so contented, so delighted—that all at once the writing began to go." He was now suddenly inspired to compose one of his loveliest works—the B minor quintet for clarinet and strings.

It happened on a visit to the Duke of Meiningen.

For several years, now, Brahms had been a frequent guest at the court of Meiningen. Duke George was an ardent Brahms enthusiast—largely through the efforts of Hans von Bülow, who had been Music Director at the Meiningen court since 1880, and who always included his friend's music on the programs he conducted. On the Master's visits there he was shown special honor and consideration.

In the Duke of Meiningen's orchestra was an exceptionally fine clarinetist named Mühlfeld. Brahms, on his visit in 1891, was so impressed by the man's playing that, as soon as he got to Ischl, where he had of late years been spending his summers, he began work on several compositions for the clarinet—sonatas, a trio, and, finest of all, the B minor quintet.

This quintet for clarinet and string quartet is one of the loveliest pieces of chamber music ever written. It has a serene and tender atmosphere radiating the quiet joy of a man who has lived through the storms of life, and who, having believed himself finished with creative work, suddenly discovers the old power within him, fresher and stronger than ever.

The first theme of the *Allegro* opening movement has a poignant, unearthly beauty. Then the mellow tones of the clarinet come in later to lend it a unique quality:

Brahms felt that no one could play the clarinet quintet as well as Mühlfeld, the artist who had inspired the work. To his friends the Master jokingly introduced the clarinetist as "Fräulein Mühlfeld, my prima donna!"

The clarinet quintet was a favorite composition of Brahms'. Once at a rehearsal of the work he was so touched by its beauty that tears came to his eyes. To cover his emotion he went over to the first violin stand, closed the music brusquely, and growled, "Stop that dreadful music!"

Brahms was, by nature, a man of strong sentiment. The tears came easily to his eyes. But he had a horror of appearing emotional. Too often he concealed his feelings under biting words and sarcastic wit. These were really a protection against his own soft-heartedness.

A beautiful old lady, in a sweeping black taffeta dress and lace cap, stood by the window of a villa in Frankfurt. In the garden outside, the wind was blowing wisps of fog through the trees. Leaves were falling and autumn filled the air.

"Like my own life," thought the woman sadly; "winter coming close." She turned, her skirts rustling like a whispered sigh. Then, going over to the piano, she sat down and began to play.

Although the years had dimmed the brilliance and facility of her technique, a master touch was still evident. The music had a plaintive, heart-reaching quality, like an echo from the past. As the woman played, dusk came creeping into the room. Presently she stopped and sat silent before the keyboard.

"Why, Mother," called a cheery voice, "what are you doing, all alone here in the dark?"

Marie Schumann lighted the lamp. Then she came over and put her arms around the old lady. "What were you playing there? I haven't heard it for years."

Frau Schumann smiled up at her eldest daughter. Marie, now a woman in her fifties, seemed more like a sister than her own child. "I was thinking of the past," she said softly. "That melody brings back so many memories. Your father wrote the theme, and Johannes wove it into beautiful variations for the piano, which he dedicated to me."

She rose from the stool and went over to an armchair by the fire. "Go to my room, will you, my dear, and fetch the box of letters on the table by the bed."

When Marie returned with the letters she found her mother staring into the fire. "What a good daughter you have been!" she said, taking the other's hand and laying it against her cheek. "You have given up your own life to stay with me."

Marie leaned forward and kissed her mother's white forehead. "The best life I could have had, being with you," she murmured.

"I only wish it could have been as good as mine!" Frau Schumann nodded her head thoughtfully. The lace on her cap threw shadows across her pale cheeks. "First," she went on, "there were those wonderful years with your father. Then, when he was taken away, Johannes remained to comfort me. What a faithful friend our Hannes has been! You know, Marie, in all these decades he and I never had but one serious misunderstanding. And that was my own fault."

Marie knew that it gave her mother pleasure to talk about the past. She drew up a low stool and sat beside her.

"It was over the publication of Robert's D minor symphony," Clara continued. "Johannes didn't agree with my ideas. This made me angry, and I wrote him a scathing letter. And he—" She lifted the lid of the box and drew out a letter. "Only listen, Marie, to what he answered." And she read:

It is hard, after forty years of faithful service (or whatever you wish to call my relationship to you), to be nothing else than "one more bad experience." Well, that must be borne. I am used to being lonely; and if one must be, I can become resigned to the thought of this great emptiness. But today you must allow me to repeat again to you that you and your husband represent the most beautiful experience of my life, that you stand for its greatest wealth and noblest meaning.

After she had finished reading, Clara Schumann was silent a moment. Then, clasping her thin hands earnestly together, she said: "Johannes Brahms is truly a good and generous man! Do you remember what he wrote when I published my concerto cadenzas, and wanted to acknowledge his share of them on the title page?"

She opened another, more recent letter.

Even the smallest J. B. would look strange. . . . Then too, by rights, I would have to inscribe my best melodies: "Really by Clara Schumann." For if I think of myself, nothing worthwhile or beautiful can occur to me! I owe you more melodies than all the passages and such-like you can borrow from me!!

"I've saved nearly all of Johannes' letters," Clara continued. "Excepting a few we thought best—" She broke off, then quickly pulled out a yellowed envelope. "How well I remember this one!" She smiled tenderly. "He was always a philosopher, our Hannes, even when he was no more than a boy. 'Passions do not pertain to man as a natural thing,' he wrote me from Detmold—and he was only twenty-four then. 'The fine, true man is calm in joy and calm in suffering and trouble. Passions must soon pass away, or else one must drive them away.' Yes," Clara nodded gravely, "one must drive them away!"

"Frau Schumann—" came the maid's voice at the door. "There is a gentleman to see you. Herr Brahms."

Clara rose so suddenly that the box and the letters fell to the floor. As Marie stooped to pick them up, her mother was already halfway across the room, her hands outstretched. "Johannes! I didn't dare hope you would find time—"

"Just long enough, dear Clara, to have a little visit with you and Marie on my way to Zürich," he said, his gruff voice full of feeling. "I've come from a music festival at Meiningen."

"Yes, of course we know all about that. Another triumph for you, my friend! I've heard they call it the 'Festival of the three B's.' "

Johannes' ruddy face grew still redder. "That Hans von Bülow! It's almost sickening the way he overestimates me. Imagine mentioning my name in the same breath with Bach and Beethoven! But, seriously, you don't know what it means to have people think my music worthy to stand beside the masterpieces of those great composers. Why, at Zürich—" He broke off to explain: "There is to be another festival there in a couple of days."

"We heard about that too," murmured Clara.

"Well, at Zürich my *Song of Triumph* is to share the program with Beethoven's Ninth Symphony!"

"Robert was right," Clara said gently. "When you were scarcely more than a boy he knew what was ahead of you. Only see what a name you have made for yourself. I wish he could have lived to witness this glorious fulfillment of his prophecies."

Johannes stared thoughtfully into the fire. "I don't understand it myself," he said. "When I think of that poor boy back in Hamburg. . . . How surprised young Hannes would have been if he could have seen into the future. Why, Clara, I'm *rich!* I have more money than I know what to do with. Now just remember, dear friend—if you ever need help. . . ."

Brahms himself hardly knew what a fortune he had piled up in the course of years. Although he spent very little on himself he gave so much away that it would have been difficult for anyone to estimate his earnings. At his death he left an estate of over $100,000—in striking contrast to the two other "B's," who died poor, and to Schubert, whose entire possessions were valued at less than fifteen dollars, and to Mozart, whose body was cast into a pauper's grave.

"I've brought you a copy of the folk songs I arranged last year," said Brahms, changing the subject abruptly. He handed Frau Schumann a thick volume. "You have no idea what fun I had doing these. I sometimes think," he continued, his eyes full of honest feeling, "that I have been most successful of all in 'arrangements' of other people's music! At any rate I have a special tenderness for this collection."

"And what are you working on now, Johannes?" asked Clara.

Brahms' face clouded over. "As a matter of fact—nothing special. Perhaps I'm getting too old. . . ."

"You—old? No, my friend, *I* am the one who is getting on." Frau Schumann sighed. "Do you realize that I shall be seventy-seven on my next birthday? While you—you are as full of strength and vigor as ever."

Johannes nodded. "Almost—that's right! The Lord blessed me with a powerful constitution. Must have been my peasant ancestors up in Dithmarsh! Why, only the other day Frau Simrock said to me, 'You're not only a God-blessed artist, but also a giant of health!'" Brahms threw back his head and laughed heartily. "And I answered her," he concluded, "'Why shouldn't I be healthy? I've never missed a meal—or taken a drop of medicine!'"

Marie had slipped away to leave her mother and old friend together. Now, as the two sat by the fire, Johannes' eyes fell on the open box. He recognized his handwriting. "Have you saved my letters all these years?"

"With the exception of those I sent back to you, Hannes. . . ."

Brahms leaned forward and took Clara's two thin hands in his own rough palms. "I sometimes think, dear Clara, that we made a great mistake. We should have married, you and I."

The old lady smiled tenderly into his eyes. "No, my dear. That was not meant to be. I was much too old for you. Besides, no woman could ever have held you."

Softly she hummed those significant notes: F—A—F.

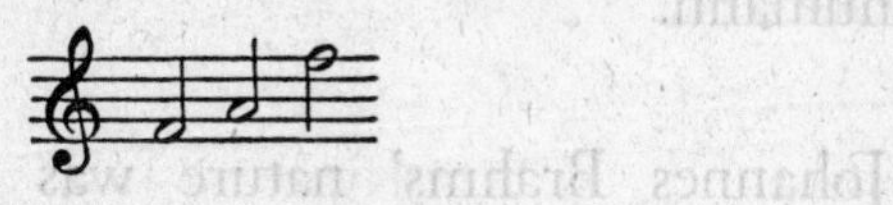

"Free, but glad of it! It was freedom that you had to have—absolute freedom. Life was not given to you for personal satisfactions, but for something greater. And because you felt this, and fully devoted yourself to a high purpose, it has been your privilege to create some of the most beautiful music the world has ever listened to."

Johannes looked at Clara with reverent affection. "My dear—you to say that! Don't you know that without you I could never have accomplished anything? You have always been my greatest inspiration." For a moment he could not speak, he was so filled with emotion. Then: "Before I go—in memory of old times, will you play for me?"

Frau Schumann rose unsteadily to her feet, and Brahms helped her over to the piano. First she played a number of his favorites. Then she said, a little tremulously: "Today I was thinking of the time when you first came to us in Düsseldorf. Here is something that will remind you of the past—of both Robert and Clara. Do you remember the Variations that you dedicated to me so many years ago?"

As Johannes listened, all those earlier days came crowding to his memory. And the future—what would it bring? Looking at the frail figure seated before the keyboard, his heart grew strangely sad. Although he did not know it, this was to be his last farewell to Clara Schumann.

Johannes Brahms' nature was usually happy and optimistic. He never liked to think of death, nor did he use it as a theme in his music. Even in the *German Requiem* he had refused to include the Lord's Passion and Death.

Now, for a reason that he could not himself explain, he was moved to write what he called *Four Serious Songs*. Most of these were based on Bible texts dealing with death.

He tried to cover up his own seriousness. "Those songs? Oh, they are just a set of *'Schnadahüpferln,'*" he told some of his friends, using the Austrian slang expression for a light, jolly song with dance accompaniment. To another friend he said, with a touch of melancholy: "I wrote the *Four Serious Songs* for my sixty-third birthday. You know, it's a serious matter, this growing old!"

Perhaps these thoughts of death were a premonition. On May 20th, 1896, just a fortnight after Brahms had gone to Ischl to spend the summer, he received word that Clara Schumann, now in her seventy-seventh year, had passed peacefully away.

Johannes was profoundly shaken. He could not imagine life without Clara. For so many years she had meant everything to him. . . . He threw a few things into his portmanteau and caught the first train to Frankfurt.

During the trip a message reached him that the funeral would be in Bonn. His old friend was to be laid to rest beside her husband Robert, who had died in that city forty years before.

Brahms' train was delayed. The journey proved irritating and exhausting. He fretted himself into a fever for fear he would be too late. At the funeral he caught a severe cold. Now for the first time his remarkable constitution showed signs of breaking.

That summer at Ischl he worked on a series of Chorale-Preludes for organ. Most of these, like the *Four Serious Songs,* had death as their subject. Just as Bach's last compositions were a group of organ preludes, these also were to prove the concluding work of Johannes Brahms' life.

He never really recovered from the shock of Clara Schumann's death. Before long his friends began to notice that the usual ruddy color of his complexion was changing to an ominous yellow.

CHAPTER XXII

FINAL CADENCE

IT WAS early in December 1896, a few months after Clara Schumann's death. Joachim's quartet—celebrated now all over Europe—had come to Vienna to give a series of concerts. The violinist had not seen Brahms for some time, and he was shocked beyond words at the change in him.

"Johannes! My God . . ." Pityingly Yussuf held out his hands towards the shrunken figure of his old friend.

Johannes laughed—a sad echo of his former throaty chuckle.

"You're surprised to see me so—slender?" he asked,

trying to make a joke of his condition. "Just a change in my architecture! From Romanesque to Gothic, so to speak. Some fool etcher wanted to do a picture of me the other day. But I told him it would hardly look natural since my 'round-arch' style has changed over to the 'pointed-arch.' "

"But your *color!*" Joachim cried, staring at his friend's greenish yellow complexion. "See here," he blurted. "What's wrong?"

Brahms rubbed his cheeks thoughtfully. "I never look in a mirror, so I wouldn't know what my color is. Fact is," he concluded, as if dismissing the matter lightly, "I've had a touch of jaundice."

Yussuf was not to be put off. "When did this start?"

"Well, as a matter of fact, it began last summer. One very hot day I set out for a walk. . . ." Brahms suddenly reached for the back of a chair. "Let's sit down," he said, dropping heavily. "I've been a bit of a walker in my time, you know, and that day I went on and on, thinking about a cadenza that wouldn't come straight, and presently I found I'd gone a good deal further than I realized. Eight miles from Ischl it was." He pulled thoughtfully at his beard, now grown scraggly and unkempt. "By the time I got home I was pretty well done in. That night I thought I was going to die. . . ."

"Did you see a doctor?" asked Joachim.

"Oh—*doctors!*" Johannes grumbled. "Never went to one in my life before, and now it's nothing but doctors, doctors and medicine! The Fellingers insisted I must go to Carlsbad and take the water cure. But the doctor there said, 'Just half a glassful, twice a day, Herr Doktor Brahms.' Didn't do a bit of good!" He sighed dismally.

When Joachim talked with the Fellingers his worst fears were confirmed. The doctor in Carlsbad had discovered that Brahms was a very sick man. Like his father, he had cancer of the liver. Nothing could be done to save him. The Master himself did not know the seriousness of his condition, and everyone tried to conceal it from him.

During his visit in Vienna, Joachim made a brave attempt to cover up his feelings. Johannes was pathetically glad to be with his old friend. He attended every rehearsal and concert of the quartet, and spent all his time in Yussuf's company.

For the first time Brahms heard Dvořák's 'cello concerto, played for him by the 'cellist of Joachim's quartet. He was greatly interested in this composition of the talented Czech whom he had earlier found struggling in obscure poverty and had started on his famous career, much as Schumann had once started a poor and unknown lad called Hannes. The concerto pleased him immensely. "If I had known that such a violoncello concerto could be written," he exclaimed, "I would have tried to compose one myself!"

Joachim and his quartet shortly left Vienna, but returned the first of January for two concluding concerts. Brahms was considerably worse now. It was all he could do to get around. Again, however, he insisted on coming to every rehearsal. After listening to his own G major quintet he nodded his head with impersonal satisfaction. "That is not a bad piece!" he murmured.

After the final concert Joachim had to return to Berlin. When the time came for the two friends to part, Johannes was more moved than he cared to admit. "Remember the first time we met?" he asked. "More than forty years ago! You had on a red Turkish fez and a gaudy dressing-gown, and I looked up to you as the greatest artist in the world. . . ."

"Now it's the other way round!" Joachim exclaimed, laughing unsteadily. "That's not only what *I* think, but what the whole world says."

"Oh, hush now," Brahms rumbled. "You know how people like to exaggerate. Well—" his voice shook a little, "good-by, Yussuf. I'll be seeing you in the spring."

The tears sprang to Joachim's eyes. He could hardly trust himself to speak. He put his arm around Johannes' shoulder. "God be with you, my friend. Farewell!"

During the earlier part of Brahms' illness he was very irascible in temper. He had always enjoyed exceptional health, and even the thought of illness annoyed him. If others asked him how he felt, he would growl, "Each day a little worse!"

By the time Christmas came the unfortunate man was suffering almost constant pain, though he still refused to admit that anything could be fundamentally wrong. The canny Frau Truxa knew what an effort he had to make to keep on his feet. She felt that he was too ill to enjoy the usual holiday festivities. A few days before December 25th, however, he stopped her as she was going out.

"How's this?" he said crossly. "I find no Christmas tree in my room!"

The good woman looked at her old lodger as if she wanted to cry. Then she pulled herself together. "There's been so much to do, Herr Doktor! But of course, I shall get the tree very soon."

"I rushed out," she related, "bought a tree, set it up as usual in there, and decorated it. That Christmas Eve we hardly noticed the terrible effort he made to cover up his own exhaustion. Not for anything would he have cast a gloom over the children's party. So good and thoughtful was the Herr Doktor!"

Christmas as usual. Brahms spent it with the Fellingers. They gave him a soft woolen house-jacket, and at once he put it on. "So warm and comfortable!" he exclaimed with a sigh of satisfaction. "Keep it here for me, so I can wear it when I come."

In that house he could sit quietly in a corner, secure in the affectionate understanding of his friends, and try to forget the terrible realization that would no longer be denied. When, at dinner a couple of days after Christmas, champagne was served, he raised his glass unsteadily. "To our meeting in the New Year!" he began—then stopped with a sigh. "But I—" he pointed to the ground, "shall soon be there."

Weeks went by, and although Brahms grew steadily worse, he refused to give up and go to bed. He had become terribly emaciated—his figure shrunken to the size of a child's and his color a dark greenish bronze.

Now his ill-temper gave way to a touching gentleness. He showed himself deeply grateful for every attention. Friends outdid themselves in trying to make him comfortable and prove their regard for him. He continued to go out, and seemed to take comfort in visiting certain of his intimates. And he still enjoyed eating and drinking.

One day when he was invited to luncheon, he was mildly surprised to find the curtains drawn and the rooms illuminated by red electric globes. He did not realize that his hostess had done this so that his terrible color would be less apparent. When one of his favorite dishes—pepper carp—appeared, he was as pleased as a child. He served himself liberally to several helpings.

"But, Herr Doktor—" his friends remonstrated gently, "are you sure it is good for you to eat so much?"

Brahms shrugged his sunken shoulders. "Oh, well," he said somberly, "it will make no difference!"

To his stepmother Frau Line, however, he kept up the pretense of a temporary indisposition. Only a few days before his death he wrote her:

I have been lying down a little, for a change, so writing is uncomfortable for me. But otherwise do not be alarmed. My condition is unchanged, and, as usual, all I need is patience.

Evenings now were spent at home. When twilight came Brahms would go to his piano and improvise softly. Then, drawing his chair beside the window, he would sit quietly until long after dark—staring in wistful silence at the familiar Viennese street. He knew now that he had only a short while left to live.

On March 7th, 1897, Vienna's Philharmonic Society gave a concert which included Dvořák's new 'cello concerto and Brahms' Fourth Symphony.

The city's music-loving public had known of the Master's illness for some time. More than once rumors had circulated that Brahms' end was near; but his amazing vitality still carried him on. Of late, however, he had been so feeble that no one expected he would ever appear in public again.

Now, at the concert of March 7th, a sudden whisper went through the hall. Incredulous eyes turned towards the artists' box. Was it really true that the Master—sick as he was—had come? Many shook their heads. They could hardly believe that this strange, emaciated figure with hollow cheeks and straggling white beard and hair, could be the round and jovial Brahms of old.

The Fourth Symphony had never been a favorite with the Viennese public. They much preferred the gay and charming Second. But today, at the close of the E minor's first movement, the whole audience broke into a wild storm of applause, and would not be quieted until Brahms dragged himself to his feet and bowed.

After each movement the applause increased, and finally at the end of the performance there was a demonstration such as even Vienna had seldom if ever witnessed. People stood on their seats waving handkerchiefs, men shouted until they were hoarse, and women wept with emotion as they looked up at the beloved, but so unfamiliar, figure in the artists' box.

Brahms himself was equally moved. His heart went out to the warm-hearted Viennese people. Always they had welcomed him, since the very first days when he came to their city, an unknown musician. Always they had taken him to their hearts with love and appreciation. For them most of his music had been written. They were his children.

Instinctively all those in the audience, as well as he who had brought them so much joy, knew that this was their final parting. The slow tears coursed down Brahms' lined, shrunken cheeks as he stood, waving his last farewell.

But they were not tears of sorrow. Rather of gratitude for all the good things life had brought him, and most of all for that power which had made it possible for him to speak—not only to the hearts of those gathered there before him, but to multitudes still to follow in years to come, wherever men have learned to find inspiration in music.

SOME BOOKS IN ENGLISH ABOUT BRAHMS

John Alexander Fuller-Maitland: *Brahms*. London, Methuen, 1911.

Karl Geiringer: *Brahms* (translated). Boston, Houghton Mifflin, 1937.

E. Markham Lee: *Brahms, the Man and His Music*. London, Sampson, Low, Marston, 1915.

Florence May: *The Life of Johannes Brahms,* 2 vols. London, E. Arnold, 1905.

Walter Niemann: *Brahms* (translated). New York, Knopf, 1929.

Jeffrey Pulver: *Johannes Brahms*. New York, Harper, 1926.

Robert Haven Schauffler: *The Unknown Brahms*. New York, Dodd, Mead, 1933. Cheap ed. New York, Crown Publishers.

Richard Specht: *Johannes Brahms* (translated). New York, Dutton, 1930.

Sir Charles Villiers Stanford: *Brahms*. New York, Stokes, 1912.

ACKNOWLEDGMENT

The authors wish to acknowledge the assistance of Mrs. Elizabeth C. Moore, who edited the text and prepared the list of Brahms' compositions, the chronological tables, and the index.

BRAHMS' WORKS AND RECORDINGS

Note—The first date following the title of a work is the date of composition; the second, the date of publication. All Brahms records now in print have been listed, following their respective opus entries. Your record dealer will quote prices. To find any record of which you do not know the opus number, consult the index under the name of the work, where—if it is recorded—you will find its page-number in this list.

OPUS NO.	RECORD NO.
1. First Piano Sonata, in C (1852-53; 1853)	
2. Second Piano Sonata, in F sharp minor (1852; 1853)	
RECORDING: by Arthur Loesser	FRM-15/17
3. Six Songs for tenor or soprano (1852-53; 1854)	
4. Scherzo in E flat minor for piano (1851; 1854)	
RECORDING: by Wilhelm Bachaus	in VM-202
5. Third Piano Sonata, in F minor (1853; 1854)	
6. Six Songs for soprano or tenor (1852-53; 1853)	
7. Six Songs (1851-53; 1854)	
RECORDING: No. 1, *Treue Liebe*, by Ria Ginster	V-8763
8. First Trio, in B major, for piano, violin, and 'cello (1853-54; 1854; new version pub. 1891)	
RECORDINGS: by the Elly Ney Trio	PD-27316/9
by Artur Rubinstein, Jascha Heifetz, and Emanuel Feuermann	VM-883
9. Variations on a Theme by Robert Schumann, in F sharp minor (1854)	
10. Four Ballades for Piano: D minor, D major, B minor, B major (1854 and 1856)	
RECORDINGS: No. 1, D minor (*Edward*)	
by Wilhelm Bachaus	V-7988
by Anatole Kitain	C-69280D
No. 2, D major, by Bachaus	V-7988

OPUS NO.		RECORD NO.
11.	First Serenade for orchestra, D major (1857-58; 1860)	
	RECORDINGS—of Minuet only:	
	by London Symphony	V-11458
	by Chicago Symphony	C-116821D
12.	Ave Maria, for female choir (1858; 1861)	
13.	*Begräbnisgesang* for choir and wind instruments (1858; 1861)	
14.	Eight Songs and Romances (1858; 1861)	
	RECORDINGS: No. 1, *Vor dem Fenster,* and No. 4, *Ein Sonett,* by A. Kipnis	in VM-522
15.	First Piano Concerto, in D minor (1852; 1861)	
	RECORDINGS:	
	by Artur Schnabel and London Philharmonic	VM-677
	by W. Bachaus and B.B.C. Symphony	VM-209
16.	Second Serenade for orchestra, A major (1857-60; new version 1875)	
	RECORDING:	
	Alumni Orchestra of Natl. Orch. Assn.	VM-774
17.	Four Songs for female choir (1860; 1862)	
18.	First Sextet, in B flat, for 2 violins, 2 violas, 2 'cellos (1860; 1862)	
	RECORDING:	
	Pro Arte Quartet with Hobday and Pini	VM-296
19.	Five Songs (1858-59; 1862)	
	RECORDING: No. 4, *Der Schmied,* by Marian Anderson	V-15409
20.	Three Duets for soprano and alto (1858-60; 1861)	
	RECORDING: No. 3, *Die Meere,* by I. and N. Kedroff with N. Boulanger	G-DB5060
21.	Piano Variations in D—No. 1, on an original theme; No. 2, on a Hungarian song (1857 and 1861)	
	RECORDING: No. 1, by W. Bachaus	V-14227
22.	*Marienlieder* for mixed choir (1859; 1862)	

OPUS NO.	RECORD NO.
23. Variations on a Theme by Schumann, for piano duet, in E flat (1861; 1863)	
24. Variations and Fugue on a Theme by Handel, for piano, in B flat (1861; 1862)	
RECORDING: by Egon Petri	CM-345
25. First Piano Quartet, in G minor (1861; 1863)	
RECORDING:	
Artur Rubinstein and members of the Pro Arte Quartet	VM-234
26. Second Piano Quartet, in A (1861; 1863)	
RECORDING:	
R. Serkin and members of the Busch Quartet	VM-346
27. Psalm XIII for female choir (1859; 1864)	
28. Four Duets for alto and baritone (1860-62; 1864)	
29. Two Motets for five-part mixed choir unaccompanied (1860; 1864)	
30. Sacred Song for four-part mixed choir (1856; 1864)	
31. Three Quartets for four solo voices (1859-63; 1864)	
32. Nine Songs for solo (1864)	
RECORDINGS: No. 2, *Nicht mehr zu dir zu gehen,* by Herbert Janssen and G. Moore	G-DB3941
No. 9, *Wie bist du, meine Königin*—	
by H. Janssen	G-DB3941
by Lotte Lehmann	C-172731
by Gerhard Husch	G-EG6779
by Heinrich Schlusnus	PD-35032
by Emmi Leisner	PD-27326
33. Fifteen Songs from *Magelone Romances,* in five books (1861-68; 1865, 1868)	
RECORDING: No. 9, *Ruhe, Süssliebchen*—	
by A. Kipnis	in VM-751
by H. Schlusnus	PD-35032
34a. Piano Quintet in F minor (1861-64; 1865)	
RECORDING: by R. Serkin and Busch Quartet	VM-607

OPUS NO. RECORD NO.

34b. Sonata for two pianos arr. from the Quintet 34a (1864; 1872)

35. Variations on a Theme by Paganini (1862-63; 1866)
Recordings: by Egon Petri — CM-X80
by W. Bachaus — V-7419/20

36. Second Sextet, in G (1864-65; 1866)
Recording:
by Budapest Quartet with Hobday and Pini — VM-371

37. Three Sacred Choruses for female voices unaccompanied (1859-63; 1866)

38. First Sonata for 'cello and piano, in E minor (1862-65; 1866)
Recordings:
by Piatigorsky and Artur Rubinstein — VM-564
by Feuermann and Th. v.d. Pas — CM-236

39. Sixteen Waltzes for pianoforte duet (1865; 1867)
Recordings: Space limitations prevent the listing of all the records of the whole series and of the individual waltzes—for solo piano, for piano 4-hands, for two pianos, for violin, and for orchestra. Consult the *Gramophone Shop Encyclopedia* (p. 87) or your dealer.

40. Trio in E flat for piano, violin, and horn (1865; 1868)
Recording:
by Adolf Busch, Aubrey Brain, and R. Serkin — VM-199

41. Five Songs for four-part male choir (1861-62; 1867)

42. Three Songs for six-part choir unaccompanied (1859-61; 1868)

43. Four Songs (1857-68; 1868)
Recordings: No. 1, *Von ewiger Liebe*
by A. Kipnis — in VM-522
by Maria Olszewska — PD-95468

OPUS NO.		RECORD NO.
	by Elena Gerhardt	V-6755
	by Lotte Lehmann	D-25806
	No. 2, *Die Mainacht*	
	by A. Kipnis	in VM-522
	by Lotte Lehmann	C-71060D
	by Marian Anderson	V-14610
	by H. Schlusnus	PD-62783
	by Ria Ginster	V-7821
	by Hulda Lashanska	in VM-612
44.	Twelve Songs for female choir (1859-63; 1866)	
45.	*German Requiem,* for solo voices, chorus, and orchestra, in 7 parts (1857-68; 1868)	
	RECORDINGS:	
	Part 1, *Selig sind, die da Leid tragen,* by Berlin Singakademie Chorus and Orchestra	G-EH257/8
	Part 2, *Denn alles Fleisch,* by the same	G-EH265/6
	Part 4, *Wie lieblich—*	
	by Berlin Singakademie Chorus and Orchestra	G-EG939
	by Irmler Chorus and Orchestra	D-25336
	by Temple Church Chorus and Orch.	G-B3453
	Part 5, *Ihr habt nur Traurigkeit—*	
	by Hildegard Erdmann, Cho. and Orch.	G-C3107
	by Emmy Bettendorf, Cho. and Orch.	D-25282
	by Florence Austral, Royal Opera Chorus and Orchestra	V-9395
	Part 6, *Denn wir haben hier,* by Irmler Chorus and Orchestra	D-25337
46.	Four Songs (1864; 1868)	
	RECORDINGS: No. 4, *An die Nachtigall—*	
	by A. Kipnis	in VM-522
	by Lotte Lehmann	in CM-453
47.	Five Songs (1858-68; 1868)	
	RECORDINGS: No. 1, *Die Botschaft—*	
	by Lotte Lehmann	in VM-419
	by H. Schlusnus	PD-62782
	by Ria Ginster	V-8763

OPUS NO.	RECORD NO.
No. 3, *Sonntag*—	
by A. Kipnis	in VM-522
by Lotte Lehmann	in CM-453
No. 4, *O liebliche Wangen,* by Lotte Lehmann	in CM-453
48. Seven Songs (1855-68; 1868)	
RECORDINGS: No. 1, *Der Gang zum Liebchen*—	
by A. Kipnis	in VM-751
by H. Schlusnus	PD-62783
No. 2, *Der Ueberläufer,* by A. Kipnis	in VM-751
49. Five Songs (1864-68; 1868)	
RECORDINGS: No. 1, *Am Sonntag Morgen*—	
by A. Kipnis	in VM-751
by H. Schlusnus	PD-62783
by Irene Joachim	G-L1055
No. 4, *Wiegenlied*. There are more than a dozen recordings of this, by soprano, tenor, baritone, and vocal ensembles. Consult dealer.	
50. *Rinaldo,* a Cantata (1863-68; 1869)	
51. Two String Quartets (1859-73; 1873)	
RECORDINGS: No. 1, in C minor—	
by Busch Quartet	VM-227
by Léner Quartet	C-LX228/31
No. 2, in A minor—by Budapest Quartet	VM-278
by Léner Quartet	C-LX163/6
52. Eighteen *Liebeslieder* Waltzes for piano duet and voices (1868-69; 1869)	
RECORDINGS:	
by quartet (Vickland, MacGregor, Hain, Calder) with G. Castagnetta and M. Kaye	MC-14
by quartet (Polignac, Kedroff, Cuenod, Conrad) with D. Lipatti and N. Boulanger	G-DB5057/9
Arr. for orch., N.B.C. String Symphony under Frank Black	in VM-455
52a. Eighteen *Liebeslieder* Waltzes for piano duet, arr. from Opus 52 (1874)	

OPUS NO.		RECORD NO.
53.	Alto Rhapsody for alto solo, male choir, and orchestra (1869; 1870)	
	RECORDING: by Marian Anderson with Univ. of Penna. Male Chorus and Phila. Orch. under Ormandy	V-1919 and V-15408
54.	*Schicksalslied* (*Song of Destiny*) for chorus and orchestra (1871)	
55.	*Triumphlied* for chorus and orchestra (1870-71; 1872)	
56a.	Variations on a Theme by Haydn, for orchestra (1873; 1874)	
	RECORDINGS:	
	by London Philharmonic, Weingartner	CM-X125
	by N. Y. Philharmonic-Symphony, Toscanini	VM-355
56b.	Variations on a Theme by Haydn, for two pianos (1873)	
	RECORDINGS:	
	by Luboshutz and Nemenoff	VM-799
	by Bartlett and Robertson	CM-X181
57.	Eight Songs (1871)	
	RECORDING: No. 2, *Wenn du nur zuweilen lächelst,* by H. Schlusnus	PD-30004
58.	Eight Songs (1871)	
59.	Eight Songs (1871-73; 1873)	
	RECORDINGS:	
	No. 2, *Auf dem See,* by H. Schlusnus	PD-62782
	No. 8, *Dein blaues Auge*—	
	by A. Kipnis	in VM-751
	by Marian Anderson with the Philadelphia Orchestra	V-15409
60.	Third Piano Quartet, in C minor (1855-75; 1875)	
	RECORDING: by Harry Cumpson, Cyril Tobin, David Dawson, Carl Stern	C-LX365/8

OPUS NO.	RECORD NO.
61. Four duets for soprano and alto (1874)	
RECORDINGS: No. 1, *Die Schwestern*—	
by Victoria Anderson and Viola Morris	C-DB1233
by quartet (Polignac, Kedroff, Cuenod, Conrad) with N. Boulanger	G-DB5060
62. Seven Songs (1874)	
63. Nine Songs (1873-74; 1874)	
RECORDINGS: No. 2, *Erinnerung,* by A. Kipnis	VM-522
No. 4, *An die Tauben,* by H. Schlusnus	PD-30004
No. 5, *Meine Liebe ist grün*—	
by A. Kipnis	in VM-751
by Lotte Lehmann	in VM-292
by K. Flagstad	G-DA1586
No. 8, *O wüsst ich doch den Weg zurück*—	
by A. Kipnis	in VM-522
by Irene Joachim	G-L1055
by Karl Erb	V-4403
64. Three Quartets for four solo voices (1862-74; 1874)	
65. Fifteen *Neues Liebeslieder* Waltzes for voices and piano duet (1874; 1875)	
65a. *Neues Liebeslieder* Waltzes arr. for piano duet (1877)	
66. Five Duets for soprano and alto (1875)	
RECORDING: No. 2, *Klänge* (II), by I. and N. Kedroff with N. Boulanger	G-DB5060
67. Third String Quartet, in B flat (1875; 1876)	
68. First Symphony, in C minor (1855-76; 1877)	
RECORDINGS: N.B.C. Symphony, Toscanini	VM-875
London Symphony, Weingartner	CM-383
Vienna Philharmonic, B. Walter	VM-470
69. Nine Songs (1877)	
RECORDING: No. 5, *Tambourliedchen,* by H. Schlusnus	PD-30004
70. Four Songs (1875-77; 1877)	
RECORDING: No. 2, *Lerchengesang,* by Karl Erb	G-EG3687

OPUS NO.	RECORD NO.
71. Five Songs (1877)	
RECORDINGS: No. 2, *Geheimnis,* by A. Kipnis	in VM-751
No. 5, *Minnelied*—	
by Karl Schmitt-Walter	T-A2539
by Herbert Janssen	G-DB3941
by H. Schlusnus	PD-90177
72. Five Songs (1876-77; 1877)	
RECORDING: No. 3, *O kühler Wald*—	
by A. Kipnis	in VM-751
by Karl Erb	V-4403
73. Second Symphony, in D major (1877; 1878)	
RECORDINGS: London Philharmonic, Beecham	CM-265
London Symphony, Weingartner	CM-493
Phila. Orchestra, Ormandy	VM-694
N. Y. Philharmonic-Symphony, Barbirolli	CM-412
74. Two Motets for mixed choir unacc. (1863-77; 1879)	
75. Four Ballads and Songs (1877-78; 1878)	
76. Eight Piano Pieces (1871-78; 1879)	
RECORDINGS: No. 2, Capriccio in B minor—	
by Wilhelm Bachaus	V-14516
by Artur Rubinstein	V-26389
by Myra Hess	G-B9189
No. 3, Intermezzo in A flat major—	
by Walter Gieseking	C-71172D
by Elly Ney	G-DA4438
by Myra Hess	G-B9189
No. 4, Intermezzo in B flat major, by Walter Gieseking	C-71172D
No. 6, Intermezzo in A major, by Eileen Joyce	D-25174
No. 7, Intermezzo in A minor—	
by Artur Rubinstein	in VM-893
by W. Bachaus	in VM-202
No. 8, Capriccio in C major, by W. Bachaus	V-7991

OPUS NO. RECORD NO.

77. Violin Concerto, in D major (1878; 1879)
 Recordings:
 by Jascha Heifetz and Boston Symphony, Koussevitzky — VM-581
 by Fritz Kreisler and London Philharmonic, Barbirolli — VM-402
 by Joseph Szigeti and Hallé Orchestra, Hamilton Harty — CM-117

78. First Sonata for violin and piano, in G major (1878-79; 1880)
 Recording: by A. Busch and R. Serkin — VM-121

79. Two Rhapsodies for piano (1879; 1880)
 Recordings: No. 1, B minor—
 by Artur Rubinstein — in VM-893
 by W. Bachaus — in VM-202
 by Egon Petri — in CM-X183
 No. 2, G minor—
 by Artur Rubinstein — V-14946
 by W. Bachaus — V-7994
 by Egon Petri — in CM-X183

80. Academic Festival Overture, in C minor (1880; 1881)
 Recordings:
 Concertgebouw Orchestra, Mengelberg — CM-X42
 Vienna Philharmonic, Walter — V-12190
 London Symphony, Weingartner — C-LX886
 N. Y. Philharmonic-Symphony, Barbirolli — CM-X200

81. Tragic Overture, in D minor (1880-81; 1881)
 Recordings:
 London Philharmonic, Beecham — CM-X85
 B.B.C. Symphony, Toscanini — in VM-507
 Chicago Symphony, Stock — CM-X214

82. *Nänie,* for chorus and orchestra (1880-81; 1881)

83. Second Piano Concerto, in B flat major (1878-81; 1882)
 Recordings:
 by V. Horowitz and N.B.C. Symphony, Toscanini — VM-740

OPUS NO.		RECORD NO.
	by W. Bachaus and Saxon State Orch., Böhm	G-DB3930/5
	by Elly Ney and Berlin Philharmonic, Fiedler	PD-67566/7
	by Artur Schnabel and B.B.C. Symphony, Boult	VM-305
84.	Five Songs (1878-81; 1882)	
	RECORDING: No. 4, *Vergebliches Ständchen*—	
	by A. Kipnis	in VM-522
	by Elisabeth Schumann	V-1756
85.	Six Songs (1877-79; 1882)	
	RECORDING: No. 6, *In Waldeinsamkeit,* by A. Kipnis	in VM-751
86.	Six Songs (1877-78; 1882)	
	RECORDINGS:	
	No. 1, *Therese,* by Lotte Lehmann	V-1733
	No. 2, *Feldeinsamkeit*—	
	by Elena Gerhardt	V-7793
	by A. Kipnis	C-7204M
	by H. Schlusnus	PD-30009
87.	Second Trio, in C major (1880-82; 1883)	
	RECORDING: Myra Hess, Y. d'Aranyi, G. Cassadó	CM-266
88.	First String Quintet (1882; 1883)	
	RECORDING: by Budapest Quartet and Hobday	VM-466
89.	*Song of the Fates,* for six-part chorus and orchestra (1882; 1883)	
90.	Third Symphony, in F major (1883; 1884)	
	RECORDINGS:	
	London Philharmonic, Weingartner	CM-353
	Vienna Philharmonic, Walter	VM-341
	Chicago Symphony, Stock	CM-443
	National Symphony, Kindler	VM-762
91.	Two Songs for alto with viola and piano (1863-84; 1884)	
	RECORDINGS: No. 1, *Gestillte Sehnsucht,* and No. 2, *Geistliches Wiegenlied,* by Marian	

OPUS NO. RECORD NO.

Anderson with William Primrose and F. Rupp — in VM-882

92. Four Vocal Quartets (1877-84; 1884)

93a. Six Songs for four-part mixed choir unacc. (1883-84; 1884)

RECORDING: No. 4, *Fahr wohl, O Vöglein,* by the Dresden Kreuzchor — PD-10282

93b. *Tafellied* for six-part mixed choir (1884; 1885)

94. Five Songs (1884)

RECORDINGS: No. 4, *Sapphische Ode*—
by Kirsten Thorborg — V-16969
by Aulikki Rautawaara — T-A2538
by Friedel Beckmann — G-EG6846
by Maria Olszewska — G-E546

95. Seven Songs (1884)

RECORDING: No. 4, *Der Jäger,* by Elisabeth Schumann — V-1756

96. Four Songs (1884; 1886)

RECORDINGS: No. 1, *Der Tod, das ist die kühle Nacht*—
by Elisabeth Schumann — in VM-383
by Lotte Lehmann — in VM-292

No. 2, *Wir wandelten*—
by A. Kipnis — in VM-751
by Lotte Lehmann — in CM-453

97. Six Songs (1884)

RECORDINGS: No. 1, *Die Nachtigall*—
by Elisabeth Schumann — V-1756
by Elena Gerhardt — V-7793

No. 2, *Auf dem Schiffe,*
by Dorothea Helmrich — C-DB1233

98. Fourth Symphony, in E minor (1884-85; 1886)

RECORDINGS:
London Symphony, Weingartner — CM-335
Boston Symphony, Koussevitzky — VM-730
Concertgebouw Orchestra, Mengelberg — T-SK2773/7
All-American Youth Orchestra, Stokowski — CM-452

OPUS NO. RECORD NO.

99. Second Sonata for 'cello and piano, in F major (1886; 1887)
    RECORDING: Pablo Casals and M. Horszowski — VM-410
100. Second Sonata for violin and piano, in A major (1886; 1887)
    RECORDINGS: by Jascha Heifetz and E. Bay — VM-856
    by Adolf Busch and R. Serkin — G-DB1805/6
    by Albert Spalding and A. Benoist — VM-288
101. Third Trio, in C minor, for piano, violin, and 'cello (1886; 1887)
    RECORDING: by Budapest Trio — D-25627/9
102. Double Concerto for violin, 'cello, and orchestra (1887; 1888)
    RECORDINGS:
    Heifetz, Feuermann, and Phila. Orchestra, Ormandy — VM-815
    Thibaud, Casals, and Casals Orchestra, Cortot — GM-85
103. Gypsy Songs, for four voices (1887; 1888)
    RECORDING: by the Madrigal Singers, L. Engel — CM-X88
104. Five Songs for mixed choir unacc. (1888; 1889)
105. Five Songs (1886; 1889)
    RECORDINGS:
    No. 1, *Wie Melodien zieht es mir*, by A. Kipnis — in VM-751
    No. 2, *Immer leiser wird mein Schlummer—*
    by Elena Gerhardt — V-6755
    by Elisabeth Schumann — V-1837
    by Marian Anderson, with Phila. Orch. — in VM-555
    No. 4, *Auf dem Kirchhofe—*
    by A. Kipnis — in VM-751
    by Lotte Lehmann — in CM-453
    by Hulda Lashanska — in VM-612
    No. 5, *Verrat*, by A. Kipnis — in VM-522
106. Five Songs (1886; 1889)
    RECORDINGS: No. 1, *Ständchen—*
    by Lotte Lehmann — C-17300D

OPUS NO.		RECORD NO.
	by A. Kipnis	in VM-522
	by Elisabeth Schumann	G-DA1620
	by Elena Gerhardt	V-7793
	No. 5, *Ein Wanderer,* by Karin Branzell	P-9614
107.	Five Songs (1886; 1889)	
	RECORDINGS: No. 3, *Das Mädchen spricht—*	
	by Lotte Lehmann	in VM-419
	by Elisabeth Schumann	G-DA1620
	No. 5, *Mädchenlied,* by Aulikki Rautawaara	T-A2538
108.	Third Sonata for violin and piano, in D minor (1886-88; 1889)	
	RECORDINGS:	
	by Paul Kochanski and Artur Rubinstein	VM-241
	by Yehudi and Hephzibah Menuhin	G-DA2832/34
	by Joseph Szigeti and Egon Petri	CM-324
	by Roman Totenberg and Adolf Baller	MC-43
109.	Festival and Commemoration Pieces for eight-part mixed choir unacc. (1886-88; 1890)	
110.	Three Motets for four- and eight-part choir unacc. (1889; 1890)	
111.	Second String Quintet, in G major (1890; 1891)	
	RECORDING: Budapest Quartet and Hans Mahlke	VM-184
112.	Six Quartets for four solo voices (1888-89; 1891)	
113.	Thirteen Canons for female voices (1863-90; 1891)	
114.	Clarinet Trio in A minor (1891; 1892)	
	RECORDINGS:	
	by Kentner, Kell, and Pini	C-DX1007/9
	by Kaye, McLane, and Hunkins	MC-15
115.	Clarinet Quintet in B minor (1891; 1892)	
	RECORDINGS:	
	by Busch Quartet and R. Kell	VM-491
	by Léner Quartet and C. Draper	CM-118

OPUS NO.	RECORD NO.
116. Seven Fantasias for piano (1892)	
RECORDINGS:	
No. 1, Capriccio in D minor, by W. Bachaus	V-14516
No. 2, Intermezzo in A minor, by W. Bachaus	V-14516
No. 3, Capriccio in G minor, by Karl H. D. von Schönberg	PD-10258
No. 4, Intermezzo in E major—	
by Walter Gieseking	in CM-X201
by W. Bachaus	in VM-321
by Grace Castagnetta	TI-1307
No. 7, Capriccio in D minor—	
by Myra Hess	G-C3226
by Eileen Joyce	D-25391
117. Three Intermezzi for piano (1892)	
RECORDINGS:	
No. 1, in E flat major—	
by Artur Rubinstein	in VM-893
by W. Bachaus	in VM-321
by Myra Hess	G-C3226
by Elly Ney	G-DB4426
by William Murdoch	D-25581
No. 2, in B flat minor—	
by Artur Rubinstein	in VM-893
by W. Bachaus	in VM-321
by Eileen Joyce	P-E11417
No. 3, in C sharp minor, by Eduard Erdmann	D-25783
118. Six Piano Pieces (1892; 1893)	
RECORDINGS: No. 1, Intermezzo in A minor, by W. Bachaus	V-7994
No. 2, Intermezzo in A major—	
by Artur Rubinstein	in VM-893
by W. Bachaus	in VM-202
No. 3, Ballade in G minor—	
by W. Bachaus	in VM-202
by Eileen Joyce	D-25782

OPUS NO. RECORD NO.

No. 4, Intermezzo in F minor—
by Luise Gmeiner T-E2220
by W. Bachaus in VM-202
No. 5, Romanze in F major—
by W. Bachaus in VM-202
by Eileen Joyce P-E11340
by Elly Ney G-DA4438
No. 6, Intermezzo in E flat minor—
by Walter Gieseking in CM-X201
by Artur Rubinstein in VM-893
by W. Bachaus in VM-202

119. Four Piano Pieces (1892; 1893)
RECORDINGS:
No. 1, Intermezzo in B minor, by W. Bachaus in VM-321
No. 2, Intermezzo in E minor—
by W. Bachaus in VM-321
by W. Gieseking in CM-X201
No. 3, Intermezzo in C major—
by Artur Rubinstein in VM-893
by W. Bachaus V-14516
by W. Gieseking C-17079D
by Myra Hess G-C3226
No. 4, Rhapsody in E flat major—
by Artur Rubinstein in VM-893
by Egon Petri in CM-X183
by Elly Ney G-DB4426
by William Murdoch D-25581

120. Two Sonatas for clarinet (or viola) and piano (1894; 1895)
RECORDINGS: No. 1, in F minor—
by Lionel Tertis (vla) and H. Cohen C-LX225/7
by David Weber (cl) and Ray Lev MC-27
No. 2, in E flat major—
by William Primrose (vla) and G. Moore VM-422
by Fredk. Thurston (cl) and M. Foggin D-25722/4

WORKS AND RECORDINGS

OPUS NO.	RECORD NO.
121. Four Serious Songs for solo bass voice with piano (1896)	
Denn es gehet dem Menschen	
Ich wandte mich und sahe an	
O Tod, wie bitter bist du	
Wenn ich mit Menschen	
RECORDINGS: by A. Kipnis	in VM-522
by Doda Conrad	G-DB5052/3
122. Eleven Chorale-Preludes for Organ (1896; 1902)	
RECORDINGS:	
No. 8, *Es ist ein Ros' entsprungen,* by E. Power Biggs	V-18292
No. 10, *Herzlich tut mich verlangen,* by Grover J. Oberlee	TA-5

WORKS WITHOUT OPUS NUMBERS

Deutsche Volkslieder—49 songs in 7 books (arr. 1854-58; 1894)

The following twelve have been recorded:

Book I—No. 2, *Erlaube mir;* No. 5, *Die Sonne scheint;* No. 6, *Da unten im Tale*

Book II—No. 12, *Feinsliebchen, du sollst mir;* No. 14, *Maria ging aus Wandern*

Book III—No. 15, *Schwesterlein;* No. 16, *Wach auf*

Book IV—No. 25, *Mein Mädel hat einen Rosenmund*

Book V—No. 34, *Wie komm' ich denn*

Book VI—No. 39, *Schöner Augen;* No. 41, *Es steht ein Lind;* No. 42, *In stiller Nacht*

Of these, the album made by Ernst Wolff contains nine: 2, 5, 6, 12, 14, 15, 16, 25, and 41	CM-X128
Others of the twelve have been recorded as follows:	
No. 2—by Elena Gerhardt	V-7795
by Lotte Lehmann	C-71059D

OPUS NO.	RECORD NO.
No. 6.—by Lotte Lehmann	C-71059D
No. 12—by Elena Gerhardt	V-7795
by Lotte Lehmann	C-71059D
No. 25—by Alexander Kipnis	in VM-751
by Lotte Lehmann	V-1857
No. 34—by Elena Gerhardt	V-7795
No. 39—by the Berlin Chamber Chorus	C-DZ18
No. 42—by Alexander Kipnis	in VM-751
by the Dresdener Kreuzchor	PD-10726
by the Madrigal Singers, L. Engel	C-9150M
Deutsche Volkslieder—14 songs arr. for four-part choir	
Volks-Kinderlieder—fourteen children's folk songs, of which the following have been recorded:	
No. 3, *Die Henne,* by Harry Hopewell	G-B8091
No. 4, *Sandmännchen*—	
by A. Kipnis	in VM-751
by Elisabeth Schumann	V-1838
No. 11, *Wiegenlied (Schlaf', Kindlein, schlaf'),*	
by Helen Jepson	in V-4289
Hungarian Dances arr. for piano duet, in 4 books. Of the 21 dances, all but 7 have been recorded, many of them several times in various versions. Consult dealer.	

Note—The above is not quite a complete list of Brahms' works, though it includes all the important ones. A good deal was published after his death—the "posthumous works." Also, he made many arrangements of other men's compositions, such as the Gluck Gavotte from Paris and Helen, *some Schubert songs, and two of Schumann's chamber works (the Piano Quartet Op. 47 and the Piano Quintet Op. 44) for piano duet. For a complete listing of all his compositions and arrangements, see the Appendix in* The Unknown Brahms *by Robert Haven Schauffler.*

THE WORLD THAT BRAHMS LIVED IN

A QUARTER of a century before the birth of Brahms, the last surviving musical genius of the eighteenth century had died—Haydn, in 1809. Weber died in 1826, Beethoven in 1827, Schubert in 1828—but their works had brought in the "Romantic Period" whose leading composers were to be Mendelssohn, Schumann, Franck, Brahms, Chopin, Wagner, Dvořák, and Tchaikovsky.

Of these, all but Tchaikovsky had already been born by 1833: Mendelssohn in 1809; Chopin and Schumann belong to 1810; in 1811 Liszt was born; in 1813, Verdi and Wagner; and Gounod's year is 1818. Schumann's wife Clara Wieck was born in 1819—the birth year also of Queen Victoria and Julia Ward Howe.

To the decade just before Brahms' own belong César Franck (1822), Smetana and Bruckner (1824), Anton Rubinstein (1829), and Hans von Bülow (1830). Brahms' friend Joseph Joachim was two years older than he—born in 1831. Three other famous composers of the nineteenth century were born during Brahms' youth: Tchaikovsky in 1840, Dvořák in 1841, and Grieg in 1843.

Now for a look at conditions outside the musical world at the time when Brahms was born. In the United States we were in the midst of the Jacksonian Era. We had little native literature or music thus far. The country was growing fast, though the West was not yet opened up. The English were busy starting the reform of Parliament. Though industry was booming, workers' conditions were bad and there was much misery and injustice.

Germany was "only a geographical expression"; not till forty years later would the dozens of German states be welded by Bismarck into the German Empire. France had driven out its last Bourbon king in 1830, and now was ruled by the "Citizen King" Louis Philippe. Italy was still split up into separate states, many of them belonging to the Church or to Austria. The real dictator of all Europe was the Austrian statesman Metternich.

But revolution was on the way. All over Europe the people were already stirring—beginning to talk and work for freedom and political rights. During the next fifteen years, thrones would totter, and in many a country the rebellious people were to obtain for themselves the constitutional rights and the elected assemblies already matters of course in the United States.

THE WORLD THAT BRAHMS LIVED IN

BRAHMS' LIFE	MUSICAL EVENTS	WORLD EVENTS
1833 Johannes Brahms b. in Hamburg, May 7.	1833 Borodin b. In London, Mendelssohn conducts first perf. of his *Italian* Symphony. Boston Academy of Music opens.	1833 Edwin Booth, A. Nobel, L. M. Alcott, b. Pres. Jackson's 2d inaug. Nullification conflict with South Carolina is ended.
	1834 April, first issue of *Neue Zeitschrift,* music magazine founded by Schumann and Wieck. Schumann starts *Carnaval,* and composes *Etudes symphoniques.*	1834 Lamb, Coleridge, d. Whistler, Mendeléyev, R. H. Stockton, Langley, b. Young Richard Henry Dana begins the voyage that he is to describe in *Two Years Before the Mast* (1840).
	1835 Bellini d. Saint-Saëns, Wieniawski, b. World prem. of Donizetti's *Lucia di Lammermoor.* Schumann meets Mendelssohn and Chopin at Wieck's in Leipzig.	1835 John Marshall d. Mark Twain and Carnegie b. Liberty Bell cracks. Business panic in U.S. Colt invents revolver. Texas proclaims independence from Mexico.
	1836 Mendelssohn conducts world première of his *St. Paul,* Düsseldorf. World prem. of Glinka's *A Life for the Tsar* and Wagner's *Liebesverbot.*	1836 Aaron Burr d. Great Trek begins in South Africa. Siege of the Alamo (Texas), garrison massacred, Davy Crockett killed. Wm. McGuffey pub. his First and Second Readers.
	1837 Schumann and Clara Wieck are engaged, but Wieck opposes the marriage. Schumann writes the *Davidsbündler* Dances and the *Fantasiestücke* for piano Op. 12.	1837 Pushkin d. Swinburne, John Burroughs, b. Van Buren becomes President. The first iron ship is built in America. Poe moves from Va. to N. Y. City. *Oliver Twist* published.
1838 Begins studying the rudiments of music under his father's direction.	1838 Bizet, Bruch, and Simrock (Brahms' publisher), b. Jenny Lind's debut at Stockholm as Agathe in *Der Freischütz.* Schumann composes *Kinderscenen, Kreisleriana,* and *Novelletten,* for piano.	1838 John Hay, Henry Adams, Count Zeppelin, b. Historic crossing of *S.S. Great Western,* Bristol to N.Y. in 15 days. *Sartor Resartus* (Carlyle), *Nicholas Nickleby,* pub.
	1839 Mussorgsky b. World prem. Mendelssohn's *Ruy Blas* Overture. He conducts in Leipzig the first perf. of Schubert's Sym. in C since its discovery by Schu-	1839 Rockefeller, Henry George, Bret Harte, b. Opium War begins in China. Belgium and Holland separate by treaty. Invention of electrotypes, photography,

			mann (1838). Bülow, aged 9, begins music study under Wieck. Schumann composes *Nachtstücke* and *Faschingsschwank*.		and rubber-vulcanizing process. Queen Victoria marries Albert of Saxe-Coburg. Longfellow publishes "The Psalm of Life."
1840	Starts taking piano lessons from Cossel.	1840	Paganini d. Tchaikovsky b. Marriage of Schumann and Clara. His "song-year": he writes the cycles *Frauenliebe und Leben* and *Dichterliebe,* and many other songs.	1840	Daudet, Zola, Rodin, Monet, Thos. Hardy, b. Bonaparte's body is brought from St. Helena, entombed in the Invalides, Paris. In England, first adhesive postage stamp is issued.
		1841	Dvorák b. Mendelssohn conducts world prem. of Schumann's First Symphony and the one in D minor—then called the Second but later rewritten and pub. as the Fourth. Birth of Marie Schumann.	1841	Pres. Wm. Henry Harrison's inauguration and death; Tyler succeeds. Edward VII, Clemenceau, Henry M. Stanley, Justice O. W. Holmes, b. *Punch* starts. *Tribune* (N.Y.C.) starts, Greeley as editor.
		1842	Cherubini d. Massenet and Sullivan b. World prem. Rossini's *Stabat Mater,* Mendelssohn's *Scotch* Symphony, Wagner's *Rienzi,* Glinka's *Russlan and Ludmilla.* Vienna Philh. and N. Y. Philh. founded. Schumann's "chamber music" year.	1842	Arnold of Rugby d. Wm. James b. Bicycle invented. In U.S., ether is first used as anesthetic. Dickens' first visit to America; "Boz Ball" in N.Y.C. Tennyson's first *Poems* pub. Washington Irving goes to Spain as U.S. minister.
1843	Cossel asks Marxsen to take Brahms for piano instruction. Marxsen at first refuses, but soon relents.	1843	Born: Grieg, Patti, Richter, and Brahms' friends Herzogenberg and Popper. World prem. Wagner's *Flying Dutchman,* Balfe's *Bohemian Girl,* Mendelssohn's *Midsummer Night's Dream* music. Mendelssohn opens Leipzig Conservatory, with Schumann on the staff. Elise Schumann born.	1843	Noah Webster, F. S. Key, d. Henry James, Koch, McKinley, b. Bunker Hill Monument completed. Wordsworth made Poet Laureate. Publication of "Ben Bolt," of "The Gold Bug" (Poe), *Past and Present* (Carlyle), *A Christmas Carol* and *Martin Chuzzlewit* (Dickens), and Macaulay's *Critical and Historical Essays.*
		1844	Rimsky-Korsakov, Sarasate, b. Weber's body brought from England for burial at Dresden. The Schumanns tour Russia. His piano quartet Op. 47 is first played, with Clara as pianist. They move to Dresden.	1844	Nietzsche, Verlaine, Sarah Bernhardt, b. Over the experimental line just completed between Baltimore and Washington, Morse sends the first telegraphic message, from the Capitol.

Year	BRAHMS' LIFE	MUSICAL EVENTS	WORLD EVENTS
1845		Fauré, Materna, Wilhelmj, b. World prem. Wagner's *Tannhäuser*. At Leipzig, Ferdinand David introduces Mendelssohn's Violin Concerto. Schumann works on his Piano Concerto in A minor.	Andrew Jackson d. Metchnikov, Roentgen, Root, b. Naval Academy opened at Annapolis. Polk inaugurated. Texas annexed as a state. Publication of "The Raven" (Poe), *Dombey and Son* (Dickens).
1846	Spends summer at Winsen, giving lessons to Lieschen Giesemann, conducting the Winsen choral society, and going home weekly for his lesson with Marxsen.	At the Birmingham Festival, Mendelssohn conducts the world prem. of his *Elijah,* and at Leipzig produces Schumann's Second Symphony in C.	Oregon Territory secured to U.S. Wilmot Proviso defeated, Free Soil party organized. Frémont starts penetration of California. Mexican War opens. Donner party crosses Rockies. Mormons, attacked at Nauvoo, flee westward. Hoe invents the rotary press; Howe, the sewing-machine.
1847		Mendelssohn d. Schumann's Piano Concerto is introduced (Vienna) by Clara. He writes his trios in D minor and F.	Hindenburg, Edison, Bell, b. Publication of *Evangeline* (Longfellow), *The Princess* (Tennyson), and *Jane Eyre* (Brontë).
1848	Continues his lessons with Marxsen. In September gives his first concert.	Donizetti d. Lilli Lehmann, Pachmann, b. Schumann writes *Album für die Jugend* and *Manfred* Overture; starts *Waldscenen.*	Popular revolutions in Europe. On defeat of Mexico, U.S. gets much new territory in Southwest. *Vanity Fair* (Thackeray) published.
1849	Makes transcriptions and arrangements under the names G. W. Marks and Karl Würth. Gives second concert, April 14. Hears Remenyi play gypsy music.	Chopin d. Wagner exiled from Germany. Joachim becomes concertmaster under Liszt at Weimar. Schumann finishes *Waldscenen.*	Poe d. Burbank b. Gold Rush to California starts. Zachary Taylor inaug. Webster-Parkman murder (Cambridge, Mass.). *David Copperfield* (Dickens) published.
1850		World prem. Schumann's opera *Genoveva* and Wagner's *Lohengrin.* The Schumanns move to Düsseldorf. He composes his 'Cello Concerto and Third Symphony. His mental ailment grows worse.	Wordsworth, Balzac, Calhoun, d. Masaryk, Kitchener, Stevenson, b. Pres. Taylor d., Fillmore succeeds. Clay's Compromise Resolutions; Fugitive Slave Law; Webster's 7th of March speech. *Pendennis* (Thackeray), *The Scarlet Letter* (Hawthorne), published.

Year	Brahms	Year	Music	Year	World events
1851	Composes earliest work to be printed: Scherzo in E♭ minor, published 1854 as Op. 4.	1851	Spontini d. Vincent d'Indy b. World prem. Verdi's *Rigoletto*. In Leipzig, Schumann conducts first perf. of his Third (*Rhenish*) Symphony. Composes G minor trio, and two sonatas for violin and piano.	1851	Fenimore Cooper, Audubon, Daguerre, d. Foch, Walter Reed, b. Crystal Palace Exhibition opens, London. Gold discovered in Australia. N.Y. *Times* starts. N.Y. Central R. R. begins operation. In France, Louis Napoleon's *coup d'état*.
		1852	Born: Rafael Joseffy, who introduced Brahms' piano concertos in America, and Hausmann, 'cellist of the Joachim Quartet. At Leipzig, world prem. of Schumann's *Manfred*.	1852	D. Webster, Clay, Wellington, T. Moore, John Howard Payne, d. Louis Napoleon is proclaimed emperor; 2d Empire begins. Otis invents brake elevator. Antioch College opens. Roget's *Thesaurus* pub.
1853	His career opens. In April, concert tour with Remenyi. At Hanover begins friendship with Joachim. To Weimar to meet Liszt. Summer at Göttingen with Joachim. To Düsseldorf to call on the Schumanns. At the Leipzig Gewandhaus, plays his C major Sonata and E♭ minor Scherzo. His first works are published.	1853	World prem. Verdi's *Traviata* and *Trovatore*. The Schumanns' friendship with Brahms begins. Schumann composes *Fantasie* (introduced by Joachim, October) and the Violin Concerto (not played till 1937). Schumann writes *Neue Bahnen* article on Brahms.	1853	Cecil Rhodes, John Drew, Bertillon, b. Boundary dispute with Mexico settled by Gadsden Purchase, adding new territory to our Southwest. Napoleon III marries Eugénie Montijo. Pres. Pierce inaug. World's Fair (Crystal Palace) opens in N.Y.C. *Bleak House* (Dickens) pub.
1854	In Hanover with Grimm, Joachim, and Allgeyer. Composes B major Trio, Op. 8. Late in February, to Düsseldorf to be near the Schumanns. Writes *Variations on a Theme by Schumann* (Op. 9) and *Ballades* (Op. 10). Summer trip with Grimm. Short concert tour.	1854	Academy of Music opens, N.Y.C. The Schumanns go to Hanover for concerts and a visit with Joachim, Brahms, and Grimm. At Düsseldorf Schumann attempts suicide on Feb. 27, and is taken to an asylum at Endenich. Late in the year is visited by Joachim and Brahms. Felix Schumann b.	1854	Kansas-Nebraska Bill starts struggle between slaveholders and abolitionists for control of new territories. Commodore M. C. Perry negotiates treaty with Mikado, opening ports of Japan to U.S. trade. Crimean War opens; siege of Sebastopol. *Uncle Tom's Cabin* (Stowe) published.

	BRAHMS' LIFE		MUSICAL EVENTS		WORLD EVENTS
1855	At the Lower Rhine Festival he meets Jenny Lind and the critic Hanslick. Begins listening twice weekly to chamber music played by Joachim and several friends. In November gives concerts at Danzig, Bremen, and Hamburg. Spends Christmas with Clara Schumann.	1855	Schumann's *Paradise and the Peri* is sung at Lower Rhine Festival, with Jenny Lind. First Brahms work performed outside of Germany is heard in N.Y.C., in November, when the Trio Op. 8 is played by William Mason, Theodore Thomas, and Carl Bergmann. First European performance, Breslau in December.	1855	Charlotte Brontë d. Florence Nightingale goes to the Crimea. Allies take Sebastopol; war ends. First transatlantic cable laid by Field, first message sent (but see 1866). Pub. of *Leaves of Grass* (Whitman), *The Age of Fable* (Bulfinch), and *Familiar Quotations* (Bartlett).
1856	In January plays at Leipzig. In early April visits Schumann, whose condition is now hopeless. Meets Stockhausen in May and gives concerts with him. Sees Schumann, June, for the last time before his death. With sister, Joachim, and the Schumanns, to Lucerne for the summer. To Detmold in October, to teach.	1856	Taneiev, Sinding, Alvary, Mottl, b. Covent Garden Opera, London, destroyed by fire. In London and Vienna, Clara Schumann plays Brahms' music early in the year. On July 29 Schumann dies. Clara moves to Berlin. With her children she goes to Switzerland for the summer.	1856	Woodrow Wilson, G. B. Shaw, S. Freud, b. Peace of Paris convention (ending Crimean War) adopts internatl. rules of war: contraband, privateering, blockade. Perkin discovers aniline dyes. Bessemer invents his steel process. John Brown in battle at Osawatomie (Kan.); antislavery party prevails. Rise of Know-Nothing party.
1857	In Detmold again in the spring, renewing friendship with Carl von Meysenbug. In the fall, engaged to teach, play, and conduct at Detmold for three months.	1857	Glinka, Czerny, d. Elgar, Nordica, Bispham, b. Brooklyn Philharmonic founded. Phila. Academy of Music opens. Bülow marries Cosima Liszt.	1857	Tesla, Hertz, Baden-Powell, Conrad, Taft, b. Buchanan inaug. Dred Scott decision by Supreme Court. Commercial depression throughout U.S. Native mutiny in India.
1858	First six months in Hamburg. Summer at Göttingen with Clara and her children. Composes the *Serenade in D* (Op. 11) and the D minor Piano Concerto. To Detmold in September. At Hanover rehearses the Concerto.	1858	Leoncavallo, Puccini, Sembrich, Calvé, Ysaÿe, b. New Covent Garden Opera House opens in London. At the marriage of the Queen's daughter to the Crown Prince of Prussia, the *Midsummer Night's Dream* march is first used at a wedding.	1858	T. Roosevelt, Booker Washington, Diesel, Goethals, b. East India Co. dissolved; govt. of India transferred to British crown. Lincoln tells Illinois state convention that the U.S. "cannot endure half slave and half free"; starts his greatest series of debates with Stephen A. Douglas.

1859 His first large work is introduced—the D minor Piano Concerto, which he plays at Hanover on Jan. 22, Joachim conducting. Repeats it Jan. 29, Leipzig Gewandhaus. Conducts the Hamburg Ladies' Choir and writes many songs for them. To Detmold in the fall; several of his works are performed there.

1859 Ilyinsky, Ippolitov-Ivanov, Melba, Victor Herbert, Frank Damrosch, b. Patti's operatic debut, N. Y. Academy of Music, as Lucia. World prem. Verdi's *Masked Ball,* Gounod's *Faust,* Brahms' D minor Pf. Concerto and Serenade Op. 11. American prem. of Schumann's Piano Concerto, played by Sebastian Bach Mills with the N.Y. Philharmonic.

1859 Metternich, De Quincey, Macaulay, Prescott, W. Irving, d. Conan Doyle, Dreyfus, Kaiser Wilhelm, Duse, John Dewey, b. First U.S. oil-well opened, Titusville, Pa. John Brown attacks Harpers Ferry; is hanged. *Origin of Species, Idylls of the King, A Tale of Two Cities, Adam Bede,* the *Rubáiyát,* published.

1860 Leaves Detmold. Second Serenade Op. 16 completed. During spring lives at home, conducts Ladies' Choir. Songs of 1859 sung by Grimm's chorus at Göttingen. At Rhine Festival, Düsseldorf, begins his friendship with the publisher Simrock.

1860 Born: Paderewski, Charpentier, Albéniz, Schröder-Devrient. Wagner is permitted to re-enter Germany after his exile. World prem. of Brahms' Second Serenade Op. 16, Hamburg Philharmonic, February; and of the Sextet Op. 18 by Joachim, Hanover, October.

1860 Barrie, Jane Addams, Chekhov, Leonard Wood, Bryan, b. Pony Express starts, St. Joseph (Mo.) to Sacramento. Garibaldi lands in Italy; King annexes the Papal States. Prince of Wales visits U.S. South Carolina secedes.

1861 Concerts with Clara Schumann, Joachim, and Stockhausen. Lieschen Giesemann calls at his house, misses him, finds four of the *Magelone Romances* on his piano. Summer at Frau Dr. Rösing's in Hamm. Finishes *Handel Variations* and begins A major Pf. Quartet Op. 26.

1861 Born: Arensky, MacDowell, and Schumann-Heink. In Paris, the Jockey Club forces withdrawal of Wagner's *Tannhäuser.* Frau Schumann, at Hamburg, introduces Brahms' *Handel Variations* Op. 24 and the G minor Pf. Quartet Op. 25.

1861 Cavour, Prince Albert, Mrs. Browning, S. A. Douglas, d. Nansen, Tagore, b. Lincoln's first inaug. Southern Confederacy formed; Sumter fired on; war opens. Gatling invents machine-gun. Mexican expedition under Maximilian undertaken by France.

1862 With Joachim in Hanover and on concert trips. Finishes A major Pf. Quartet. In March goes to Oldenburg to give concerts. Spends summer at Frau Dr. Rösing's, composing. On Sept. 8 leaves for Vienna. There meets leading musical figures. Begins friendship with Hellmesberger and plays with his quartet. Gives successful concerts.

1862 Born: Debussy, Delius, Walter Damrosch. St. Petersburg Conserv. opens. First concert of Theodore Thomas' Orchestra, N.Y.C. First Brahms orch. work to be played outside of Germany is the 2d Serenade Op. 16 (Amer. prem.), in February, N.Y. Philharmonic. In Vienna, first perf. of Brahms' A major Pf. Quartet Op. 26 by Brahms and three members of Hellmesberger Quartet.

1862 Van Buren, Thoreau, d. Maeterlinck, Schnitzler, Hauptmann, O. Henry, Mary E. Wilkins, b. Battles: *Monitor* and *Merrimac,* Shiloh, Antietam. Napoleon III declares Mexico a monarchy under Maximilian. U.S. Bureau of Printing and Engraving opened. Burning issue of government land grants settled by passage of Homestead Act.

Year	BRAHMS' LIFE	Year	MUSICAL EVENTS	Year	WORLD EVENTS
1863	At a Jan. concert, produces some new songs, sung by Marie Wilt. Trouble with clarinetist in March. Goes to Hanover to see Joachim and his fiancée, and to Hamburg for summer. Apptd. cond. of Vienna Singakademie, returns to prepare next season's concerts.	1863	Born: Mascagni, Ternina, Weingartner. American prem. of Mozart G minor Symphony and Gounod's *Faust*. Joachim marries the opera singer Amalie Weiss, who retires from opera but continues concert work.	1863	Thackeray, Gen. Houston, d. H. Ford, Lloyd George, b. Emancipation Proclamation. Battles: Chancellorsville (Stonewall Jackson d.), Gettysburg, Lookout Mountain. At dedication of Gettysburg field, Lincoln's address.
1864	A Singakademie concert includes early version of what will be the Piano Quintet Op. 34—now a two-piano sonata, played by Brahms and Tausig. His father and mother separate. Summer at Baden-Baden, making new friends in Carlsruhe nearby. Writes birthday serenade for Mme. Viardot-Garcia, sung by her pupils.	1864	Richard Strauss b. Wagner's friendship with Ludwig II of Bavaria begins. World prem. of Bruckner's Mass in D minor. Joachim's son, born in June, is named for Brahms, who stands godfather.	1864	Hawthorne d. Austria and Prussia attack Denmark over the Schleswig-Holstein question. Internatl. Red Cross founded by Dunant at Geneva. Clerk Maxwell of Cambridge proves existence of electromagnetic waves. Battle of the Wilderness; Shenandoah Valley campaign; Sherman's march through Georgia.
1865	On mother's death, goes to Hamburg. The *Magelone Romances* and Piano Quintet Op. 34 are pub. At Lichtenthal for the summer, near Frau Schumann. Carlsruhe concert in Nov. Writes Horn Trio Op. 40. Concerts in Switzerland and Germany.	1865	Born: Glazunov, Eames, Sibelius, Dukas. Liszt becomes an abbé. World prem. of Schubert's *Unfinished* Symphony—long lost and just rediscovered—by Friends of Music, Vienna; and of Wagner's *Tristan and Isolde*.	1865	Palmerston, Cobden, Edw. Everett, Lincoln and his assassin Booth, d. Yeats, Kipling, George V, b. Lincoln's 2d inaug. Lee surrenders at Appomattox. Assassination of Lincoln; Johnson inaug. The 13th Amendment abolishes slavery.
1866	Works pub. this year include *Paganini Variations;* Second Sextet; First 'Cello Sonata; 16 Waltzes for piano 4-hand Op. 39; Horn Trio. Works on *German Requiem*. Father remarries. Brahms spends summer at Zürich; friendship with Billroth begins. Completes the *Requiem* (except for Part V). Concert trip with Joachim.	1866	Born: Busoni, Scotti. Moscow Conservatory opens under N. Rubinstein. First all-Norwegian concert, in Christiania, given by Grieg. World prem. Smetana's *Bartered Bride;* Thomas' *Mignon;* Brahms' Horn Trio Op. 40, at Oldenburg.	1866	H. G. Wells, Sun Yat-sen, b. The 14th Amendment makes freedmen citizens. Bismarck attacks Austria; battle of Sadowa. Transatlantic cable (Newfoundland to Ireland) permanently established after breakdown. Wood-pulp paper, Whitehead torpedo, invented. First nickel (five-cent piece) issued.

1867	Successful concert tour in Austria. In July sends *Requiem* ms. to Dietrich. Takes his father on walking tour, Austrian Alps. Autumn, concerts with Joachim in Austria. At a Friends of Music concert in December, parts of *Requiem* are sung in Vienna.	1867	Born: Granados, Toscanini. Opening of Cincinnati and N. E. Conservatories and Chicago Acad. of Music. In Vienna Sir George Grove and Sullivan find lost Schubert works. World prem. of *Blue Danube* and of Brahms' G major Sextet Op. 36—both in Vienna.	1867	Maximilian shot in Mexico. Wilbur Wright, Arnold Bennett, Mme. Curie, b. Lister publishes first description of antisepsis. Nobel invents dynamite. Dominion of Canada estab. U.S. buys Alaska from Russia. Reconstruction Act passed. Ibsen's *Peer Gynt* published.
1868	Plays several times with Hamburg Philharmonic and at Oldenburg. Then with Stockhausen in Dresden, Berlin, and Copenhagen. In April to Bremen for prem. of *German Requiem*. In May writes Part V of *Requiem*. Autumn, at Oldenburg with Frau Schumann and Marie.	1868	Rossini d. Joachim becomes director of Royal Music Acad., Berlin. World prem. Wagner's *Meistersinger* and of Brahms' *German Requiem* at Bremen, his Piano Quintet Op. 34 (by Louise Japha in Paris), and his Waltzes Op. 39 (by Brahms and Frau Schumann, Oldenburg).	1868	Kit Carson d. Gorki, Capt. Robert Scott, Wm. Allen White, b. Andrew Johnson impeached, acquitted. Christopher L. Sholes patents typewriter. First *World Almanac* pub. Colleges founded: Cornell, Univ. of California, Univ. of Minnesota.
1869	Besides the *Rinaldo* production, Brahms gives three concerts with Stockhausen in Vienna, early spring. Goes to Julie Schumann's wedding. Writes the *Liebeslieder* Waltzes and *Alto Rhapsody*. His works now being heard in all European musical capitals.	1869	Berlioz d. Joachim organizes his quartet. Vienna State Opera opened. World prem. Wagner's *Rheingold,* and Brahms' *Rinaldo* (Vienna Sängverein, Brahms conducting) and *Liebeslieder* Waltzes (at Carlsruhe, Frau Schumann and Hermann Levi, with singers).	1869	Gandhi b. Grant's first inaug. Suez Canal opened. First American transcontinental railroad completed. Westinghouse invents air brake. American Museum of Natural History opens. First apt. house in U.S. built, N.Y.C. *Lorna Doone* (Blackmore) published.
1870	In March goes to Jena for the first public perf. of the *Alto Rhapsody*. Publ. the first two books of *Hungarian Dances* in their original form as duets.	1870	Wagner marries Cosima Liszt. World prem. Wagner's *Walküre* (Munich) and of Brahms' *Alto Rhapsody* (Jena, with Mme. Viardot-Garcia as soloist).	1870	Dickens, Dumas père, Lee, Farragut, d. Lenin b. 15th Amendment passed. Kingdom of Italy estab. under Victor Emmanuel II. Franco-Prussian War begins, July; ends Sept. 2; siege of Paris. Diamond mines opened in the Transvaal. Dogma of papal infallibility proclaimed.

BRAHMS' LIFE	MUSICAL EVENTS	WORLD EVENTS
1871 Begins work on *Song of Triumph,* whose first chorus is sung in Bremen Cathedral on April 7, Good Friday. In May, finishes the *Song of Destiny.*	1871 Royal Albert Hall opened, London. World prem. Verdi's *Aïda* (Cairo) and Brahms' *Song of Destiny* (Carlsruhe). Leopold Damrosch and his family come to live in the U.S.	1871 Orville Wright, Dreiser, Rasputin, b. Paris capitulates; German Empire established. Chicago Fire. Stanley finds Livingstone in Tanganyika. Mendeléyev founds table of chemical elements.
1872 Moves to Karlsgasse 4, the Vienna rooms that will be his home for the rest of his life. After his father's death, he sends Frau Brahms to the country. Completes *Song of Triumph.* Is appointed chorus cond. of Vienna Friends of Music.	1872 Born: Scriabin, Gadski, Vaughan Williams. Wagner lays the foundation stone of the Bayreuth Theater. Amer. concert tour of Rubinstein and Wieniawski. First May Music Festival, Cincinnati. World prem. Brahms' *Song of Triumph,* Carlsruhe.	1872 Deaths: Mazzini, Seward, Greeley, S. F. B. Morse. Births: Amundsen, Blériot, Diaghilev, Paul Dunbar, Coolidge, Gertrude Stein. Great fire in Boston. Finding of the *Mary Celeste,* abandoned.
1873 Successful season as F. of M. conductor. Goes to Schumann Festival, Bonn, where he and Frau Schumann play his new *Haydn Variations* to their friends. Finishes the two string quartets Op. 51, which are published this year, as is the two-piano version of the *Haydn Variations,* Op. 56b.	1873 Born: Rachmaninoff, Caruso, Chaliapin. Colonne Concerts started in Paris. N.Y. Oratorio Society has its first concert. World prem. Franck's *Redemption;* Bruckner's Second Symphony; and Brahms' *Haydn Variations,* orch. version Op. 56a, and the two Op. 51 quartets: A minor by Joachim in Berlin, and C minor by Hellmesberger in Vienna.	1873 Deaths: Napoleon III, Livingstone, L. Agassiz, Landseer, Liebig, Bulwer-Lytton, W. H. McGuffey. Births: Lee De Forest, Proust, De la Mare. Financial panic in U.S.; many business failures; Stock Exchange closed. Grant's second inauguration.
1874 Besides Friends of Music concerts in Vienna, Brahms is kept busy conducting his own works at concerts and festivals in Germany and Switzerland, including several at Leipzig, where he has not appeared publicly since 1860. Composes 2d set of *Liebeslieder,* songs and vocal quartets, and the Pf. Quartet Op. 60.	1874 Born: Koussevitzky, Tetrazzini, Holst. World prem. Verdi's *Manzoni Requiem,* Mussorgsky's *Boris Godunov,* Lalo's Violin Concerto. Amer. prem. Wagner's *Lohengrin;* and Brahms' *Haydn Variations* Op. 56a by the Brooklyn Philharmonic under Theodore Thomas.	1874 Born: Winston Churchill, Marconi, Herbert Hoover, Norman Angell, Amy Lowell. In England, Tichborne claimant sentenced after sensational trials. Boss Tweed convicted in N.Y.C. Charley Ross kidnapped. At St. Louis, bridge over the Mississippi is completed.

1875	At close of concert season he gives up Friends of Music conductorship (though continuing active in the Society's work) and devotes himself to composing. In November (with Hellmesberger, Bachrich, and Hilpert) introduces the Pf. Quartet Op. 60.	Bizet d. Born: Ravel, Glière, Kreisler. Paris Opera opened. World prem. Bizet's *Carmen;* Tchaikovsky's Concerto in B♭ minor; his Third Symphony; Lalo's *Symphonie espagnole;* and Brahms' Piano Quartet in C minor Op. 60, in Vienna.	Deaths: Kingsley, Hans Chr. Andersen, Corot, Millet, Andrew Johnson, General Pickett. Births: Thomas Mann, Sabatini, Robert Frost. Gold discovered in South Africa. Great Britain obtains control of Suez Canal.
1876	To Holland to conduct the *Haydn Variations* and play the D minor concerto. At Rügen for the summer, completing his B♭ String Quartet Op. 67, pub. and produced this year. Attends first perf. of his First Symphony in C minor, Carlsruhe. Conducts it himself at Mannheim and Munich, and in December at Vienna. Induces Simrock to publish Dvořák's music.	Born: Wolf-Ferrari, Falla, Casals. First *Ring* Cycle is given at Bayreuth. World prem. Ponchielli's *Gioconda;* Goldmark's *Rustic Wedding* Symphony; Grieg's *Peer Gynt* Suite; Franck's *Les Eolides;* and Brahms' B♭ String Quartet (Joachim in Berlin) and First Symphony in C minor (Carlsruhe under Dessoff).	George Sand, Harriet Martineau, d. Litvinov, Jack London, Sherwood Anderson, Willa Cather, b. Bell patents telephone. Centennial Exposition at Phila. Ashtabula train disaster. In Montana, massacre at Little Big Horn; Custer killed. In disputed election, presidency goes to Hayes over Tilden.
1877	Conducts the C minor Sym. at Leipzig on Jan. 18 with notable success. Declines invitation from Cambridge University to receive a degree, but sends over the ms. of the symphony by Joachim, who in March conducts it there. During summer, works on Second Sym. in D Major, produced in December by Richter. Songs Opp. 69-72 published.	Born: Dohnanyi, Cortot, Mary Garden. World prem. Brahms' Second Symphony in D, Vienna Philharmonic; Saint-Saëns' *Samson and Delilah;* Borodin's Symphony in B minor; Tchaikovsky's *Francesca da Rimini.* Amer. prem. Brahms' First Symphony and *German Requiem.*	J. L. Motley d. Wm. Beebe, Trotsky, Sir James Jeans, b. Hayes inaug. Edison patents gramophone. Great Britain annexes Transvaal. Russo-Turkish War begins; "Bulgarian atrocities." Queen Victoria proclaimed Empress of India. "Molly Maguire" murders in Pennsylvania coal region.
1878	In early spring he enjoys a holiday trip to Italy with Billroth. During the summer spent in Carinthia he grows his famous beard. In Sept. to the 50th anniversary celebration of the Hamburg Philharmonic, Marxsen being present when the new D major Sym. is played. It is pub. this year; also *Ballads and Romances* Op. 75.	Dr. Leopold Damrosch founds the N.Y. Symphony Society Orch. World prem. Tchaikovsky's Fourth Symphony. Amer. prem. Wagner's *Rienzi* and *Siegfried Idyll,* and Brahms' Second Symphony in D.	Cruikshank, Daubigny, Bryant, Bayard Taylor, d. Isadora Duncan, Molnar, Masefield, Sandburg, Upton Sinclair, b. Victor Emmanuel II d., Humbert I becomes King of Italy. Russo-Turkish War ends; Congress of Berlin settles Balkan question. Edison patents incandescent lamp. First Chinese minister to U.S. (Yung Wing) arrives.

BRAHMS' LIFE	MUSICAL EVENTS	WORLD EVENTS
1879 At Leipzig, on New Year's Day, Brahms conducts the first performance of his Violin Concerto, with Joachim as soloist. In November, at Vienna, he plays the Violin and Piano Sonata in G with Hellmesberger.	1879 World prem. Grieg's Piano Concerto, Grieg as pianist; Tchaikovsky's *Eugen Onegin;* and two Brahms violin works: the Concerto and the Op. 78 Sonata in G major.	1879 Stalin, Stefansson, Nazimova, Einstein, Vachel Lindsay, b. Zulu War in South Africa. In U.S., specie payments resumed. The Arctic ship *Jeannette* sails, is caught in the ice north of Siberia (see 1881).
1880 At Crefeld he makes many new friends and at a concert there plays his Rhapsodies in B minor and G minor. Goes to Bonn in May for the unveiling of the Schumann Memorial. Composes the *Tragic* and *Academic Festival Overtures*.	1880 Offenbach, Ole Bull, Wieniawski, d. Teatro Costanza opens in Rome. World prem. Tchaikovsky's *Italian Caprice;* Franck's Piano Quintet; and Brahms' *Tragic Overture,* Vienna Philharmonic.	1880 Flaubert, George Eliot, d. Queen Wilhelmina, Helen Keller, H. L. Mencken, b. Jesuit order disbanded by proclamation in France. Invention of the storage battery.
1881 Gets degree in Jan. from University of Breslau and conducts there the prem. of his *Academic Festival Overture*. Meets Liszt again at Budapest in Feb. Then to Sicily with Billroth. At Ischl for the summer, working on *Nänie* and the Second Piano Concerto in B♭. In Nov. at Meiningen, where Bülow conducts an all-Brahms concert.	1881 Mussorgsky, Vieuxtemps, d. Boston Symphony Orchestra founded. World prem. Tchaikovsky's Violin Concerto; Bruckner's *Romantic* Symphony; Brahms' *Academic Festival Overture* (Breslau) and Second Piano Concerto (Stuttgart). Amer. premières of both the Brahms overtures.	1881 Carlyle, Disraeli, Dostoevski, Sidney Lanier, d. Tsar Alexander II assassinated. Garfield assassinated; President Arthur succeeds. Picasso, Kerenski, F.P.A., b. St. Gothard railway opened across Alps, through tunnel. Great Ring Theater fire in Vienna. Survivors of crushed *Jeannette* land on Siberian coast.
1882 At Hamburg early in the year. Summer at Ischl; then a trip to Italy. Starts friendship with the Fellingers. Introduces the Trio in C and the String Quintet in F, and in Dec. goes to Basle to conduct the first performance of *Song of the Fates*.	1882 Stravinsky, Kodaly, Schnabel, Stokowski, b. World prem. Wagner's *Parsifal;* Tchaikovsky's *1812 Overture* and Trio in A minor; Rimsky-Korsakov's *Snegurotchka;* MacDowell's First Piano Concerto; Brahms' *Song of the Fates,* Trio in C, Op. 87, and Quintet in F, Op. 88.	1882 Garibaldi, Darwin, Rossetti, Trollope, Longfellow, Emerson, d. De Valera, Eddington, James Joyce, S. Undset, Van Loon, F. D. Roosevelt, b. Panama Canal begun by the French. Koch discovers tubercle bacillus. U.S. signs Geneva Convention, initiating the Red Cross in this country.

1883	In April goes to Meiningen, where Bülow is ill, to take over temporarily part of his conducting. To Hamburg for an all-Brahms concert. Celebrates his 50th birthday. Writes Third Symphony in F. Produced in December, it wins instant popularity.	1883	Wagner d. Concertgebouw Society of Amsterdam founded. Metropolitan Opera House opened, N.Y.C. World prem. Chabrier's *España* Rhapsody; Brahms' Third Symphony, Vienna Philharmonic under Richter. Amer. prem. Brahms' *Alto Rhapsody,* N.Y. Philharmonic.	1883	Marx, Manet, Turgenev, Doré, FitzGerald, d. Mussolini b. Triple Alliance formed (Germany, Austria, Italy). Eruption of volcano Krakatao. Brooklyn Bridge opened. Civil Service Reform Act passed.
1884	Publishes the Third Symphony and many songs. Works at the Fourth Symphony in E minor. Is joined by Hanslick at Mürzzuschlag in Styria. Concert trips during the winter.	1884	Smetana d. Russian Symphony Concerts at St. Petersburg begin with an all-Glazunov concert. World prem. Massenet's *Manon* and Debussy's *Enfant prodigue*.	1884	Wendell Phillips, Abbé Mendel, d. Eduard Benes b. Mergenthaler invents linotype. Waterman patents fountain pen. Hadfield invents manganese steel.
1885	Again at Mürzzuschlag. Finishes the Fourth Symphony. In October conducts its first performance, Meiningen. Goes on tour with it, conducting Bülow's orchestra.	1885	Lowell Mason and Leopold Damrosch d. Present Gewandhaus in Leipzig opened. In Boston, Kneisel org. his quartet. World prem. Bruckner's *Te Deum,* and Brahms' Fourth Symphony in E minor.	1885	V. Hugo, Grant, King Alfonso XII, d. D. H. Lawrence, Sinclair Lewis, b. Siege of Khartum by Mahdi; General Gordon killed. Grover Cleveland inaugurated President.
1886	Writes the 'Cello and Piano Sonata Op. 99, the Violin and Piano Sonata Op. 100, and the Trio Op. 101—introduced in the fall, Brahms playing in all three. Frau Truxa becomes his housekeeper.	1886	Liszt d. World prem. Mussorgsky's *Khovantchina,* and three Brahms works: 'Cello and Piano Sonata in F (Vienna), Violin and Piano Sonata in A (Vienna), and Trio in C minor (Budapest).	1886	Chiang Kai-shek b. Statue of Liberty unveiled. A.F. of L. organized. Haymarket (Anarchist) Riots, Chicago. Earthquake at Charleston, S.C. Hertz identifies and produces electromagnetic waves.
1887	The three new chamber-music works are pub., and Songs Opp. 96-97. Another Italian journey in the spring. Composes the Double Concerto in A minor, and conducts its first perf. in October at Cologne, with Joachim as violinist and Hausmann as 'cellist.	1887	Borodin, Jenny Lind, and Brahms' teacher Marxsen, d. "Franck Festival" in Paris. World prem. Rimsky-Korsakov's *Caprice espagnole;* Verdi's *Otello;* Brahms' Double Concerto.	1887	Deaths: H. W. Beecher, Mark Hopkins, Krupp, Eads, Emma Lazarus. Births: A. Zweig, Edna Ferber, Elinor Wylie. Interstate Commerce Act passed. Monotype invented by Lanston.

	BRAHMS' LIFE		MUSICAL EVENTS		WORLD EVENTS
1888	Op. 103, published this year, is the 11 four-part Gypsy Songs, sung in Vienna in April. Third summer at Thun. Writes the Violin and Piano Sonata Op. 108.	1888	In Leipzig, Grieg and Tchaikovsky meet each other and Brahms for the first time. Kreisler's American debut (N.Y.C.) at 13. World prem. Tchaikovsky's Fifth Symphony and *Hamlet Overture.*	1888	Kaiser Wilhelm and his son d., Wilhelm II succeeds. L. M. Alcott d. Australian secret ballot introd. in U.S. Historic blizzard in N.Y. and eastern U.S. Adding machine, photo film, electric meter, inv.
1889	City of Hamburg bestows honorary citizenship on him. Emperor Francis Joseph gives him the Leopold Order.	1889	World prem. Franck's D minor Symphony; MacDowell's Second Pf. Concerto; Strauss' *Don Juan;* Brahms' Violin and Piano Sonata in D minor.	1889	Browning, d. Hitler b. Benjamin Harrison inaugurated President. Eiffel Tower opened, Paris World's Fair. Okla. opened for settlement. Great flood at Johnstown, Pa.
1890	Rewrites early Trio in B major Op. 8 and plays it privately. To Italy in the spring. At Ischl writes the String Quintet in G, produced in Nov. Spends Christmas with the Fellingers.	1890	Franck d. Melchior, Gigli, Myra Hess, Ibert, b. World prem. Mascagni's *Cavalleria Rusticana;* Franck's Str. Quartet; Strauss' *Death and Transfiguration* and *Hamlet;* Brahms' Quintet in G, Op. 111.	1890	Cardinal Newman, Sitting Bull, d. Nellie Bly's trip around the world in 72 days. McKinley Tariff Act. Bismarck resigns chancellorship. Mormons stop plural marriages.
1891	At Meiningen hears the clarinetist R. Mühlfeld and decides to write for him. At Ischl composes the Clarinet Trio Op. 114 and the Clarinet Quintet Op. 115, played privately at Meiningen in November.	1891	Brahms' friends Felix Dessoff and Marie Wilt d. Prokofiev, Elman, b. Chicago Orchestra org. Tchaikovsky visits U.S. for opening of Carnegie Hall, N.Y.C. At a Joachim Quartet concert, Berlin, Dec., Brahms' Clarinet Trio and Quintet.	1891	Lowell, Gen. Sherman, Moltke, Barnum, d. Dom Pedro d., Brazil becomes federal republic. Rotary turbine invented. U.S. passes first International Copyright Act.
1892	Takes part in arranging a Joachim Quartet concert in Vienna at which the two clarinet works are introduced there. Pub. this year, as are the piano pieces Opp. 116-117.	1892	Born: Honegger, Milhaud, Szigeti. World prem. Leoncavallo's *Pagliacci;* Tchaikovsky's *Nutcracker Suite;* Bruckner's Eighth Symphony.	1892	Tennyson, Whittier, Walt Whitman, Renan, Cardinal Manning, d. Peary makes new Polar record. Borden murders at Fall River. "Pledge to the Flag" written and first used. Homestead strikes. Tesla invents AC motor.

1893	In the spring goes on his last trip to Italy, spending his 60th birthday in Naples. His visit to Hamburg when his sister dies is his last there. Works at editing Schumann's papers and music. Pub. piano pieces Opp. 118-119.	1893	Tchaikovsky, Gounod, and Brahms' friend Billroth d. World prem. Dvořák's *New World* Symphony; Tchaikovsky's *Pathetic;* Verdi's *Falstaff;* Humperdinck's *Hänsel and Gretel;* Franck's *Les Béatitudes;* Debussy's String Quartet.	1893	Taine, Maupassant, Tyndall, Edwin Booth, Parkman, d. Cleveland's 2d inaug. World's Columbian Expos., Chicago. Agitation for "free silver" begins. Ives invents halftone engraving process. Edison patents motion-picture machine.
1894	Assembles and pub. his seven volumes of arrangements of German folk songs. At Ischl composes the two Sonatas for clarinet and piano Op. 120. In Nov. at Frankfurt visits with Frau Schumann, now 75 years old.	1894	Bülow, Anton Rubinstein, Chabrier, d. World prem. Debussy's *Prelude to the Afternoon of a Faun;* Massenet's *Thaïs;* Bruckner's Fifth Symphony.	1894	Stevenson, Kossuth, Helmholtz, Lesseps, Hertz, O. W. Holmes, d. Duke of Windsor b. Simon Lake invents submarine. Pullman (Ill.) strikes and riots. Coxey's Army marches on Washington. *Trilby* (Du Maurier) pub.
1895	Concerts in Germany with the clarinetist Mühlfeld, playing the new sonatas. In Sept. attends a Meiningen festival devoted to the works of Bach, Beethoven, and Brahms. A visit with Frau Schumann in October; she plays for him; they never meet again.	1895	Born: Iturbi, d'Aranyi, Hindemith. Cincinnati Orchestra founded. World prem. Strauss' *Till Eulenspiegel;* Ippolitov-Ivanov's *Caucasian Sketches;* Brahms' Clarinet Sonatas Op. 120.	1895	Pasteur, T. H. Huxley, Frederick Douglass, Eugene Field, d. Nansen, in *Fram,* gets "Farthest North." Rebellion in Cuba. Roentgen discovers X-ray. Ramsay discovers helium.
1896	In Jan. conducts for the last time. On his 63rd birthday finishes the *Four Serious Songs* Op. 121. In May goes to Clara Schumann's funeral at Bonn. Attacked by jaundice, he takes the cure at Carlsbad.	1896	Deaths of Clara Schumann and Bruckner. World premières of Puccini's *La Bohème;* Albéniz' *Pepita Jimenez;* Strauss' *Also sprach Zarathustra.*	1896	Nobel, Verlaine, Du Maurier, Wm. Morris, H. B. Stowe, d. Marconi signals by wireless across 2 miles, England. R.F.D. of mail started in U.S. Bryan's "Cross of Gold" speech; he is defeated on a "Free Silver" platform.
1897	Though worse, he attends the Joachim concerts (Jan.) and the Philharmonic concert (March) at which his Fourth Symphony is played. Death on April 3.	1897	Cassadó, Korngold, b. World prem. Leoncavallo's *La Bohème;* d'Indy's *Istar Variations;* Dukas' *Sorcerer's Apprentice.*	1897	Daudet d. McKinley inaug. Dingley Tariff Act. Venezuela boundary dispute settled by arbitration. Paris Charity Bazaar fire. *Quo Vadis?* (Sienkiewicz) and *Cyrano de Bergerac* (Rostand) published.

GENERAL INDEX

INDEX

INDEX

INDEX TO BRAHMS' WORKS

(*Note—A capital* R *preceding a page number indicates that a recording of the work will be found listed on that page.*)

INDEX

92

235